Communicating and Relating

Jacquelyn B. Carr

Foothill College

The Benjamin/Cummings Publishing Company, Inc.
Menlo Park, California • Reading, Massachusetts • London
Amsterdam • Don Mills, Ontario • Sydney

Sponsoring editor: Larry J. Wilson
Production editor: Margaret Moore
Cover designer: Michael Rogondino
Book designer: Michael Rogondino
Artist: Barbara Reinertson

Library of Congress Cataloging in Publication Data

Carr, Jacquelyn B. 1923-
 Communicating and relating.

 Bibliography: p.
 Includes index.
 1. Interpersonal communication. 2. Self-perception.
3. Interpersonal relations. I. Title.
BF637.C45C36   158'.2   78-58969
ISBN 0-8053-1820-8

ISBN 0-8053-1820-8
abcdefghij-HA-782109

The Benjamin/Cummings Publishing Company, Inc.
2727 Sand Hill Road
Menlo Park, California 94025

Communicating and Relating

Acknowledgements

Grateful acknowledgement is made to the following people for the photographs used in this book.

Tom Tracy, cover.

Elihu Blotnick (© Elihu Blotnick 1978. All rights reserved), pp. 4, 12, 24, 26, 35, 114, 143, 148, 181, 349.

Joy Davis, pp. 246, 293, 372.

Lise Giodesen, p. 278.

David Houle, pp. 10, 42, 47, 54, 86, 96, 131, 175, 187, 200, 208, 213, 229, 243, 261, 265, 302 (right), 362, 394.

Steven P. Mangold, pp. 16, 221, 250, 264, 284.

Susan Martin, p. 236.

Neil Rappaport, p. 311.

Russ Rogers, pp. 27, 72, 322, 324, 347.

Patricia Stammer, pp. 60, 302 (left).

Robert Wilson, pp. 122, 160, 164, 198, 380.

David Cherkis from The Stockmarket, Los Angeles, p. 300.

Mark Jones from The Stockmarket, Los Angeles, p. 179.

Jean-Claude Le Jeune from The Stockmarket, Los Angeles, pp. 2, 21, 39, 52, 80, 104, 109, 337.

Marshall Licht from The Stockmarket, Los Angeles, pp. 99, 150.

Robert Pacheco from The Stockmarket, Los Angeles, p. 89.

Lory Robbin from The Stockmarket, Los Angeles, p. 92.

To the Reader

If I could give all of us one gift to make our lives more meaningful, it would be the ability to communicate more effectively so that we could experience deeper, more fulfilling relationships.

C.G. Jung said, "The best of truths is of no use unless it has become one's most personal inner experience." If this book affects *your experience* of communicating or relating, I would appreciate your sharing those experiences with me.

Jacquelyn B. Carr

Preface

FOCUS AND PURPOSE OF THE BOOK

This book is based on the concept that given enough information, both theoretical and experiential, we can choose relevant, satisfying ways to communicate with and relate to other human beings. The underlying assumption is that the subjective human being has importance and value—that he or she can make the best of all possible choices and be responsible for them without knowing in advance how they will turn out. This humanistic-existential approach has particular relevance for communicating and relating in the 1980s.

We are all students; and we are all teachers. My intention in writing this book is to provide us all with theory, practice, and experiences that will help us to create our own communication systems, to find our own ways to improve communicating and relating with others. The interactions in the interpersonal communication class provide a learning and growing environment for both teacher and students.

The field of communication has yet to establish any sharply defined boundaries or uncontested theories or principles, yet some theories are more useful and helpful to one person than to others. In its complexity, the subject of interpersonal communication is ultimately a personal subject. It needs to be experienced, used, and applied by each individual in his or her own style and manner.

ORGANIZATION

Part One, "The Basis of Interpersonal Communication," provides the foundation upon which the other two parts are built. It defines communication, both intrapersonal and interpersonal, as processes of creating meaning. It helps students explore personal perceptual processes, self-images, and their interactions with the perceptual processes of others. Part Two, "Aspects of Communication," analyzes how language, thoughts, body, emotions, and actions interact in complex, sometimes ambivalent ways. Part Three, "Growth through Communication," integrates and unifies the concepts in the first two parts, applying them to interpersonal relationships, resolving differences in perception, and exploring ways to improve the quality of communication.

SPECIAL TOPICS/FEATURES

Making the assumption that communicating is a *people process*, I emphasize the person and his or her use of language, mind, body, emotions, and behavior. After experiencing these separate aspects of communicating, we must synthesize the parts into a unified whole. Special topics include ways of enhancing self-esteem, exploring personal values and goals, awareness of emotions and the part they play in communicating, empathy and conflict in developing significant relationships.

In other texts, activities are separated from theory, often appearing at the end of chapters. In this book, activities appear at specific points throughout the chapters. They are primarily group experiences, and serve to expand the central concepts and ideas in the text. Participation in these activities gives us personal experience of the theoretical concepts underlying interpersonal transactions. Personal involvement in classroom activities is essential in effective skill development which can then be applied in daily living.

Additional activities appear in *Communicating with Myself: A Journal*, a supplement which accompanies this text. The journal contains a wealth of exploratory ways to become better acquainted with aspects of the self which may be hidden from consciousness. The paradox is that although communicating and relating rest on a foundation of personal exploration and development, self-clarification depends upon our transactions with other human beings.

Both this book and the journal employ self-directed learning approaches that are open-ended and unlimited. They require an active commitment to exploring and discovering one's own unique communication processes. Therefore, each of us will discover and create our own human communication systems in direct proportion to the degree of commitment we make to the process.

I want to thank Helga, Denos, Tom, David, Sharon, and all the individuals close to me who listened and made suggestions. And I especially want to thank Larry, who "held my hand" for a year; and Margaret, who worked nights and weekends. Without their support, I never would have completed this project.

Jacquelyn B. Carr

Contents

Communicating and Relating

Part One

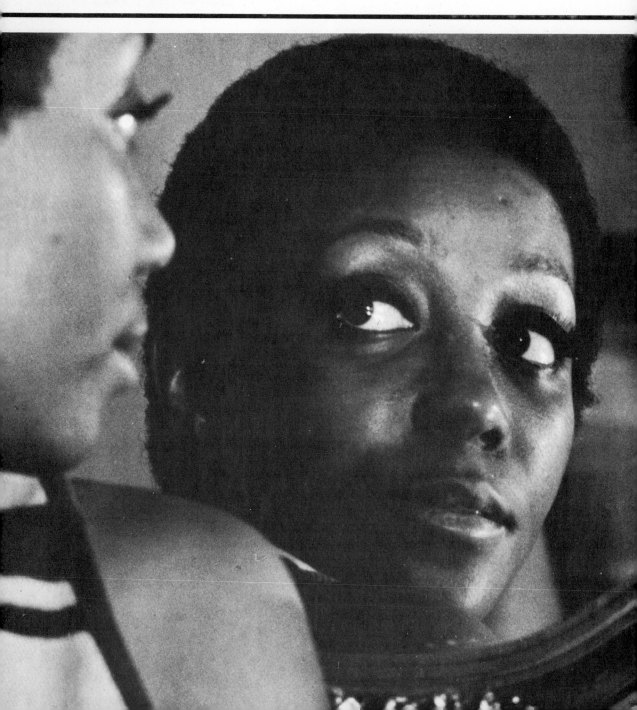

The Basis of
Interpersonal Communication

Each of the twelve chapters in this book is a small unit. Several of these units together make up the three parts. In Part One, The Basis of Interpersonal Communication, Chapter 1 defines communication as both an intrapersonal and interpersonal process. Chapter 2 explores the processes of personal and social perception. Chapter 3 involves creating a self-concept, and Chapter 4 suggests ways to communicate acceptance and support to others.

When we take things apart, analysis leads to some answers. But insights alone are not enough. We must synthesize the smaller units and parts into a larger whole. Finding meaning in life is similar to putting separate notes into chords and chords into symphonies.

Your life will reveal to you its unique meaning and its personal goals, its purposes and directions, as you integrate the events and relationships that occur. Every event, situation, and relationship in your life is open-ended, part of a process. The content of your life can only be given form and meaning from inside through intrapersonal com-

munication. You will feed thoughts and images back into the stream of your life. Then it will begin to settle at some new level. We all work in our own place, in our own time, in our own way. No outside source or force can give meaning to an individual. You must create your own meaning.

Only you can work with the content of your life. Yet there are valuable methods for working with these intangible, inner processes of creating meaning, perception, and self-concept. An unfolding occurs when we work together to reflect back to each other what we discover. The multiple interplay of insights from reading, writing, discussing, and experiencing these units of interpersonal communication has a cumulative effect which generates energy within each of us.

We come together in a social setting to give one another support. We descend into the well of our own life until we come to an underground spring—a stream containing the experiences of all humanity. Each of us must capture the meaning of our personal life before we can reach beyond our personal realities to find unity with all others.

The creative process is a living thing, implanted, as it were, in the souls of men.

Jung

1

Creating Meaning

COMMUNICATION AS CREATING MEANING

Since time began, human beings have devised religions, philosophies, and social systems to answer questions about the meaning and the processes of being human. Ultimately, each of us must create his or her *own* answers; the answers other people find do not fit you or me. Yet often we cannot find our answers alone, so we learn to communicate and relate to others. Your ability to "create" yourself, to answer your own questions, is limited primarily by your awareness of your choices as well as by how well you communicate. Thus: *You can shape your life by expanding your awareness and knowledge.*

Knowledge and information added to experience can lead you to discover and develop your special talents and individual capacities, help you make decisions, and guide you in finding your own answers to what it means *to you* to be human.

Human communication is the process of creating meaning. Because we communicate constantly, giving the process little more attention than we give to breathing, we are often unaware of all the complexities inherent in the process of creating meaning. *Talking* involves knowledge of linguistic meaning. *Thinking* results in attitudes, beliefs, judgments, and differing points of view that involve intellectual meaning. Our bodies communicate nonverbally, often expressing *feelings* or emotional meaning. And our *behavior* not only communicates our real intentions but also coordinates and reflects all these aspects of communicating.

Meaning is created simultaneously on many levels—talking, thinking, being, feeling, and behaving—much of which occurs unconsciously. In the process of creating meaning, we have an *intention*. Whether you are conscious of it or not, you intend to produce some kind of result or get something you want when you communicate. Therefore: *Creating meaning involves intention.* When we are aware of our intentions, we can be more responsible for the results.

You undoubtedly have some personal theories about communicating (creating meaning). You may use these theories without being aware of them. These theories are constructed from your experiences of yourself as a unique individual, as a member of the human species, and as a part of the universe. Education in communication can help you expand these theories by helping you find answers to such questions as:

1. What is the special meaning of my life?

2. In what ways can people share their meanings with each other?

3. What is the purpose of human existence?

Creating meaning in your life, in your interpersonal relationships, and in your world is the subject matter of interpersonal communication.

In this introductory chapter, we will examine the roles that awareness and consciousness play in both intrapersonal and interpersonal communication; we will look at the components and purposes of interpersonal communication; and we will explore what lies beyond our present levels of communicating. Although defining terms and discussing how they are to be used leads to more responsible use of language, communication confusions may still occur because of differing realities, a subject covered in Chapter 2.

The study of interpersonal communication provides a learning opportunity, a tool for self-discovery, a social environment, and a "space" to explore oneself in relationship to the world. You will have chances in this book to look inward, to observe social interaction with others, to become aware of both verbal and nonverbal communication, and to see yourself and others in relationship to the culture.

Because most of us give communication little conscious thought, we often fail to communicate the message we intend. Awareness can make communicating more effective and relationships more fulfilling. Communication is the process through which we develop our individual humanness and our relationships with others. Every aspect of our lives from birth to death is affected by our desire to relate to others. We cannot relate well until we recognize that *everything affects communication and communication affects everything:* our environment, other people, ourselves.

As we explore communicating and relating, we will experience "having been here before." One student said to me, "I am enjoying just about everything, but I am increasingly aware that I am merely relearning what I already know." Becoming aware is not the creation of a new state but the recognition of what always has been.

When you read what is written here, you may often feel that you already know it. *Yet to know the words or to "know" the experience is not necessarily to know the meaning.* While the meaning may be inherent in your responses, it may not be explicit in your consciousness. Studying and experiencing communication can help us bring this information to awareness. Becoming fully aware of what we already know allows us to *choose* our direction in life instead of simply drifting along or allowing others to choose for us.

Basically this is a course in *creating.* Each of us has the ability to create our life. When we realize that we create our problems, we are more willing to learn to create the solutions. When we let go of the negative past, we let go of who we were. Then we gain energy and power to concentrate on who we are and who we are becoming. Creating new and positive patterns takes time and intention. You have the power to change and the freedom to create your own reality.

We shall not cease from exploration
And the end of all our exploring
Will be to arrive where we started
And know the place for the first time.

T. S. Eliot

Creating Meaning through Awareness

You cannot teach a man anything. You can only help him discover it within himself.

Galileo

A synonym for awareness is consciousness, two words we will be using interchangeably. *To be conscious is to be awake to one's own existence, sensations, feelings, and actions.* People are never either wholly aware or wholly unaware. At any given moment, we are more aware of certain parts of ourselves, of our intentions, than of other parts or intentions. And it is often difficult to recognize, measure, describe, or observe ourselves.

Awareness (consciousness) increases an individual's freedom of choice. Being aware or conscious does not *guarantee* that you will put that information to use. Yet ultimately a great deal of value will come from directly experiencing what is true for you from your interactions with people, from your interactions with information shared, and from your responses to the diversity in the world around you.

This book offers a guide for becoming more conscious. It also offers a source of motivation—a collection of experiences and ideas that can serve as models for improving communication. As students and instructor respond, share experiences, and offer each other helpful suggestions, they will be creating both individually and as a group their own consciousness—their own directions. Developing communication skills is an ongoing process throughout our lives.

The interconnections between language and human relationships are very complex. No theory has yet been developed that can encompass the multiple facets involved. Many techniques have been developed for exploring these interconnections, however. And much can be learned that will enrich our relationships and our lives. Only you can choose from the theories, general principles, skills, activities, guidelines, and suggestions offered here. Then you can adapt this information for use in your personal relationships with yourself, others, and your culture.

Although knowledge and information can help you understand your personal experiences, you cannot learn to communicate simply by reading *about* communication any more than you can learn to play the piano by reading about it. The whole process includes reading, listening, observing, questioning, writing, experiencing, and relating.

Every human being is constantly evolving. At times, in this course, you may feel that you are in a hall of infinite mirrors. You will be looking at yourself to observe how you appear. You will be confirming this perception by noting how you appear to others. You will be looking at others and sharing with them how they appear to you. In this sharing of perceptions, we embark upon a joint venture of expanding awareness.

At times you may be filled with a feeling of unreality. When you put your perceptions into words, you "know" *that description* is not you or the other person. Like taking a still photograph, you will be freezing a moment from a motion picture that really is as long and varied and continuous as an individual life. Yet the still photograph can be very useful. It gives us a chance to slow down, to become fully conscious of individual aspects of the process. Then, like a symphony when we reintegrate the parts, the whole composition will be experienced on a much higher plane with more fulfillment.

Some people feel that thinking and writing about the self may be an "ego trip"—that using the words *I*, *me*, and *mine* is self-centered, selfish, or conceited. But our growth develops outward from the self. To grow, then, it is appropriate that we continually return to the self. Ultimately our goal is to find a balance between commitment to ourselves and commitment to others and to society.

The complex process of communicating is intimately connected to language. *Language is any set or system of symbols used by people to communicate with one another.* The study of communication explores the ways in which language can be used to expand one's ability to define self, to relate effectively to others, and to make a personal contribution to our culture. Before we can tackle the problems of humanity, however, we must find some answers to the many questions in our own lives, and we must move toward a clearer understanding of our own complex personalities. Describing and exploring personal realities and experiences—and then *sharing* them—is a valuable part of this process.

Sharing *involves taking a perception or an experience and recreating it by putting it "out there" to look at.* Every time I share something, I make it more real. And I gain more mastery over it. Sharing helps me to overcome barriers to my awareness of my experiences. When I make my experiences more real, I can defuse the painful ones and recreate and share the joyful ones. I can look at them; I can move around, through, and beyond them. I can get in touch with what works in my life.

When I feel confused or troubled, I often find another person and ask him or her to listen. I say, "I'm stuck in something. I want to get unstuck. Will you listen while I work to get out of it?" My intention is to work out my problem for myself. When I share, I give another person a chance to give me support. I find many people asking me to listen in return. And when I listen, I get a chance to give them support. If I can't find another person, I write. Writing is a form of sharing with myself. It makes what I am trying to understand more real and more tangible—I can look at it. And sometimes in the process of writing, the communication problem solves itself.

Activities are offered throughout this book so that you can experience parts of yourself in tangible ways and share them with others. You *always* have the right to pass. You can always choose to share or not share at whatever level you wish.

We share meaning with other people.

This exercise is designed to help you identify the strongest aspects of your self—the foundations on which you can build.

These are ten of my strengths:
-         •
-         •
-         •
-         •
-         •

I can use these strengths to build on in my growth toward these three personal goals:
-
-
-

Take some time to think about how you personally view communication. Athletics, movies, and reading are often used as subjects of communication. What kinds of subjects are important to you? How would you like to communicate better?

- How effective am I in "talking to myself"? Are my thoughts often confused or disquieting? Are they clear and insightful? How do I reach conclusions, solve problems, or resolve uncomfortable feelings?

- How effective am I in communicating with one other person? How do I express myself in a one-to-one situation?

- How effective am I as a communicator in a small group or in a class? Am I primarily a listener or a talker? Can I hold my own? Do I try to control? Do I hope that others will not notice me?

- How do I share myself with others? How do I feel about sharing? Do I like it when others share themselves with me?

Intrapersonal Meaning

Intrapersonal communication is the process of creating meaning within the self. Before we can explore communication with others, we must have some understanding of how we create meaning

This above all: to thine own self be true.

Shakespeare

We create meaning patterns within the self.

patterns within the self. If we are unaware of how we process information, we will be less conscious of how we attach meaning to the external world—which includes other people as well as the environment and the situation. Knowing how I as a unique individual communicate with myself and how I can expand my consciousness of that process will enhance my ability to create meaning for myself and share that meaning with others.

We have a "memory bank" of experiences from which, at any given moment, we can select, interpret, and evaluate incoming information. Outside each of us, in the form of external stimuli, something occurs that we process through our sensory equipment (eyes, ears, skin, nose, mouth). How we deal with much of this information depends on our cultural and social environment. We select certain stimuli and block out others. We spend a great deal of energy considering, reacting to, and making *sense* out of what comes to us through our senses. In the process, we develop our own realities, our own impressions of what the world is like—we develop a "personal consciousness."

Intrapersonal communication, communicating with the self, occurs when we think, feel, or act, as well as when we verbalize to ourselves. By exploring intrapersonal communication, we observe ourselves and become more aware of our personal consciousness—our self-concept. We get in touch with what reality means to us and what is real to us about ourselves. We get to know ourselves better through experiencing body, emotions, and mind. As you become aware of the language you use, you will begin to hear how you talk to yourself. Moreover, observing your behavior will give you more information useful for improving communication.

Each thought we have is part of our personal consciousness. And our thoughts are always changing. We may see the same object, hear the same tone, taste the same food, but our consciousness of these experiences changes each time. This changing series of experiences is always modified by previous experiences. We often feel strange about our subsequent views of the same things. We sometimes wonder how we could have responded the way we did the first time. We all experience pluralistic thinking, duplicity, contradictions, paradoxes, and inconsistencies. We are always in flux, never the same person we were before. We continue, moment by moment, to add to what we were a minute ago.

How do we get to know who we are? In Chapter 2 we will examine how we create reality through selective perception. In Chapter 3 we explore our self-concept. We learn in Chapter 4 about communicating with others. Then in Chapters 5 and 6 we concentrate on how we use language and how our minds work. In Chapter 7 we study our body to become more aware of how it functions and what it can tell us. In Chapter 8 we concentrate on awareness of feelings and how to express them. And in Chapter 9 we gain some insight into our behavior patterns. Through the study of these processes—language, mind, body, emotions, behavior—we will see that communication involves our whole being. Although it is necessary to divide up the subject matter in some meaningful way, you and I are not so divided. The interplay of all these aspects of ourselves is infinite. And, with so many possibilities to explore, it is exciting.

Some fields of study such as psychology, sociology, and anthropology deal with human behavior in the aggregate; yet you and I want to know how we differ as individuals. *There is only one person in the world exactly like you.* You are truly unique. There never has been and never will be a person exactly like you. A genetic code gives instructions that tell each cell its process: its sequence of development. As the embryo develops the cells differentiate. The baby at birth is an individual, a new and original arrangement. You are a very special creation, and you have the capacity to develop or "create" yourself. Your ability to create yourself is limited primarily by your awareness of the possibilities. Expanding your awareness, knowledge, and experiences can lead you to discover and develop your special talents and individual capacities, help you make decisions, and guide you in finding your own answers to what it means to be human.

The process of communication is easier when you know something about another person. The information you provide can help others in your class begin to know you.

Personal data

Name:

Birthplace:

Family (race, religion, father's/mother's occupation, number of brothers and sisters and their ages):

Marital status:

Activities/hobbies/sports:

Travel/vacations:

Education:

Major areas of interest:

Descriptions

Describe yourself:

Describe your father:

Describe your mother:

Describe another person who is important to you:

Describe what really makes you happy:

Describe what really makes you angry:

Describe any health or family problems:

Describe tentative future plans:

Choose a partner. Exchange your personal information sheets. Ask each other questions. Let the questions and answers evolve into a personal dialogue about yourselves. Then move into groups of five or six people in the class. Share whatever personal information you choose. Allow the discussion to include information about yourself beyond what is listed.

Interpersonal Meaning

Every facet of our life from birth to death is affected by our ability to relate to other people, which in turn is affected by how well we know ourselves. *Interpersonal communication is the complicated process of sharing meaning with others.* Meaning exists, sometimes, beyond an individual; yet not beyond people. Together we create meaning. We can create meaning without being able to experience meaning (as in the case of pain)—we can talk about cancer or a heart attack, for example, without experiencing them. Furthermore, there are experiences for which we are unable to create meaning in the form of language or even thoughts. Therefore, the study of communication is not the experience itself. Yet the experience can be a source of illustration, a way of sharing. When we become more conscious of the many aspects of communication we can choose among the many alternatives to find those which work best.

Who is it who can tell me who I am?

Shakespeare

We are born into human relationships. No human being has ever been born "alone." Part of our personal identity is formed by these relationships. We experience ourselves through the responses of others. These images of ourselves, reflected back from others, may often be inconsistent or contradictory. The study of interpersonal communication can help us deal with these discrepancies. It can lead us to find and establish and foster close relationships; exert influence; express and evoke love. Or, conversely, we can erect barriers, block communication, put others on the defensive. And we can function anywhere between these two extremes. Since interaction with others is unavoidable, becoming aware of our choices can change the quality of our relationships. To understand how people do or do not communicate successfully may be the most important objective of your life.

Interpersonal communication is communication that occurs between two or more persons in the process of relating. Communication becomes more effective when each participant recognizes his or her own uniqueness and acknowledges the uniqueness of the other person. Interpersonal communication is itself unique each time one person interacts with another.

Components of Interpersonal Communication   In the interpersonal communication process, three components—people, messages, and environment—are interwoven in **transactions.** When two people are communicating, they are *sending and receiving* messages simultaneously. We often operate under the illusion that one person is sending (talking) and the other is receiving (listening). The sender continually searches the face and body for the reactions of the listener, who is sending conscious and unconscious nonverbal messages. If the listener looks confused, the sender may repeat or add information. The listener's reactions (attention or distraction, understanding or confusion, approval or disapproval) often cause the sender to alter the message. This reciprocal interaction is circular. It is a process of simultaneous

People, messages, and environment are interwoven in transactions.

influences that create meaning and recreate meaning and create and recreate experiences.

People—unique and complicated individuals, each with self-perception, beliefs, attitudes, and self-esteem—in transactions with other unique beings would be complicated enough. But we also have to deal with their messages, which are couched in both verbal and nonverbal symbols. People are able to create messages and meanings because of their ability to use symbols, usually words that represent actions and things. Often we are unaware of the effect of these symbols on ourselves and others in relationships. Finally, the *environmental* component—which includes all our institutions, the social context, and the total culture, in addition to the physical setting and location for each

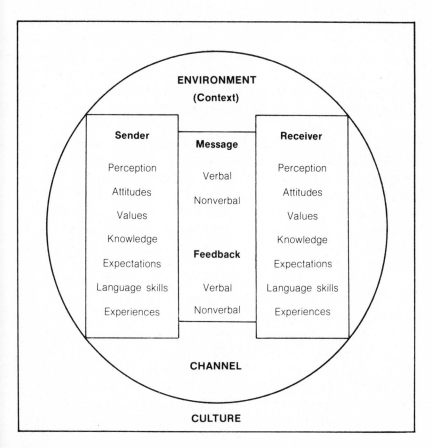

Figure 1–1 A communication model.

transaction—interacts with the people and their complex messages.

There are several major elements in the process of communicating. Figure 1–1, a communication model, will help you to understand material covered in later chapters. *A communication model is a blueprint of how communication works.* In Chapter 11 you will be asked to create your own model to illustrate your understanding of the communication process. Creating your own model will mean much more to you than accepting one devised by someone else.

Communication includes our environment, other people, and ourselves. Communication is **continuous**—coming from the past, occurring now, and moving into the future. Another characteristic of interpersonal communication as a process is that it is **irreversible.** If you say or do something, you cannot take it back. You can add to it, but added remarks only continue the process—they do not erase or reverse it. Moreover, we have little control over what others perceive, what interpretations they make of our messages, or how they are going to feel about what we say. Thus we can see that interpersonal communication is more than its components. It is a dynamic process like life itself.

Purposes of Interpersonal Communication   Interpersonal communication has many purposes. First, as we will see in the next chapter, we continually search for **reality** by testing or measuring our personal reality against the reality of others. Through the process of feedback, we use others to check our impressions of ourselves and others in the world. Through communication, we organize our physical environment, get information about it, adapt to it.

In addition, we try to achieve a **personal identity** by communicating with others. We experience ourselves through the responses of others to us. We hope to obtain a clear reflection of our image from others who can help us evaluate inconsistent or contradictory images. As we will learn in Chapter 3, we want to achieve **self-esteem**—a positive self-image reflected back from interaction with others. Each time we meet another person, we implicitly seek validation of ourselves as acceptable persons. We seek to enhance our personal growth through our relationships.

We also want some **control** over our social environment. To function socially and securely, we need to relate to others. In our attempts to control our social environment, we negotiate with others. Sometimes we cooperate; at other times, we compete. Sometimes in order to achieve control we even conflict with others. We often work with others to improve human life and existence on this planet. When we cooperate to improve human life, our goal in communicating may be to **share information**—to transmit a specific message in order to create a product or give a service in our daily work. But in relationships our goal is more often simply to communicate with others in a way that ensures a sense of mutual well-being. We simply come together to enjoy the company and conversation of others. If we repeatedly find that communication with a particular person is not enjoyable, we tend to avoid that person. Therefore, one purpose of communication is to **experience pleasure** in the company of others.

Today we are very much concerned about human transactions. Increasing automation and complexity have created a growing condition of impersonality—a climate in which many people yearn for closer personal ties with other human beings. We need to improve our relationships for our personal fulfillment as well as for achieving harmony and surviving among our fellow human beings. Interpersonal communication is the foundation on which we can build *relationships*.

In effective *intra*personal communication, a person evolves a concept of something, develops a feeling about it, and names it. In this sense, we create a picture for ourselves out of our experience of something. In effective *inter*personal communication, that picture (concept, name, feeling) is shared with another person in such a way that the other person can also create in his or her mind a similar picture (concept, name, feeling). Thus: *Effective interpersonal communication includes creating and sharing intended meanings with others.* If I can physically point out a referent (chair, desk, book) to you, we have a good chance of sharing accurate meaning because the object is *concrete* and *specific;* we can both look at and experience the same object. However, most of the things—feelings, hopes, plans, experiences—we talk about are impossible to point to. How, then, do we create similar pictures to share when we cannot look at what is being referred to?

The answer is that it is difficult. Communication is a process that is not easy to control. If you say something to me, I hear your words, interpret your behavior, watch your body for nonverbal messages, and respond to each word, expression, and body movement. As I react and respond to each unit of your message, you are also watching me. Then, if I respond verbally to your concept, the responding and reacting in both of us become intertwined in a **complex transaction** composed of the concepts, messages, words, feelings, and pictures that we exchange and experience. And all this is connected to all the preceding communication experiences in our lives. Moreover, humans have cultures that affect and are affected by the values of all their members. Thus much of what happens between two people in a single communication event is related to all the communication values of the culture. Yet somehow we do communicate—and often quite well.

So the process is complex, and sometimes it may seem very difficult to communicate effectively. But the search for better communication is definitely worthwhile. Not only can better communication help us develop more pleasurable social relationships, but the process of searching helps us grow.

Interpersonal communication includes getting to know others.

- *Getting acquainted:* The class sits in a circle. A volunteer gives his or her first name. The person to his left says, "This is Ann (pointing to the first person); I am Joe." The person to his left says, "This is Ann; this is Joe; I am Mary." Once every person has had a turn, volunteers can repeat the exercise.

- At the next class meeting, repeat the preceding exercise; this time, each person can add a descriptive word or statement. For example: "I'm Mary and I'm nervous."

- *Interviews:* Choose a partner. Each of you has five minutes to talk about yourself to your partner. Each couple decides who will talk to the group about the other one first. Introduce your partner and tell what you know about that person. Then your partner will do the same for you. Mention nonverbal impressions that you got.

    As your partner introduces you, notice what he or she chooses to say, what he or she remembers of the interview, and how he or she presents you to the class. Write down (a) how accurately you feel your partner presented you, (b) how you feel about what you said about yourself and what you liked or disliked about what you said, and (*c*) how you feel about what your partner selected to tell the class about you. Give your partner feedback on your observations and feelings.

BEYOND INTERPERSONAL COMMUNICATION

The growth of interpersonal awareness precedes the development of social conscience at community, national, and world levels. The search for self often leads to a search for a world view. We are becoming increasingly aware that knowledge and understanding at these levels have their origins in nonrational intuition, unpredictable imagination, and the creativity inside each of us.

Many scientists in leading universities around the world today are studying altered states of consciousness. Even the "hard" sciences such as physics are in a revolutionary process of changing theories and concepts about their perceptions. Newtonian reality dealt with absolute space, absolute time, and gravity. Einstein's theory of relativity suggests that travelers carry their own space and time. Today many scientists agree that we can perceive reality fluidly in a multiplicity of dimensions.

The meaning which a being has to fulfill is something beyond himself. It is never just himself.

> *Viktor Frankl*

Social conscience appears at community, national, and world levels.

Culturally we are experiencing a communication revolution. At the same time, each individual is also in a process of personal evolution to a higher state of awareness than he or she now experiences. Related to individual awareness in communicating are an individual's purposes, intentions, choices, and responsibilities. Expanded consciousness of purpose, intention, free choice, and responsibility can lead to a higher quality of communication.

Purpose *and* **intention** *in communicating are often unconscious in sender and receiver.* These words are often used interchangeably, but we are going to make a distinction between them. Purpose implies a direction that we put before ourselves. Our purpose in studying interpersonal communication is to become better communicators, and as we proceed through this course we hope to move in that direction. But our intention will communicate itself through our behavior. If I intend to lose weight but keep eating more food than my body can use, I must question my *real* intentions. Usually we state our intentions by saying "I want . . . ." For example: "I want to stop smoking." "I want to learn to play the piano." "I want to exercise more." I can check my intentions by looking at my behavior to find out whether I do it or not. Intentions can be strong or weak and have to do with *intensity.* As we proceed through this text, the process of becoming more aware will include looking at our behavior as a measure of our intentions.

Choice *and* **responsibility** *are also related to expanding consciousness.* We only have as many choices as we are aware of. If we can think of three possible solutions to a problem, we have only three choices. If we can think of five, we have five choices. And in this book we will *assume* that we are responsible for our behavior whether or not we have all the information we need and whether or not we are aware of all the choices. We also assume that some individuals will intend to avoid taking responsibility for their behavior—which is their choice. The advantage is that they can blame others or find fault outside themselves. When we take responsibility, we choose ownership: to own up to our choices.

This network of themes will be expanded throughout the book. In our movement to get beyond where we are today, in this process of growing and expanding, at times some of these concepts will be a little beyond our grasp. We are struggling with assumptions rather than the truth. There is nothing here for you to *believe* in the sense that it is either true or not true. You do not have to believe or disbelieve these assumptions about expanding awareness, purpose and intention, choice, and responsibility. You can choose to test them through your experiences to see if they work for you and if they improve the quality of your communication.

As you explore this book, be as creatively skeptical as you can. It is your own experience of reality that will show you the path for you rather than any theory or concept presented here. Listen to your own inner voice. Now we will explore how each of us can expand our perceptions of reality beyond current boundaries and, in doing so, dramatically increase the quality and the effectiveness of our communication.

FOR FURTHER READING

Cronkhite, Gary. *Communication and Awareness.* Menlo Park, Calif.: Cummings, 1976.
> One of the author's main points is that communication is largely a process of becoming aware of what we have been doing all our lives . . . communicating.

Jung, Carl. *Man and His Symbols.* New York: Dell, 1968.
> Jung's last published work delves deeply into the symbolic processes and their effects on thinking, feeling, behavior, and communication with both the self and others.

Miller, Gerald R. *An Introduction to Speech Communication.* 2nd ed. Indianapolis: Bobbs-Merrill, 1972.
> The author presents a thorough coverage of the basic theory of the communication process.

Ogden, C. K., and I. A. Richards. *The Meaning of Meaning.* New York: Harcourt Brace, 1956.
> The authors study the influence of symbols on thought and human affairs.

Stevens, John O. *Awareness: Exploring, Experimenting, Experiencing.* Lafayette, Calif.: Real Press, 1971.
> This book of exercises is designed to expand self-awareness.

Wilmot, W. W., and J. R. Wenberg. *Communication Involvement: Personal Perspectives.* New York: Wiley, 1974.
> The authors stress the personal interactions that occur in the communication process.

2

Perception and Communication

PERCEPTION

Perception *is the process of sensory stimulation being translated into organized experience.* The key words are *sensory* and *experience.* The senses respond to stimuli, yet these stimuli would have little meaning if they were not interpreted by the individual who organizes them into a personal framework of experiences. Thus perception is affected by past interpretations that build on each other.

People often perceive what is in accord with their personal needs, motives, and interests. We screen what the senses receive and determine how sense perceptions get organized into experience. We tend to see what we *think* we will see. The mind keeps insisting on evidence to support what it thinks, and it rejects evidence that goes against it. Often, in fact, it will not even let our eyes see such evidence. If we wish to see in new ways, we must change the way we think. This change takes practice and patience. It also takes *intention,* or will. By changing our thinking and altering our concepts of things, we bring fresh experiences and fresh insights to whatever we see.

25

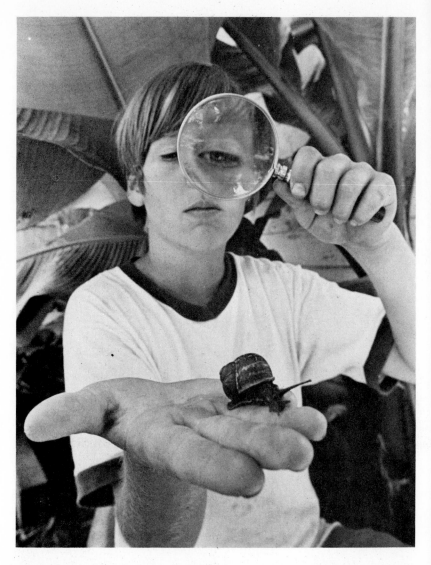

Perception is the process of translating sensory stimulation into organized experience.

To change our ways of perceiving reality, we must become aware of how we limit our present perceptions. For example, we can learn how **selectivity** affects perception. And we can become aware of **illusions** and **preconceptions** that distort reality. And finally, through the study of the effects of **environment** on perception, we can expand our awareness of the perceptual processes.

Selectivity of Perception

Perception is selective. We choose what we see and put what we see into a coherent pattern to fit our needs. We organize and interpret along personal lines. We respond selectively to establish some predictability in an otherwise confusing world. Selective perception is based on:

1. *Physiological differences:* One person is color-blind, another needs glasses to read; another hears notes in harmony while his brother is tone-deaf. Biological rhythms, hormonal balances, and health affect perceptual selection.

2. *Spatial differences:* Position in space differs for each person in a room. Each one is the center (the "I") of his or her field of vision and hearing. No other person in the room sees all the objects or other people in the same spatial order or distance.

3. *Psychological differences:* Individual values, emotions, and personalities make every person see differently.

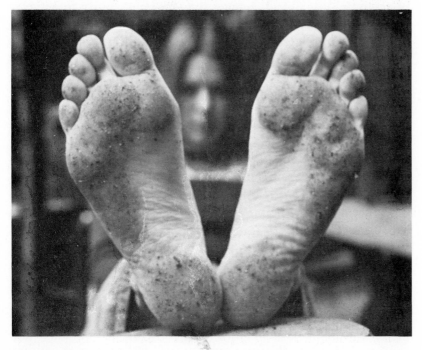

The observer's position in space affects his or her perception.

4. *Experiential differences:* Birth order in a family (first, middle, or last), education, past learning, cultural differences, differences in income, and language differences affect perception.

5. *Contextual differences:* Time of day, age, relationship, and all the other variables that make each situation different change perception.

Every minute we are literally bombarded with stimuli, but it is physically impossible to respond simultaneously to all of them. When we concentrate on what is being said (for example, when we take notes for an exam), we often lose touch with our bodies. Then, when we stand up, we may experience pain or find that one foot has gone to sleep.

As we have noted, past experiences also influence our selection of perceptions. A child may have great affection for an old doll given her by her grandfather and may see the doll as beautiful no matter how discolored and hairless it may be. Another child might throw the doll away.

Emotional predispositions accompanied by characteristic actions and physiological changes influence our ability to perceive clearly what goes on around us. Depression usually fatigues us while pleasure elates us both mentally and physically. "Seeing red," "flying into a blind rage," and "love is blind" are common phrases that express the effects of emotion on perception.

We never experience the "reality" of an outside stimulus directly. We perceive only a small fraction of what physically exists. Robert Ornstein says that in one-thirtieth of a second we translate what is "out there" in the process of **physiological selection.** Moreover, the values of our culture have further reduced what we see. If we expand our awareness of all these variables, we can become more conscious of how they affect our perceptions. Then we will better understand how our differences in perception influence our ability to communicate and relate.

Illusion and Perception

Absolute truth cannot be arrived at through our perceptions because no two people perceive things identically. Perception does not literally reveal the environment. And experiments show that our perceptions are often illusory—one study found that poor children see a coin as much larger in size than do rich children.

Illusions occur for many reasons. In the first place, we tend to perceive things as complete and unified—if parts are left out or repeated, we fill them in. In addition to this tendency, we often see things as constant. As you move your hand close to your face, for example, it will appear larger. Yet you perceive the size, shape, and color of your hand as constant.

Context also affects our perception. If we put a gray square inside a black one, it will appear lighter than the same gray square inside a white one. In Figure 2–1, 13 appears as the *letter* B or as the *number* 13, depending upon context.

Figure 2–1 Effect of context.

Surrounding conditions affect our perceptions. Each of us perceives reality in different ways, and this fact often presents us with difficulties when we try to communicate with others. If we forget that each human being has a unique "reality," communication can break down.

Figure 2–2 Closure: Filling in the gaps.

The term **closure** is used to explain our tendency to perceive certain figures as if they were complete or closed rather than incomplete or unclosed. In Figure 2–2, we see a square, a triangle, and a circle; yet all three figures are incomplete or unclosed.

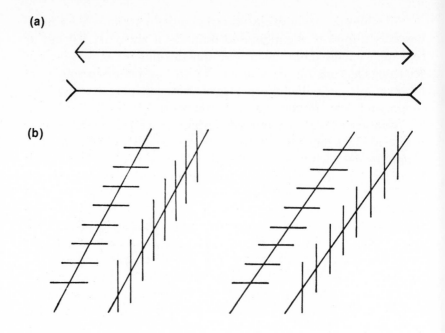

Figure 2–3 Perceptual illusions.

Our world is a spatial world, yet our perceptions do not necessarily correspond with the physical dimensions of objects. For example, in part (a) of Figure 2–3, both lines are the same length. In part (b) there are two sets of parallel lines. **Illusion** occurs in the relationships of objects due to the total organization of the surrounding patterns of objects. Context, closure, and total organization of lines, figures, and objects often result in perceptual illusions. If such simple perceptions as lines can be illusions, it is understandable how our more complex perceptions of ourselves, others, and our world are seldom the same.

Preconception and Perception

An old fable tells about six blind men who went to "see" an elephant. Each man approached the elephant from a different direction. One man felt the broad side and said, "The elephant is like a wall." The second, feeling the tusk, said, "The elephant is like a spear." The third touched the trunk and said, "The elephant is like a snake." The fourth felt the knee and said, "The elephant is like a tree." The fifth touched the ear and said, "The elephant is like a fan." The sixth man seized the swinging tail and said, "The elephant is like a rope." Each was partly right, but all were partly wrong.

Like these blind men, each of us comes from a different direction and looks at life in a different light. Past experiences and values create individual mental sets. A **mental set** is formed by conditioning—by a combination of experiences and values— and is the tendency of a person to pay attention to certain features of a situation. Just as an alarm clock is set to ring at a certain time, so people are "set" to perceive certain changes in their environments. This preconditioning may be a result of individual occupations or interests. At the scene of an accident, for example, a doctor will try to find out if anyone is injured; a policeman will be concerned with the cause of the accident; a mechanic will focus on the damage to the cars. Each of us responds to stimuli in accordance with individual interests and conditioning.

In one experiment, subjects were shown nonsense words flashed rapidly on a screen. One group of subjects was told the words were in categories of birds and animals. Another group was told the words were connected with travel. Both groups were shown the same nonsense syllables, such as *pasrot* and *chack*. Those subjects conditioned to expect animal words perceived the words *parrot* and *chick*. The others expecting travel words saw *passport* and *check*.

Perception is not a simple process, but by acknowledging the complexity of preconception and attempting to understand mental sets, we may be able to accept other people's perceptions and communicate our own more effectively. The process of receiving information through sensory stimulation is subject to error when translated into experience because of selective perception, the various effects of past experiences, optical illusions, and psychological and emotional states. What an individual "receives" is not necessarily what any other individual "perceives" nor what is actually present. In our attempts at both intrapersonal and interpersonal communication, an awareness of perceptual problems can result in improved relationships and understandings.

- Form groups of three to five.
- Hold up one of the signs shown in the figure below for several seconds and then remove it.
- Ask the group what they saw.
- Continue presenting the sign for several seconds until all participants discover the errors.

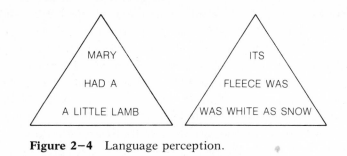

Figure 2–4   Language perception.

The preceding exercise illustrates **mental set.** In our culture, most of us have learned this little nursery rhyme. Language is conditioned, thus we often fill in missing words or do not see added words where they do not ordinarily occur. **Preconception** is a form of conditioning which affects our perceptions not only of language but of our world and the people in it.

Environment and Perception

People, events, or things in our current environment also influence our perceptions. Our attention is drawn by such external variables as the following:

1. *Changes:* changes in color, noise, size, movement
2. *Repetition:* repeating a stimulus (such as a dripping faucet) over and over
3. *Intensity:* a loud noise, a strong perfume, a large object
4. *Contrast:* anything different such as a dark spot on white
5. *Novelty:* anything new or strange in contrast with the familiar
6. *Distraction:* anything that changes the focus of attention (such as noise)

In a research study of distraction, a group of typists worked for one day under very noisy conditions. The next day they worked inside quiet, soundproof partitions. By measuring oxygen intake, experimenters concluded that the energy cost of attention under distracting conditions was significantly greater than when there was no noise. Becoming aware of these many environmental influences on our perceptions can broaden our choices of control over these external variables.

By expanding our consciousness of the complexity of human perception, we improve our ability to communicate and relate. *Knowing that perception is selective, that we fit new perceptions in preset patterns, and that external variables affect perception, we are better able to remove limits to our perceptions of our world.* We are also able to understand more easily why others perceive the world the way they do. This facilitates communication by tearing down perceptual differences and finding areas of similarity between ourselves and others.

These suggestions are intended to help you expand your perceptual awareness.

- Imagine you are a photographer. Today, when you leave class, look for "new" photographs—open your senses to new ways of perceiving what you ordinarily see. Look at the front of the place where you live. Look up and down the street with the intention of seeing something new. Walk into your house, apartment, or room. Notice things you have not noticed before and note how they might appear from different angles, with different lighting, coloring, and focusing. Imagine that you are going to take pictures with the intention of creating something new from a familiar object or situation. Then write about this experience.

- Changes in our perceptions can show us how selective perception works:

  1. Think of something that used to have great meaning for you.

  2. Give an example of selective perception from your personal experience.

  3. Tell how your perceptions have changed in regard to the way you viewed your home and family as a child.

- Describe a situation in which your mind set interfered with your perception. The following situations may stimulate recollections of a personal experience:

  1. A first encounter with a person who later became a close friend, lover, or business associate
  2. A repulsion to something done by a close friend you admired
  3. An attraction to someone who later turned out to be quite different from your first impression
  4. A reaction to a movie, book, or person that a friend had discussed with you beforehand
  5. A taste in music, food, or drink that prevented you from sampling something

- The following suggestions offer ways to explore individual differences in perception:

  1. Play a record and ask each person to write for five minutes about what he or she hears and feels about the music. Take turns sharing these responses.
  2. Show three different abstract paintings or photographs. Ask each person to write a paragraph about what he or she sees and feels. Share what you have written.
  3. Go to a movie in a group of three or more (or watch a TV program). Do not discuss the movie or program. Sit down and write your reactions to the experience. Then share what you have written.

These activities demonstrate that perceptions are not in objects—songs, paintings, stories, or movies—but inside people. You may not like a person or a painting someone else likes; or you may like a person or painting someone else dislikes. The liking or disliking is inside you rather than inherent in the person or object you perceive. When we really *experience* this concept, we become far less vulnerable to the approval or disapproval of others because we can see that *we are not the creation of some other person's perceptions.* Our perceptions and those of others can be deprived of their power to erect barriers between us.

Perception of Others

Perception, *the process of organizing sensory stimulation into patterns, affects our experience of other people.* Our perceptions are highly selective—we categorize into sets, classify people according to size and shape, and then create some stability about them. We have a tendency to freeze people into our original impressions of them. Some structure and stability are probably necessary for meaning to exist. We could not deal with a world in which, with every experience of a person, we had to begin again with first impressions. The world of people must be ordered into some kind of meaningful experience. Thus past experiences play a necessary role in our perceptions of others.

The world of people must be ordered into some kind of meaningful experience.

We know there is a great deal more to our experience of other people than simply appearance. We make inferences about *characteristics* that cannot be seen, such as "ambition," "intelligence," and "honesty." We also look for *intentions* and make value judgments about others in terms of what they intend. We perceive *feelings* in other people. We observe *behavior*, and we carve it up into units in order to label the other person's behavior. We perceive people as "causes" of their behavior. We assume that others intend to do certain things and attempt to cause certain effects. Then, because we assume they are the source of their actions, we consider them capable of varying their behavior to achieve intended effects. This intentionality leads us to organize actions into **intent-act-effect** units.

We perceive others as having enduring personality traits. A man who talks loudly, seems unconcerned about the feelings of others, and talks mostly about himself we might label "egocentric." If we notice that a certain woman usually remains emotionally stable, we might classify her as "a happy person" or a "depressed person" according to her usual state of feeling.

We create patterns in our perceptions of people in a vast number of ways. Our past experiences and our present motives affect the categories we use. Some of these categories are created by our experiences in a common culture; others depend on the perceiver. Furthermore, when a person interacts with different people on different occasions, his or her behavior changes. How we categorize people influences their behavior, and their behavior in turn influences our own.

A person's behavior may vary greatly in even a brief period of time. Yet we focus *not* on changing behavior, but on invariant characteristics. If a woman smiles, talks softly, and says pleasant things about others, for example, we infer that her *intent* is to be friendly. We then assume that we can predict her behavior in the future. If we observe this woman behaving in a similar manner with others, we label her "a friendly person." When we classify a person according to certain traits, we try to increase the predictability of our interpersonal world.

We perceive people as organized entities, behaving in ways that make sense. If certain people puzzle us or confuse us, we may avoid further interaction with them. As we observe intent-act-effect behavior units, we develop hypotheses about other people to explain the enduring personality traits we see. Moreover, we derive meaning from our own experiences and assume that other people are similar to us—that other people behave, think, and feel as we do. In so doing we develop personality *theories:* We find correlations between certain traits and certain behaviors. An honest person usually doesn't steal; so we trust someone we perceive as honest.

We also simplify the complex world of other people by organizing them into groups. We classify people: Jews, Asians, Blacks, Germans, Italians. We classify people into blue-collar, white-collar, and executive groups. We classify people as salespersons, politicians, and police; then we correlate what we know about these categories with certain traits. In addition, we correlate certain kinds of behavior with all the people we have classified into a certain group. Therefore: *Our perceptions of others are influenced by categorizing into groups based on inferences about character and personality traits, race, religion, age, occupation, and other classifications.* Although such **stereotyping** distorts and restricts our awareness of people as individuals, the process creates stability and meaning.

Perceptions of others are affected by language and culture, by experience and knowledge, by emotions and needs, by beliefs and attitudes, by expectations. They are affected by age and sex, by race and time, by physical and psychological health. *There are so many separate influences affecting perception that we can never be aware of them all.* The result is that each human being selects, organizes, and interprets all the separate influences in his or her life in a totally unique way. To understand these unique processes we will learn a great deal if we look at the society in which we live. Each of us is, to some degree, a product of our culture. Our perceptions of our social world are made up of certain social agreements, conscious or unconscious, that we have made with others.

PERCEPTION OF OUR SOCIAL WORLD

Social reality includes the realization that another person, no matter how different from us, is just as real, as worthy and as worthless, just as much a center of the universe as we are. We then join hands as members of humanity, recognizing that although we are unique and individual there are many ways in which we are alike. What unites us is much greater and deeper than what divides us. We need not lose our self-centeredness, our feeling of being the center. We can, though, accept the perceptions of other people and regard them as equally important.

Socialization is a product of intrapersonal and interpersonal communication within a culture. Rules, values, and attitudes of the culture are understood, acted out, and expressed in both verbal and nonverbal ways. Communication plays a vital role in creating our personal identity and the perceptions of our social world. We can look at the content and style of our communication and see our reflected selves. But socialization and communication never stop. We continue to grow through both. Integrating personal and social perceptions through communication is a constantly changing process that we will engage in throughout our lives.

The ways of tradition inevitably lead to mediocrity, and a mind caught in tradition cannot perceive what is true.

J. Krishnamurti

Social Agreements

Social reality includes all the **agreements** *we are taught in order to live in our society and culture.* These agreements include clothes (what we agree to wear), time (when we agree to meet), greetings ("Hello," "How are you," "I'm fine"), and all the other rituals we perform. Children learn they may not eat at the table with their hands; they may not take their clothes off at school; they may not urinate on the grass at the park.

One experimenter studied the development of *group reality* by having people sit in a darkened room. He placed a very small, stationary light on a far wall. Now if you sit in a darkened room with no visible walls, floor, or ceiling, you will get the feeling that the light is moving around. These subjects were asked to estimate the distance that the light moved. At first their estimates varied, but soon the group of subjects agreed on the distance it moved. By the end of the experiment, all members were experiencing the same reality. Although other groups arrived at quite different amounts of movement, each group reached an agreement about "reality."

Most of our social agreements and institutions become so totally a part of our everyday lives that we lose sight of them as agreements; instead, we experience them as reality. A society cannot function without agreements. For each social agreement there is a gain and a loss. We gain the products of other people's labor: education, houses, food, cars. We gain love, respect, and affection. But there is no gain without a payment. We must pay for houses, food,

Social agreements include rituals we perform.

cars, and education. And we also pay something for love, respect, and affection. We simply cannot live together in groups without it costing us something.

Some of the social agreements made for the benefit of the whole group may not make sense to an individual. We may see no reason why we cannot take off our clothes at the beach. There may be many rules or laws that do not make sense to us. Yet we can choose between obeying the rules or being ostracized, obeying the laws or going to jail. *Agreements offer the group safety, predictability, security from chaos, feelings of belonging and identity, economic security, and political order.*

Sometimes social agreements serve the society as a whole at the expense of the individual. We often lose sight of the fact that we have been taught agreements. Too often agreements become rules, and we no longer realize that we have a choice. If we do not take off our clothes, for example, we are choosing to abide by an agreement.

When children begin to realize they are doing many things simply because they have been told what to do, some of them become rebellious. Other children comply for the sake of being "good" or to get approval. Ideally, as adults we eventually come to the conclusion that we cannot live together without agreements and each of us is responsible for those agreements. But we must first recognize that they are agreements, what they consist of, how they are formed, and how they operate.

Agreements are not absolute. In a whole system of agreements many become outdated and are revised. *We can choose our positions in relationship to laws or agreements.* We can defy them, obey them, ignore them, or try to change them. We can resist an agreement, break it, or blame others for it. We can talk about why an agreement is not working. We can change agreements and end relationships. We can also take responsibility for accepting an agreement. We agree to get to class on time and to be there every day. We can choose to see these agreements *not* as the instructor's rules but as an agreement with ourselves. We can say: "I am responsible for my own agreements. And I can choose to end these agreements by dropping the class. I am in control of my own agreements."

There is only one reality: the act of freeing ourselves in the process of making choices.

Erich Fromm

When I keep my agreements, "my life works." I feel I am in control of my own life. No one else is setting the rules for me. As more and more of us understand this kind of choice, social reality will become more aligned with personal reality. *Social reality provides choices for creating our personal realities.*

- Write about or discuss some social agreement that really bothers you. How would you feel if everyone could take off their clothes; if people performed sex on the sidewalk; if people urinated on lawns?

- What do you gain and what do you pay for social agreements? Think of specific agreements you have made and examine the costs and benefits.

- Choose a common social agreement, such as the agreement not to litter, and show how accepting this agreement could help build a bridge between your self-interests and the interests of others in society.

- What social agreements do you no longer want to accept? What would be some creative ways that would permit you to respond or act in new ways? What are the costs and benefits of the changes?

Conflicting Perceptions

One of the basic struggles we confront is the conflict between our own view of ourselves and the view others have of us. Some people decide to risk the conflict of these perceptions and choose to be involved with others. Other people may choose to be "safe" when the conflict between two realities is more than they wish to struggle with. But conflict exists—and we cannot live in the world without conflicting perceptions. *To live a life accepting all the perceptions of others is to give up self-awareness and choice. To live a life without considering others is to live in isolation.*

We can handle conflicting perceptions in many different ways. One person may say: "Let's not say who we are. Let's be kind to each other instead. I will take responsibility for your feelings and censor what I have to say to you, if you will be just as careful with me." But if we deny our own reality too often, we may lose a clear sense of who we are and what we really feel or think. We may lose contact with ourselves. *It is important to know what is true for the self, for if we do not, we give up our freedom to create our life.*

Another person may say: "I struggle with ambiguity, with my own subjectivity, and with the intrusion of your subjectivity, which threatens my own. I am aware that you are a free self. I want to respect you as such, be aware of you as a person, not use you as an object to be manipulated for my needs."

Fritz Perls wrote: "I do my thing, and you do your thing. I am not in this world to live up to your expectations and you are not in this world to live up to mine. You are you, and I am I." Many people find this statement too strong to live with. Recognizing that we are each ultimately responsible for the way we confront others with our personal perceptions, we can also allow others to express their perceptions. We write our own biographies in the process of creating our own worlds. Yet we cannot exist without relating to other perceptions.

"Let's not say who we are."

Another way to handle conflicting perceptions is through **direct confrontation.** Confrontation involves a challenge from one person to another—a challenge of two different perceptions. Responsible confrontation does not force or manipulate the other person; it does not offer threats or false encouragement. Our responsibility to others is to communicate spontaneously, truthfully, and realistically: to say what we think and feel, and then to trust others to respond with whatever is real to them. *In communicating responsibly we maintain our self-identity and allow others to do the same.*

Some communication breakdowns occur because of differences in perception. A college student once told me: "My mother makes me work all the time. I don't even have time to do my homework after I do *her* housework and take care of my little brother." Her mother said: "I work all day. When I come home she's sitting in front of the television instead of fixing dinner. After dinner, she does the dishes, yes, but she leaves the stove and refrigerator dirty and *always* forgets to sweep the floor. I can't get her to do anything." Each person perceives a different reality of the same relationship. And for each the perceptions are very "real."

Recognizing and accepting differences in perceptions can help us overcome communication breakdowns between ourselves and others—especially when we communicate acceptance of those differences.

- Describe a personal situation in which you and another person have different perceptions that are causing problems in communication.

- Describe a situation in which you said to another person "You are wrong," and a situation in which another person said to you "You are wrong." Can you now expand your perception and describe the interaction in a way so that no one is "wrong"? Does "wrong" mean "seeing it differently"? "Understanding it differently"?

- Describe a time when you were surprised by another person's perception of a situation that involved both of you.

We often make the mistake of thinking our own perceptions are "reality" or The Truth and the facts about life or the world. We guess, make inferences, and state opinions—and think we are describing facts. When we describe these "facts," we treat the event, our perception of the event, and the words describing the event as if they were all the same. *Once we really experience that our perceptions are inside us, not in objects, situations, or people outside us, we can choose our attitudes and values rather than shape them to fit old patterns.* One way we can accept other people's differences in perception is through empathy, a process that enhances our relationships.

Empathy

A word often used in discussing interpersonal communication is **empathy.** There are many reasons for our difficulties in communicating with others—we perceive the world differently than does any other person; we have different attitudes, beliefs, and values; we have different personalities and experiences of the world. We use our words differently. We think differently. We feel differently. Thus as both senders and receivers we can never really re-create the same meaning in our own minds as that in the minds of others. We can, however, have empathy—we can imagine that we *are* the other person and respond accordingly. *To be empathetic or to have empathy for others is to imagine how they might be feeling or thinking and attempt to see things from their point of view.*

Empathy is not the same as sympathy. We can sympathize with people without really feeling or understanding their situation. If a friend's father dies, you can feel sympathy without imagining how you would feel if your own father died. You can feel *sorry* for your friend without entering into his or her experience of pain. Thus there is a difference between feeling *sorry* for (sympathy) and feeling *with* (empathy).

Although basic emotions such as love and fear are universal, their varieties and nuances are unique. No two people experience love or fear in the same way. Empathy helps us transcend the limits of the mind. When we empathize, we give up our stock labels for others in favor of experiencing their experience. Empathic abilities are more appropriate in interpersonal communication, in relationships, and in the study of persons than in the study of things. In relating, feeling often transcends reason. When we explain, we classify *quantities* in terms of regularities or physical laws. But understanding between persons involves appreciation of *qualities*. When we want to comprehend the other person's actual experience, we empathize. In entering this fantasy, however, we take the risk of relaxing our self-control and being caught off guard. To empathize is to trust one's own feelings and instincts—and that can be frightening.

If we empathize with others, we may not be able to regain our objectivity. Once we identify in our imagination, we become one with the other person. Empathy is the best antidote for blind spots in a relationship. It places you in a position to predict and become aware of the other person's attitudes, behavior, and feelings. In imagination, you experience a tolerance and sensitivity you may not be willing to handle. Thus you may prefer to stay preoccupied with your own emotional position. Until we have worked out many of our own ambivalences, we may not have the energy and strength to experience empathy.

We can communicate empathy for another human being in the way we listen to that person. We listen to others differently at different times. Much of our listening involves simply the enjoyment of being in the company of others. Or it may involve trying to understand what they say or what they want us to do, just as we listen to an instructor or read a textbook. Some situations require critical listening, which may result in a decision, such as which record or book to buy. But when your intention is to improve relationships with others, to understand what is individual and distinctive in them, to share their experiences, then **empathic listening** is appropriate.

Empathic listening requires that we listen to understand not only the entire message the sender is trying to convey but also the person's emotional experience. Empathic listening requires sensitivity to nonverbal as well as verbal clues. It requires withholding judgment or criticism. We do not need to approve or disapprove of what others say. Suspending judgment does not mean that we agree; it only implies that we hear others and confirm them as human beings. Empathic listening does not include agreement, sympathy, or "friendly advice." It does require being wholly attentive to others. It results in reduced defensiveness, and provides a supportive atmosphere in which trust increases and self-disclosure is possible. It requires a willingness to *give* ourselves to others at that moment in time.

Most genuine communication between people requires the ability to empathize. To be good listeners, we need the elusive quality of empathy. When we say "If I were you . . .," we are also saying "If you were me in your situation," which is the process of **projection**—the tendency to attribute to another person what is actually within the self.

Empathy involves risk. When we identify with others and imagine ourselves to be them, our imagination projects us out of ourselves and into them. The risk is that we may become so involved in their experience that we cannot see alternatives. Empathic understanding, then, requires subjective involvement. But at the same time it requires our detachment or withdrawal to an objective position that allows the use of reason and analysis. Empathic understanding requires a personal involvement with that person at the same time it requires objectivity. To risk empathic understanding, we must be strong in self-knowledge, self-trust, and self-acceptance—we can only deal well with others' anxieties and give them a sense of security when we come from a place of strength ourselves. Empathy takes energy, of course, and we may choose at times *not* to exert our energy in the direction of another person's experiences.

A certain amount of personal creativity is involved in empathy along with the risks and gains involved. Empathy requires that we experience a similarity between ourselves and others, to understand their experience, to identify with them. Empathic communication is an attempt to achieve a similarity of *experience*, as contrasted with intellectual communication, which is an attempt to achieve similarity of *meaning*. Emotional understanding involves appreciating the quality of another person's actual experience.

One method for developing empathy is **role-playing,** which intensifies likenesses through imagination. Most of us in our imaginations have played the roles of movie star, space explorer, teacher, parent, pilot, pioneer, adventurer. One of the best ways to get in touch with how others feel is to imagine yourself playing their role.

• Practice role-playing in your groups. Choose a person you have met or perhaps have seen on television; let that person talk and move through you. You may want to prepare for the role

Genuine communication between people requires the ability to empathize.

you play by writing down a "speech" beforehand. You may also want to try taking the role of a person you do not understand very well; if you do, notice how your understanding of the person may change as you play out the role.

• Write down a personal problem. Name the people involved and describe the situation fully. Ask the class for volunteers to play the roles of the people in the situation so that you can see how others might act out your problem.

Another technique used to learn empathy is called the **"Hot Seat" dialogue,** developed by Fritz Perls. Perls would invite a student to come to the front of the group. He would place two empty chairs facing each other and ask the student to take one. Then he would say, "Sit down. Now imagine your father sitting in this other chair facing you. Take some time to really 'see' him in front of you. What is he wearing? What kind of facial expression does he have? Notice all the details of his posture. How do you feel as you are facing him? Tell him how you are feeling." The student tells the imaginary father. Then Perls would say, "Now move into the other chair. Be your father and respond to what you just said."

This dialogue allows people to be completely honest with their parents—to express all the things they have never said, all the resentment and anger they have held back, all the love they have never expressed and questions they never asked. As the student became the parent and responded to the child, Perls would say, "Be aware of how you feel as your child is talking to you. How do you feel toward your child? Tell your child how you feel—what kind of relationship you want, how much you love him or her, your feelings of frustration and sadness. Tell your child what you need from him or her." To conclude the dialogue, the student would tell the "father" what he or she appreciated in him. No matter how difficult the relationship, there is always something about the parent the child can appreciate. Then the "father" tells the things he appreciates in the child.

As the dialogue progresses, many people are able, for the first time, to really experience their parent—the frustrations, needs, emotions, blocks, and all the parts of their parent that prevent them from communicating or loving or relating. Perls' "Hot Seat" technique is very powerful, and can be used in dialogue between husband and wife, teacher and student, friend and friend.

Perhaps you would prefer to practice this technique in your own room or in your imagination. Simply sitting at a desk, imagining the dialogue with another person or writing it down can also help you experience a great deal of empathy toward someone with whom you are having a difficult relationship. Role-switching is especially effective when you're having an argument with someone and communications have broken down. It may take many sessions of struggling, in your imagination, with an imagined partner in dialogue before you can fully empathize with the other person.

The gain and the threat in this experience of empathy is that you may eventually abandon your demands that other people be different. You will "feel" them as they are and accept them as they are. If you can empathize deeply with others, you can stop demanding that they be who you want them to be and can allow them to be who they really are. When this letting go happens, your relationship with them will change. Letting go actually results in change in both persons in the relationship. When you abandon your demands, you often let go of your resentment, anger, resistance, or dislike of the other person. Many of us cannot *will* to let go, but in an imaginary dialogue we can *experience* letting go.

Only you can decide how much you are willing to risk. The paradox is that the less you fear losing the self, the more you find the self. Risking empathy can result in self-fulfillment, expanded awareness, and creative change. To encounter other people's viewpoints, perceptions, and values can challenge and modify our own experiences of the world. But the basis of relationship at any level is to find a place to meet and touch the other person. By finding common points of experience, feeling, and understanding with others, we can perhaps *deal with the conflicting areas more creatively.* This is what the commitment to communication is about.

BEYOND TODAY'S REALITY

When we realize we are creating our day-to-day existence and the life we know, we can begin to alter our mental patterns and thus change our daily environment. As we begin to expand our awareness of selectivity and illusion in perception of both objects and people, we learn to trust our own reality and begin to take responsibility for creating our own experiences. *We can see that we create reality according to our own emotions, values, and beliefs.* And the processes of our communicating and relating begin to change with these realizations.

It is almost impossible to go back mentally and perceive the world as you experienced it as a child. A boy of six imagines himself building and playing in a tree house. He has no concept of tools, the cost of materials, the processes of building. Yet he dreams about a clubhouse where he can meet with all his friends. Like that little child, each of us will go beyond today's reality as our perceptions expand.

At any given moment we have many possible choices of actions, some trivial and some of the utmost importance. We may sit or stand, walk to the window or the door, pick up a book or scratch our head, save a child from fire, commit suicide, or go to the park. It often seems to us that reality is composed of those actions we choose to take. *We construct physical reality from what seems to be a series of physical acts, and the nonphysical acts usually escape our notice or judgment.* Yet other acts, thought but not chosen, have been carried out mentally. All actions are initially mental acts and are part of the nature of reality.

Therefore: *Mental acts exist and cannot be negated.* They are part of our perception of reality and affect our communication. They are part of all those serial happenings that compose our normal existence. Our lack of conscious perception of them cannot destroy their validity. Beginning with an act of imagination, we can sometimes follow for a short way one of the many "roads not taken." The possibilities are many and they are real. The slightest thought gives birth to new worlds.

Some philosophers believe our destiny is to reach a higher and higher consciousness of reality itself. This evolution is a *process*, not a static condition, and must stand the test of experience. To the extent that we are open and receptive to these many possibilities of perception and communication, we can gain knowledge. The dimension of consciousness that makes this evolution possible is to *assume* that we can go beyond today's limitations—that we can develop greater perceptual awareness and go beyond present experiences of reality.

A working premise is an idea to use as if it were true for the moment. There is a direct relationship between what goes on in our consciousness and what goes on in our life. We don't have to "believe" the premise of expanded perception, but if we change what is going on in our consciousness, our life experiences change in a corresponding way. We can open these lines of communication to help us make the many exciting choices that we now recognize as part of our present reality and lead to our future reality.

This is my way...
What is your way?
The Way *doesn't exist.*

Nietzsche

FOR FURTHER READING

Bandler, Richard, and John Grinder. *The Structure of Magic.* Palo Alto: Science & Behavior Books, 1975.
> The authors suggest that when people change their representations or images of the world, they expand their life choices.

Burke, Kenneth. *Permanence and Change.* Indianapolis: Bobbs-Merrill, 1965.
> The author presents a study of selective perception and how it affects our sense of reality.

Fabun, Don. *Communications: The Transfer of Meaning.* Beverly Hills: Glencoe Press, 1968.
> This booklet illustrates with drawings and text how pictures in one person's mind can get distorted in the transfer process to the mind of another.

Hastorf, Albert H., et al. *Person Perception.* Reading, Mass.: Addison-Wesley, 1970.
> The authors present a thorough exploration of research and theories in the field of perception.

Laing, R. D., et al. *Interpersonal Perception.* New York: Springer, 1966.
> This book is a comprehensive study of perception problems due to the various perspectives held by different people.

Vernon, M. D. *The Psychology of Perception.* Baltimore: Penguin Books, 1962.
> Vernon offers a clear exposition of the psychological aspects of human perception.

The true vocation of man
is to find his way to himself.

Hermann Hesse

3

Creating Self-Concept

THE CONCEPT OF SELF

The problem of defining the "self" is essentially that of defining the word I. We assume that we know who we are, yet we find it difficult to describe the self. Although we may create self-concept through the process of intrapersonal communication, we depend on others to reflect back to us some confirmation beyond our own sense perceptions. The self, expressed by the word *I*, has to do with more than simply our appearance and behavior. We cannot fully explain this concept, yet we do experience it.

Some people claim that the self embraces both mind and body. Others include actions and feelings. Yet others say the self is more than the body, mind, actions, and feelings. John Locke said, "Self is that conscious thinking thing which is sensible or conscious of pleasure and pain, capable of happiness or misery, and so is concerned for itself, as far as that consciousness extends." The philosopher William James gives us a wider definition. He said that an individual is "the sum total of all that he can call his," which includes the people he loves and his personal property such as tools, clothes, house and furniture, beloved books and paintings.

The self is that aspect of you that determines your uniqueness as a separate entity from "not-self"—from the environment and all that is outside self. The self can never be known completely because it is constantly in flux. Moreover, there is no *single* self. It consists of many roles that manifest themselves in many modes of behavior relevant to a situation. Most of us experience many selves, depending on the situation, time of life, age, and past experiences.

Many child psychologists believe that the newborn infant does not differentiate between self and environment. The infant is aware of events, but not of his or her *self* as a separate entity. *The universe and the self, in the consciousness of the newborn, are one.* The small child as yet knows no firm boundaries between self and not-self. The formation of those boundaries is a gradual process, spreading over several years until the child becomes fully conscious of his or her own, separate, personal identity.

The self is more than the sum of its parts: language, mind, body, feelings, and actions.

There are so many factors involved in the development of self-concept that it is impossible to provide a complete definition and explanation of them. However, self-concept does involve at least the following:

1. your past self (how others have seen you)

2. your present self (self-image)

3. your future self (what you want to be)

4. multiple selves (different voices)

5. self-esteem (how you feel about yourself)

Self-concept, then, refers to a collection of perceptions about the self: physical, mental, social, and psychological selves. It is a composite picture formed through interaction with others in the past and present in the process of communicating. These self-concepts affect our behavior and determine the messages we send to others about ourselves.

The Past Self

Self-concept is a product of an individual's past communication and relations with others. *To a large extent we create ourselves from what we believe others have perceived of us.* The ways others react to us, as well as how we interpret and are influenced by those reactions, constitute our self-image. When we look into a mirror, we see a reflection. And if there is a flaw in the mirror, we may see ourselves with a flaw. The same is true when we rely on others—who all have flaws—to reflect us. On the basis of these reflections, we make judgments and we create a self-image. We also decide whether we like or dislike ourselves, whether we are valuable or not.

Although we are always in the process of developing a self-image, the period of greatest development occurs in childhood. To manufacture a self, children often imitate others. They learn by example; they learn what is expected and allowed; they learn what they can and cannot do (or what others reflect back to them that they can and cannot do).

Yet it would be an oversimplification to say that self-concept is learned. Although self-concept begins to develop early and takes place in a social context through interaction with others, adults do *not* have the power to control a child's perceptions. The same behavior exhibited by the same parent can be interpreted in different ways by different children. Moreover, each child *selects* from all the actions, emotions, attitudes, and behaviors expressed toward him or her by a parent. As a result, we cannot predict how a child will decide to behave in response to those variables.

Exploring your past self can help you discover how you developed your present self-image.

- Each of us has thousands of hours of "memory tapes" that were "recorded" when we were children. Can you remember a voice (your mother, father, or a grandparent) that recorded a word in your memory? (Some examples are "stupid," "smart," "pretty.") What do you say to yourself when you do something "stupid"? How does that echo from your childhood affect you now? Play the role of this voice with some members of the class.

- Choose a critical incident in your childhood and trace the effects it had on your self-image.

- Write about a compliment you remember receiving, or describe a moment in which an older person told you something positive about yourself and how you felt about that.

- Write about a major conflict with a person of authority in your childhood. How did it make you feel and think? Do you recognize any carry-over from that time?

The Effects of Position (Birth-Order) in the Family

A good deal of research has been done that indicates certain characteristics, personality traits, and ways of responding to the world occur as a result of birth-order in the family. The class will now divide into four groups:

#1. The first group will be made up of all students who are the first-born child in their family. It will be called "the *oldest child*" group.

#2. The second group will be made up of all students who were born after the first child and before the last child. It will be called "the *middle child*" group.

#3. The third group will be made up of all students who were the last-born child in the family. It will be called "the *youngest child*" group.

#4. The fourth group will be made up of all students who are the only child in the family. It will be called "the *only child*" group.

After forming your groups, have one student-recorder take out a piece of paper and write on it the following:

Group #1: "What are oldest children like?"

Group #2: "What are middle children like?

Group #3: "What are youngest children like?"

Group #4: "What are only children like?"

Take as much time as you need in your groups to agree on a list of at least five items or more. Then reconvene as a class; each group will share its list with the entire class. Discussion can follow. For example, "What are the advantages of being the oldest (middle, youngest, only) child?" "What are the disadvantages?" Do you like what you are? Would you change position if you could? How?

The Present Self

The structure of the self is constantly changing. At any given moment, we are only partially aware of it. Although the self-image is not the total self, we base much of our behavior on our perceptions of ourselves. Therefore: *Awareness of self-image is essential to growth and change.*

You can't go home again.

Thomas Wolfe

Each of us forms judgments which become the bases for our decisions. We consider our choices and try to make logical decisions about what to do and what to say, what goals to pursue, and how to spend our lives. But in communicating we often create problems when we act as judges who pass judgments on ourselves and others. Carl Rogers says, "The major barrier to mutual interpersonal communication is our very natural tendency to judge, to evaluate, to approve (or disapprove) the statement of the other person."

It seems only natural to label an action we admire as "courageous," one we deplore as "foolhardy." We use words not only to give information but also to express our attitudes and to influence others. But in interpersonal communication, *descriptions* of behavior are often more valuable for the purpose of creating images of ourselves and others than judgmental labels. To get to know your self-image better, it would be more useful for you to explore the following questions than to engage in a general discussion.

Exploring your present self can give you valuable guidelines for future growth and development.

- Describe your present self (do not judge or give reasons):
  1. How do you see your body? Your hair and facial features? How do you feel about your physical abilities?
  2. How do you feel about your social abilities? Are you "popular"? Do you have friends? Are they "good" friends? Are friends important to you?
  3. How do you feel about your mental abilities? Are you satisfied with your intellectual performance in school? What are your strong areas of interest? What are your weakest school subjects? Which is more important to you, common sense or intelligence? How do they differ?
  4. How do your values affect how you feel about your body, your mind, and your ability in the social world?
  5. Imagine yourself as one of your grandparents (or great-grandparents). Go back three generations. What were they like? Is this image part of your self-image today?

- Choose from the words listed below or choose your own words to describe yourself. Notice that once you label yourself, you have a tendency to act out a self-fulfilling prophecy.

persuasive	gentle	humble	original
aggressive	fearful	defensive	life of the party
dogged	sweet	God-fearing	attractive
determined	good-natured	cautious	convincing
bold	charming	docile	loyal
high-spirited	agreeable	willing	eager

easygoing	cheerful	open-minded	obliging
assertive	sympathetic	confident	tolerant
persistent	generous	animated	well disciplined
competitive	merry	considerate	harmonious
forceful	admirable	kind	resigned
unconquerable	obedient	fussy	playful
pioneering	respectful	optimistic	accommodating
brave	timid	inspiring	submissive
argumentative	adaptable	nonchalant	lighthearted
self-reliant	gregarious	patient	soft-spoken
positive	contented	trusting	peaceful
adventurous	receptive	cordial	moderate
vigorous	lenient	aesthetic	good mixer
controlled	talkative	conventional	decisive
accurate	restrained	outspoken	companionable
audacious	diplomatic	polished	satisfied
restless	popular	neighborly	devout
even-tempered	precise	nervous	jovial

- Each of us has layers of self-perception and, like an onion, these layers can be peeled off one by one. These layers may be positive or negative to you. Some of the layers are like masks behind which we sometimes hide parts of ourselves we do not want to look at. Somewhere in the core lies the innermost essence of our natural being, covered by layers of family, social, and cultural programming.

1. Take a sheet of paper and write the date at the top. Title the paper "Who Am I?" Then write freely and honestly until you are ready to stop.

2. Sit in a relaxed position; close your eyes and clear your mind. Ask yourself: "Who am I?" Look for the answer in the form of an image on a screen. Let your mind wander, and write down whatever you see. Write down the feelings that go with this image and what it means to you.

3. Ask yourself: "Who do I pretend to be?" Write whatever comes to your mind, without censoring or judging.

4. Ask yourself: "Who do I wish to be?" Fantasize an ideal image. Write about that person.

This exercise, when repeated at intervals, can lead you to look deeper and deeper into yourself. It may also be used to indicate change and provide valuable insights into the direction in which you are growing.

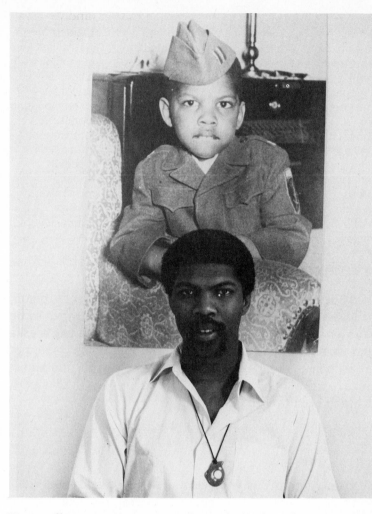

We are all in transition, moving from who we have been through who we are to who we are becoming.

The Future Self

In our culture the past, present, and future are compartments of time. Americans have a tendency to think of time as a road stretching into the future along which one progresses. The expression "One thing at a time" is an attempt to keep time in discrete little units. We value time schedules and get annoyed with people of other cultures who do not value time the way we do. In some cultures, there is no concept for future. Not only do we segment time, but we are future-oriented. We like new things, and we value change. We want to know where we are going. Our view of the future is often limited to our "plans"—to what is foreseeable in the future.

Time is a major form of communication. It often eludes our consciousness. We tend to think of time as fixed, something around us and from which we cannot escape, part of our environment like the air we breathe. Even though we can study how other cultures use time, our own perceptions of time resist change.

Through our own transitions, changes, and growth we can learn to increase our ability to control and shape our lives. Each of us has our own "true nature" which only we can experience for ourselves. Your true nature can also be called the true self, a personal and unique source of inner wisdom, insight, perception, and intuitive power. Clarity, focus, and a greater feeling of purpose can be developed as you direct your own life. *Self-expansion through learning is a process of planting the seeds and directing the creative process.*

We are all in transition: moving from where we have been, through who we are, to who we are becoming. Ways of exploring our future self can put us in touch with our transitions.

- Close your eyes and imagine yourself ten years from now. Look at where you are, how you are dressed, what you are doing, where you live, and what your environment is like. How do you feel about this person you are ten years from now?

- Now close your eyes and create an image of what you would like to be doing twenty years from now. See yourself very clearly and exactly. Notice what you are wearing, what you are doing, how you move and talk; see your face and the expressions on it. Act out, in your imagination, the kind of person you would like to be.

As we proceed through this course, you will have many opportunities to explore your past, present, and future selves. We will be examining personal and social values, outlining goals in relationships, and exploring life goals. Through the process of communication, we define the self.

Multiple Selves

All the world's a stage;
And all the men and
*   women merely players;*
They all have their exits
*   and their entrances;*
And one man in his time
*   plays many parts.*

William Shakespeare

Many of us recognize that the question "Who am I?" implies a single self. Yet each of us plays many parts in life: student, teacher, child, parent, friend, stranger. The roles are limitless. Every relationship seems to add a new aspect to the self. The self is reflected in different relationships, different professions, different experiences, and in significant choices and expressions of values. In addition to a physical self, we have intellectual and emotional selves, private and public selves. This multiplicity of identities can make communication difficult, but self-awareness can help us sort out who is really speaking.

Exploring multiple selves.

Eric Berne, author of *Games People Play*, calls the voices within us The Child, The Adult, and The Parent. Each of these voices is important. If we can become conscious of them, we will be able to choose the one that best expresses our feelings at a particular moment. Sometimes The Child in us expresses rebellion by saying, "You can't make me do what you say. No! I won't!" At other times, The Child voice expresses the "fun-loving, creative child," the one that loves to run and play. When grown-ups act out The Child, they joke, laugh, and act childlike. Their facial expressions and posture visibly change. Intuition, spontaneity, and enjoyment flourish when we allow The Child in us free expression. The creative drive to paint, play music, take photographs, to allow our imaginations to roam and build worlds of beauty expresses itself through the joy and excitement of The Child.

The Parent state of mind, like The Child, also has two aspects. One is the scolding authoritarian parent who tries to tell us what to do. "You should do this." "You shouldn't do that." "This is bad." "That is good." At other times, The Parent voice is the nurturing, loving parent who takes care of us, tells us to be careful while crossing the street so that we won't get hurt, tells us to eat properly and get enough sleep so that we will be healthy and strong. The Parent voice, according to Eric Berne, is one we learned from our actual parents, but now that we are older we still continue to replay these voices from the past.

The Adult voice is necessary for survival. It processes data and computes probabilities for dealing effectively with the outside world. When I was making a decision about whether to learn to fly a small, one-engine plane, My Child voice said, "I'm afraid," and My Parent voice said, "Don't be silly." But my Adult voice said, "Flying is eight times safer than driving on the freeway. Since I am intelligent and learn easily, I will base my actions on logic." Thus The Adult voice mediates objectively between the parent and the child and it regulates their activities.

Our multiple selves become fascinating when we consciously choose that self most appropriate to the situation and the unique communication event. We can learn to be free, loving, and affectionate with positive feelings when that is appropriate. In another situation, we can control our feelings and take care of ourselves. Thus we can deal with the world in a balanced manner. The multiple self will be explored later in the book when we look at the different roles we play and how they affect *behavior*.

Listening to your different "voices" can help you choose the most appropriate self for a particular communication event.

- Listen carefully to yourself and to others this week. Can you hear The Child voice in yourself? In others? Watch for changes in voice and posture. Write about an example of observing the "rebellious" child or the "fun" child in yourself or another person.

- Listen to The Parent voice in yourself and others. When you go out in public, notice how children speak to each other. You will sometimes see a child as young as three or four years old scolding a younger child. Listen to the voices, the authoritarian tone, the words: "Don't do that. It's not nice. You're a bad girl." Watch the expressions on the children's faces. At a very young age, we have The Parent voice within us. We use it to manipulate ourselves and others. Saying "good girl" is an attempt to manipulate. Write down other examples of what The Parent voice says, including what you say to yourself.

- Describe some of your various other selves: big sister, good guy, wage earner, friend, and so on. What do those different selves have in common?

Self-Esteem

I celebrate myself, and sing myself. And what I assume you shall assume.

Walt Whitman

Self-esteem is an individual's personal judgment of worthiness or unworthiness. To have *high* self-esteem is to have a favorable opinion of self. To have *low* self-esteem is to have a negative opinion of self. These feeling/judgments are intimately related to an individual's behavior and self-concept.

Self-esteem is not a constant quality or state. It changes with time, situation, and people. But generally you have a basic attitude or feeling about yourself—either somewhat negative or positive.

Self-esteem is not the same as success but may be related to success or failure. Success/failure feelings come early in life. When we get approval or disapproval from parents, teachers, and other significant adults, it tends to affect our feelings of self-worth. High or low self-esteem patterns begin in early childhood as children begin to evaluate themselves as good or bad, smart or dumb, successful or unsuccessful. As children develop their self-images, they may develop patterns through self-fulfilling prophecies. Adults can change their self-images. Adults can choose their own personal values, set their own goals, and define what success means to them.

Our feelings of self-worth and self-esteem come from two sources: *our perceptions of our personal progress and our perceptions of how we compare to other people.* It is usually more productive to compare ourselves as we are today with where we were at an earlier stage of personal growth. Expectations can also affect our feelings about ourselves. If our ideal selves are too high above our real selves, this discrepancy can be a source of unreasonable disappointment. Perfectionists, people who expect themselves to be excellent in most ways, find most things in the world to be faulty or imperfect—including themselves. They constantly find themselves less worthy than they had hoped to be.

Most of us learn to cope with negative self-images by using defense mechanisms or self-deception. These defenses become habitual patterns of responding when we feel threatened, and they block self-awareness and growth. Becoming aware of these protective devices can help us give them up. If we like ourselves, if we have a basic faith in our ability to handle failure or a bad experience, we are apt to like other people more and be liked by them. Most research indicates that *people who are highly self-critical are more anxious, more insecure, and possibly more cynical and depressed than people who accept themselves.* Researchers have found a high correlation between low self-image and vulnerability to criticism, judgment, or rejection either by the self or by others. Moreover, people with low self-esteem can be easily flattered or pleased by positive comments because they see themselves as inadequate or inferior. They are not sure of their ideas or their abilities, so they often accept uncritically what others say.

This checklist will help you become more aware of how you view yourself. Although self-esteem changes with time and setting, mark an × on each line to describe how you feel about yourself most of the time.

- *As I Really Am*

Good ——————————————————— Bad

Pleasant ——————————————————— Unpleasant

Active ————————————————— Passive

Successful ————————————————— Unsuccessful

Strong ————————————————— Weak

Secure ————————————————— Insecure

Rational ————————————————— Emotional

Social ————————————————— Unsocial

- *As Others See Me*

Good ————————————————— Bad

Pleasant ————————————————— Unpleasant

Active ————————————————— Passive

Successful ————————————————— Unsuccessful

Strong ————————————————— Weak

Secure ————————————————— Insecure

Rational ————————————————— Emotional

Social ————————————————— Unsocial

- *As I Wish I Were*

Good ————————————————— Bad

Pleasant ————————————————— Unpleasant

Active ————————————————— Passive

Successful ————————————————— Unsuccessful

Strong ————————————————— Weak

Secure ————————————————— Insecure

Rational ————————————————— Emotional

Social ————————————————— Unsocial

Self-esteem and self-acceptance can be learned. Evidence indicates that people who are self-accepting are also more accepting of others. There are variations among individuals, of course, and for the same individual depending on the situation. Nevertheless, when your self-image is positive:

1. You have values and principles you believe in, and you are secure enough to modify them when necessary.

2. You are capable of acting on your own best judgment even when others disapprove.

3. You do not worry much about the future nor do you think much about past mistakes.

4. You feel confident in your ability to deal with problems.

5. You feel *equal* to others (not superior or inferior).

6. You feel that you are a person of interest and value.

7. You can accept either praise or criticism without much emotion.

8. You are inclined to resist the efforts of others to dominate.

9. You experience a wide range of feelings without needing to act them out.

10. You enjoy a wide variety of activities: work, play, creative expression, companionship, and relaxation.

A sense of self-worth creates internal energy. When you feel that you are worthwhile, that you are valuable and important to yourself, you have more energy. You feel more competent and believe in your own decisions. Appreciating your own worth, you are able to see and respect the worth of others. Self-trust creates a climate in which you will be able to accept other people even though they are not like you, do not value what you value, and do not do what you do.

When people lack a sense of personal value, they tend to manipulate others. They feel that asking openly for what they want would result in a refusal; therefore they are afraid to ask. They often feel they do not deserve to get what they want. *People with high self-esteem usually know what they want and can simply state both what they want and what they do not want, without expecting the other person to either give or withhold what is requested.* They rarely do what other people expect of them or what they think other people want simply to get others to think they are "nice." They deal with their own feelings and what feels right for them, not what they believe other people want. They are in touch with their emotions and often tell others what they want to do.

Self-esteem can be learned.

People usually feel more comfortable around a person who has high self-esteem because such a person is less likely to "play games," manipulate, or make other attempts to be liked. *People who have a sense of their own value know they cannot meet all the needs of others.* Such a person can say "No! I am unwilling to do that. I value you and like you, but I prefer to do it differently." The paradox is that the person of high self-esteem who is willing to lose friends gains them instead. Such a person says, "Look, I can't have everyone in the world love me. I have to let those go who do not value me."

People of high self-esteem often want more time alone. They like people, but they also have their own projects. They spend time with themselves, recharging their energy, getting new ideas, getting in touch with their feelings and thoughts. By spending time alone they "balance" themselves and find a greater sense of personal direction. In short, they find the time to communicate with themselves.

By becoming aware of self-judgments, successes, and strengths, we can gradually raise our self-esteem.

- Spend a day noticing whenever you judge yourself. ("Why did I do that stupid thing?" "What an idiot I am!" "I'm not very smart!") Then write down a balanced view of each situation. ("That didn't work out—but in general I am quite intelligent." "Now that I have more information, I can make a better decision next time.")

- Write about:
  1. A time when you felt very competent about something you did or accomplished.
  2. Something about which you feel highly skilled.
  3. A subject about which you feel well informed.
  4. A discussion in which you were able to offer some facts or insights.
  5. A time when you felt that your discussion of a topic was both logical and well presented.

- Write down ten verbal compliments for yourself. Keep this list where you can see it every day—perhaps tucked into the corner of a mirror frame or in a diary or journal. You may also want to trade lists with a friend; ask your friend to write you compliments and vice versa. Notice how you feel about receiving these compliments.

- Choose a partner and tell that person qualities you like about yourself, things you do well, things other people say they like about you. Then tell your partner things you like about him or her. Take turns. Now discuss how you feel about telling your positive qualities.

Self-concept, then, is the product of how others perceive us, how we perceive ourselves, and how we feel about these images. It is made up of our past self, present self, future plans, multiple selves, and our self-esteem. It can be defined as our total perceptual appraisal of our self—a private picture we carry that evolves out of who we think we are, what we think we can do, and how well we think we can do it. We then communicate messages that are consistent with the person we perceive ourselves to be. This self-concept even includes an evaluation of the self as communicator.

How we view ourselves as communicator is transmitted through behavior. If our self-concept includes being an effective and skilled communicator, we will act out that perception. How we talk and listen, how we think and feel, how we act and relate—are founded upon self-concept as a communicator. Self-concept grows, develops, changes, and expresses itself in both the verbal and nonverbal ways we communicate. *The more deeply we study the self, the more freedom we have to choose and to change our self-concept.*

Self-Assertion and Personal Power

To know oneself, one should assert oneself.

Albert Camus

The experience of self-esteem leads to a sense of personal power. Carl Rogers, in his book *On Personal Power*, writes: "There is in every organism, including man, an underlying flow of movement toward constructive fulfillment of its inherent possibilities, a natural tendency toward growth. It can be thwarted but not destroyed without destroying the whole organism." Each of us has this personal power to make decisions and assert oneself. When we come in contact with and accept our inner strength, we can experience intense excitement. We can learn to trust our choices, be responsible for our decisions, and change our personal world. Through personal power, we create ourselves.

Alexander Lowen says, "Self-awareness depends on self-assertion." *Self-assertion is a declaration of one's individuality.*

Without the ability to express opposition, we lose the experience of what we are and what we want for ourselves. As children, some of us found it difficult to say no to parents, teachers, and other authority figures. As adults the inability to look (lack of courage for self-awareness) and to say no (make choices) gives away personal power.

People who are afraid to say no to others may have difficulty saying no to themselves. Saying no to oneself is the source of self-discipline, the root of commitment to goals. It expresses a growing consciousness of choice, of individuality, of identity: "I am me. I am not you. I have a mind of my own. I can see the world through my own eyes."

The rebellious need to say no to everything is *not* choice, however. It comes from fear and is a child's defense against being controlled. A child or adult who is overly obedient lives with fear and carries that fear into adulthood. Finding the proper balance is finding one's personal power, finding the courage to use that power, and finding the strength to live with the consequences.

Power struggles between individuals in a relationship develop over the issue of control and operate through control. At times a child must be controlled. We cannot allow a two-year-old to run into the street in front of an oncoming car. We do not give children a choice about whether to drink the bleach under the sink. There is no way that a child can be brought up in a culture without adults (big persons) using their power to control children (little persons). But whenever two adults in a relationship get into a power struggle, the relationship may be in trouble. If the weaker person feels threatened and uses an undercover struggle to win, good feelings and affection may become corroded. Power struggles can destroy the pleasure experienced in a relationship. Individuals can become conscious of their choices, of knowing what they want and who they are, of when to say no and when to say yes. Personal power is not power over others. *Ultimately, personal power is the power to create the kind of life you want.*

Recognizing our personal power can help us exercise our freedom of choice.

- How did you learn to use power in relationship with your father? Your mother? A brother or sister? With other adults? With teachers? Who is the most and least assertive in your family?

- Are you more assertive in some relationships than others? What factors influence you?

We all attempt to obtain, possess, share, or surrender our power over ourselves and others. To gain control over our own lives and the lives of others, we use maneuvers, strategies, and tactics (conscious or unconscious). Carl Rogers believes that we *gain* personal power when we *give* others personal power, when we

How old were you when you discovered you could say "No!"?

trust others to make decisions for themselves, when we allow others to move in their own directions, when we create a growth-promoting climate. *Genuineness, trust, acceptance, and empathy are ways to share power and control.* Rogers suggests that influence is gained as power is shared and that self-control is more constructive than control of others.

Most of us do not see ourselves as being powerful. We think of power as outside us, an external force that comes to people by accident (being born into the right family) or by association (having a job in a powerful organization). Such concepts alienate us from our own power. Moreover, we do not need to be strictly rational, task-oriented, or aggressive to be powerful. To experience the power within, we can be intuitive, receptive, and creative. We can base our concept of power on our individual potential. Personal power is experienced as a quiet strength with inner firmness, determination, and flexibility—a strength that keeps us in balance, headed toward our own goals, and in line with our own values.

PERSONAL VALUES

Before we can freely make choices in our lives, we need to know who we are and what we value. We have explored the notion of self-concept to become more aware of who we are. Now we examine values in order to know what is important in our lives. We live in a world of confusion and conflict. Many of us are finding it increasingly difficult to cope with life. In our natural striving for emotional and spiritual balance and maturity, we need values to guide us.

We all have value systems. If you have admired or envied another person, cringed at a news report, or felt joy in an experience, your values have been involved. *Your values are the standards you use to evaluate things, events, people, and yourself.* Values can give your life more meaning if you understand what they are and how you acquire them. In this section, you will examine many questions about your own personal values. In addition, we will consider the value of self-disclosure, which is intimately connected with your ability to *risk* disclosure and your ability to *trust* others when communicating with them. In the next chapter we will discuss interpersonal values when communicating with others.

What would you do if you could do anything you wanted for a whole day without worrying about money? (Write the answer.) If you had six months to live, how would you spend that time? Some of our personal values are derived from what we want in life.

- Make a list of five things you want out of life.

- Order the list according to priorities, with the most important first.

- Put the list away for a week and revise it. Have any items changed?

- List on paper the five most important things about yourself that you want others to know. Choose a partner; read and discuss both your lists. Then join two other pairs forming groups of six. Each original partner is to introduce the first person he or she shared with and tell about the partner's five items. After all six individuals have been introduced with their values, the group can discuss differences and similarities in the lists.

- *The Values Collage:* Using a large sheet of paper or cardboard and several magazines, cut out pictures, words, and titles or phrases that represent things you value or tell something about you. Paste all these separate items into a creative pattern that represents you and your values. You can be as original as you like using photos, yarn, cloth, pieces of wood, buttons, or any other objects you wish. You may draw lines or designs or symbols to connect the various parts. Share your collage with the class or with a smaller group of classmates.

One problem with thinking about values is that people often think of values as they ought to be rather than as they really are. Try to be realistic; remember that personal values change. You may be listing values you wanted a few years ago rather than ones you want today. You have been bombarded from all sides by many points of view and have been in contact with others living different life-styles from your own. The family, community, school, and church all differ. In earlier generations, traditionel ideals and values were handed on from one generation to another. Today many young people are accepting the responsibility for creating their own personal values.

Before you are free to choose your own values, you need to be conscious of the values of your culture. Here is a partial list of American values. Get together in small groups and discuss these questions. Do Americans:

- Respect science and reason?

- Believe in a college education yet want it to be "practical"?

- Measure success chiefly by economic means (money)? And believe it is achieved through hard work and perseverance?

- Respect efficiency, thrift, and competition?

- Value physical activities such as sports, hunting, and fishing?

- Respect neatness, cleanliness, and good grooming?

- Value honesty, sincerity, kindness, generosity, and friendliness?

- Admire fairness, justice, aggressiveness, ambition?

- Prize loyalty to America, democracy, the Constitution, liberty, equality, the individual above the state?

- Believe in Christianity, church membership, God, life after death, charity?

In a small group, discuss which of these values *you* personally accept. How do members of your group differ?

Sometimes the responsibility for creating our own values may produce anxiety, frustration, rage, or emptiness. At moments, we may feel as if our lives are meaningless. Or perhaps we see others who appear valueless, aimless, or empty of commitment. It is difficult to live in a drifting state as if life had no purpose. Peter Koestenbaum, a philosopher, suggests that "meaninglessness" tells us we can choose our own values, our own nature, and our own self-definition. The feeling of emptiness can be the beginning from which to create a value system.

A value system, if clarified and verbalized, can provide us with criteria for choosing what to do with our time and energy. It can help us create the kinds of human relationships we want. If we make choices, order priorities about how to live our lives, and develop our own guidelines, then we must accept responsibility for them. We must also accept responsibility for *not* developing our own guidelines. Choosing guidelines developed by others is also a choice. In any case, we cannot escape responsibility.

A value system involves many different areas. Here are some areas where you may experience confusion or conflict in values. Choose those that are not clear; then think and write about them.

politics	love	material possessions
religion	family	aging and death
work	friends	war and peace
leisure time	money	law and authority
education	health	culture: art, music, literature

Where do you want to live? What kind of life-style do you want?

The Process of Valuing

Today we are confronted with many more alternatives than in previous times. We are surrounded by a bewildering array of choices. This has made the act of choosing values infinitely more difficult and perhaps more vital than ever before. Bombarded by outside influences, by groups and individuals who mouth "shoulds" and "shouldn'ts," we must sort out what fits us as individuals. Too many important choices in life are made on the basis of peer pressure, unthinking submission to authority, or the power of propaganda.

Another problem is that there is often a dichotomy between theory and practice—between what we say we value and what we do (lip service versus behavior). Moralizing frequently influences only what people say and has little effect on behavior. The process of valuing, therefore, is more complicated than simply stating your values. One approach that helps people not only to become aware of what they value but also to put those values into effect in their lives is to follow a series of steps:

1. *Choose freely* from all the alternatives after you carefully consider the consequences of each choice.

2. *Publicly affirm* your values by sharing them with others.

3. *Act out* your values consistently.

4. *Reassess* your values periodically.

The purposes of clarifying values are multiple—to give you experience in thinking critically, to give you the opportunity to share your perceptions and yourself with others, to learn cooperative problem-solving skills, and to help you learn to apply valuing processes in your own life. It is a never-ending quest to sort out what is important in one's personal life.

After considering alternative values and the consequences of each choice, the next step is to *affirm* your values publicly by sharing them with others in your small groups. Group discussions of values not only affirm them but give us a chance to make them more specific and to find people who have similar and dissimilar values.

After choosing your values and stating them to others, the next step is to think of ways to *act out* your values—to make changes in your behavior leading to the kind of life you want. If you find you want to spend less time socializing, ask yourself: "how many friends do I want? What kinds of friends and what kinds of relationships do I want?" Think about where and how you want to live. Ask yourself: "What kind of living environment is important to me? What can I do to create that kind of environment?" The following suggestions can help you to act out your values:

List three areas in your life you would like to change.

Determine three or four clear, short-term objectives for each of these areas.

List any obstacles you can think of.

Name a creative solution for overcoming each obstacle.

Make a schedule for putting your changes into action.

Break the plan up into small steps.

Make a commitment to yourself and complete one step at a time.

In Chapter 9, Behaving: How Actions Communicate, we will explore several ways to modify behavior and act out our values. And at the end of this chapter we will talk about values that conflict as well as values which are constantly in transition, which change and grow as you grow. An awareness of these transitions can make us more effective communicators as well as help us in our relationships.

Self-Disclosure and Trust

Self-disclosure *is the communication of personal or private information to another person.* It is closely related to self-concept and self-esteem. Self-disclosure involves trust and risk. The greater the disclosure, the greater the risk. When we reveal something private about the self to another, we must be prepared for that person to criticize or judge us. Therefore, we have a tendency to conceal those things about ourselves which we believe another person might not accept.

In our culture, self-disclosure seems especially difficult because we value privacy. In other cultures where families, including grandparents, aunts, and uncles, all live in a single room, privacy as a concept does not exist. As a result, self-disclosure in our culture must be learned and experienced as valuable.

One research study indicates that many men are unable to reveal themselves to other men. As men today become more flexible in their sexual roles, however, more of them are willing to accept the vulnerability of self-disclosure in order to relate more fully. The cultural bias against self-disclosure as a weakness is likewise changing.

Some people have an intense fear of intimacy—of someone getting inside them and seeing who they are. To them that risk seems intolerable. They prefer an isolated, private existence invulnerable from others. *The paradox is that fear of intimacy and rejection, fear of being judged or criticized, often results in rejection and criticism.*

Sidney Jourard says that "Men keep their selves to themselves and impose an added burden of stress beyond that imposed by . . . everyday life." Men have a shorter life expectancy, possibly because of the alienation and stress that come from keeping to themselves. People of either sex who are totally unable to reveal their feelings to others tend to function less adequately in life. Suspicion, lack of trust, isolation, and fear all contribute to the need to maintain a "secret" life.

Although each individual has the right to decide what areas are private and to resist self-disclosure, flight from self-knowledge means less chance to know the self. To communicate with the self, we need the responses of others. *The more trust and risk we act out, the more freedom we have in communicating.*

There are many different levels and types of self-disclosure.

- Disclosing biographical information—age, past experiences, family background, hobbies, interests—is one kind of self-disclosure. In your group, share three items of biographical information.

- Personal ideas, attitudes, and values constitute another sort of disclosure. In your group, share five of your personal values (about religion, politics, ethics, morality, ambitions, goals, money, friendship, or love).

- Sharing personal feelings, although most threatening, may be our most important kind of sharing, because it allows someone to really know us. In your group, tell each member how you

There are many different levels of self-disclosure.

feel about him or her. (Do not ask for or give reasons.) For example: "I feel threatened by you" or "I feel comfortable with you."

• Tell others how you feel about yourself. For example: "I worry about being . . ."; "I feel anxious about . . ."; or "I feel attractive."

Self-disclosure can improve a relationship when it is appropriate and mutually shared. We can be sensitive to cues showing that another person is bored, threatened, or offended by our level of disclosure, and we can readjust that level or not, as we choose.

Self-disclosure tends to be reciprocal. The more I disclose to you, the more likely you are to disclose yourself to me. People look to each other for cues as to what is appropriate. If a person talks about the weather, baseball, politics, or cars, you are likely to keep the conversation at a superficial level. However, you can also choose to lead your partner away from superficial conversation to a personal level of dialogue.

Self-disclosure plays an important role in the quality of our relationships. Sidney Jourard, in *The Transparent Self*, says: "Alienation from one's real self not only arrests one's growth . . . it also tends to make a farce out of one's relationships." He suggests that people who do not disclose themselves can never love or be loved by another person. Loving and caring for another person requires knowing that person.

Yet there are too many people in our lives for us to love all of them. We do not have enough time in our lives to disclose ourselves truthfully and fully to everyone. Thus self-disclosure as an act is not a matter of "good" or "bad" behavior but a matter of *appropriateness* to the other person, the situation, and the purpose of the disclosure. A person who reveals too much too fast may frighten another person; therefore, being self-disclosing is a way of selecting or eliminating relationships.

We tend to disclose more about ourselves when we accept ourselves—and self-acceptance is increased by self-disclosure and subsequently results in being accepted by others. The greater our self-acceptance, the easier it is to risk self-disclosure. When we hide information about ourselves or try to create a certain impression on others, we feel liked for the lie, not for our real selves. When we realize how empty we feel in being liked for something that is not real, we may risk rejection and be ourselves.

Some people hold back by disclosing only safe things about themselves—past experiences, experiences with others, facts rather than feelings. Some people hold back because they think that if they share themselves, they will somehow end up with "less." Yet the more of ourselves we share, the more of ourselves we get in touch with and the more we have.

Self-disclosure results in people finding out they are similar to one another at the same time they find ways in which they differ. They learn about another person's needs—which then means that they can *choose* to cooperate in meeting those needs as they also have their needs met. Love and trust follow when we devote ourselves to each other's well-being.

The following suggestions offer opportunities to explore self-disclosure in small groups.

- **Tell your group something about yourself that is difficult for you to reveal.**

- Suppose the person on your left wants to be with you, but you want to be alone. What could you say? (Discuss.)
- Tell one person in the group a way in which you feel that the two of you are similar.
- Describe a way that you "use" a friend or manipulate someone.
- Repeat to the group a lie you often tell about yourself, in the way that you usually tell it.
- Say something to someone in your group that you have never said but would like to say.
- Tell each person in your group a way in which you would like to know that person better.
- Describe the way you are when *you* like yourself best. Now describe the way you are when *others* like you best.
- Choose one person to be your father (or mother) and ask that person for something that is difficult for you to request.

When to open the door, and to whom, and when to keep it closed depends on the time and situation. Voltaire said: "The secret of being a bore is to tell everything." By being selective, by sharing only what is worth sharing, we approach intimacy. A confession may devastate someone you love; it may be insensitive or cruel. There simply is not enough time for two intimate people to tell each other every thought, every emotion, every possibility that crosses their minds. A relationship is built primarily by disclosing reactions to events that two people both experience or responses to what the other person says or does.

To like you, to be involved with you, to be your friend, a person must know who you are. If you cannot reveal yourself, you cannot be valued by others for who you are. To be closely involved with others you must also know them. Intimacy involves not only selecting individuals, since we do not have time in one life to be intimate with everyone, but also selecting what to share. Reactions to people and events are not facts as much as unique perceptions, personal feelings. We select those things we feel about events that are especially relevant to the person and to the relationship.

Timing is important in self-disclosure. Sharing reactions as soon as they occur is the ideal—for example, "I feel upset now. . . ." Yet it may not always be *appropriate*, as in certain situations where you are not alone with the other person, to share your reactions at the moment. Self-disclosure does not mean revealing intimate details of your past life. Making highly personal confessions about your past may lead to a temporary feeling of intimacy but has little to do with the present relationship. A person comes to know you not through your past history but through your present reactions—that is, by knowing the person you are in this relationship at the present time. Past history is only relevant when it clarifies why you are reacting in a certain way *now.*

Hiding the self in an intimate relationship takes energy and adds stress to the relationship. It dulls your experience and leads to self-alienation. It decreases your ability to disclose your reactions even when it is perfectly safe and appropriate to share yourself. Hiding your reactions from others through fear of rejection or conflict or through feelings of shame and guilt leads to alienation and loneliness. Strength is the willingness to take risks—to disclose yourself with the intention of building a better relationship.

Self-disclosure can improve a relationship under certain conditions. Above all, the disclosure must begin with a desire to improve the relationship. Only when you care about others and the relationship is sharing effective. You want them to know how you feel about their actions. At the same time, you want to know how they feel about you. You must be willing to risk being rejected or hurt by others; they must be free to be themselves, whatever they feel and think. And you must be willing to trust them to handle what you really think and feel. Although your interaction may involve pain or anger, it must not be coercive. Manipulation to change the other person is to be avoided—it does not work. There is no right/wrong issue. All choices must be freely and responsibly made. *Shared understanding, risk-taking, and trust are all elements of self-disclosure for the purpose of creating better relationships.*

The appropriateness of self-disclosure depends on timing, the situation, and the relationship.

- List three situations (for example, a party, at home with the family, with a boyfriend or girlfriend, on the job, or in this class). Name a person in each situation (for example, new acquaintance at a party, your mother, or your boyfriend). Name the topics most appropriate to each situation.

- Describe and share some specific situations or people, and explain how self-disclosure worked or didn't work for you.

- Rate your self-disclosure in this class (1 is low, 10 is high):
  1. I ask for feedback: I want to know how others see me.   always (10) _____ never (1)
  2. I am open (10) _____ closed (1).
  3. I give feedback to let the group and others know how I see them.   always (10) _____ never (1)
  4. I am trusting (10) _____ not trusting (1).
  5. In this class I have risked a lot (10) _____ a little (1).

- Rate each person in your group on the following (10 high; 1 low):
  1. Asks for feedback.
  2. Open to closed.
  3. Gives feedback; does not give feedback.
  4. Is trusting.
  5. Risks evaluation by others.

We cannot say that risk-takers are better than others, or more courageous, or more foolhardy. Choosing risk over safety is, in the final analysis, a personal choice. Risk-taking is a more attractive choice when the risks are taken in a supportive environment where everyone agrees to confirm each other as in an interpersonal communication class. The rules are different outside the classroom. Yet once we use this class environment to change ourselves, trust and risk become easier to experience out in the world.

What do we risk when we disclose ourselves? Above all, we are afraid of what we will find. To expose the self is to become transparent. It takes courage to look. Another risk is when others disclose themselves. If we listen and accurately receive messages from others, we run the risk of having our own thoughts and feelings changed. We do not want to expose ourselves to ideas and views that are different. We have invested ourselves emotionally in our own defense of ourselves as represented by our biases. Honest sending and receiving expose us to the possibility that we might become different. We fear finding out about ourselves, exposing the way we really are, and the possibilities of change. *In this sense, communication requires self-trust, inner security, and personal courage.*

Trust is often a self-fulfilling prophecy. A person who expects to be disliked and rejected acts suspicious and guarded. Others withdraw, and the person says, "See, I knew they would reject me. I was right." Those who expect to be liked behave with warmth and friendliness. As a result, others find them congenial and trustworthy. People often conform to the expectations of others.

The other side of trusting is to be trustworthy. Trustworthy people respond to others' risks in responsible ways. They confirm and support others who risk sharing themselves and disclosing their feelings. Trusting, like self-disclosure, is often reciprocal.

A friend is a person with whom I may be sincere. Before him, I may think aloud.

Ralph Waldo Emerson

The following activities can help us explore trust with others.

- *Trust cradles:* In groups of six or eight, move to an area where you have enough room. One person volunteers to lie down. The rest of the group divides into two and stands on each side of the person. They slip their hands under the person lying down and then, slowly and carefully, lift him or her up (not higher than the shoulders of the shorter members of the group). Then they rock the person slowly and smoothly in silence. After a minute or 50 seconds, they slowly lower the person to the floor. Each person who volunteers to have this experience can be cradled. After those who wish to be cradled have had the experience, talk about it and tell about your feelings.

- *Trust walk:* Choose partners. One person at a time closes his or her eyes and pretends to be blind. The other person will act as a guide and lead him or her around outside for ten minutes. The guide's intentions are to take good care of the blind partner and also to have the partner experience a full range of sensory impressions such as touching, hearing, and smelling. Then switch roles. After the trust walk is completed, come back to class and share the experience. Those who do not want to share can write about their experiences. What were some of your thoughts? Feelings? Sensations? Were you able to trust your partner? How much?

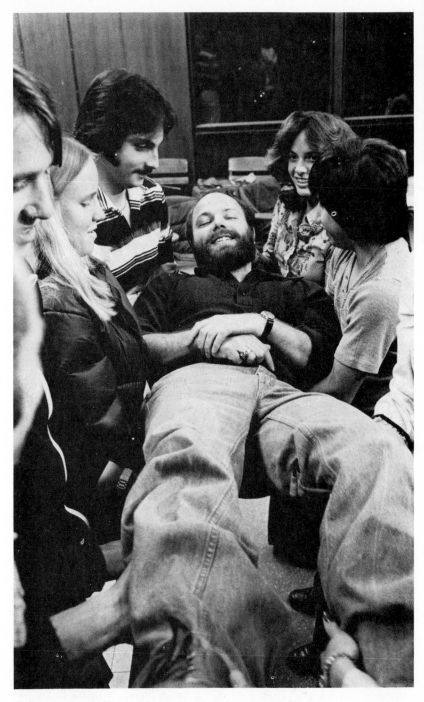

Trust cradles help people explore trust with others.

The quality and experience of trust are difficult to define. Yet we can list some important aspects of a trusting environment. In a relationship we feel safe when we are with sensitive, responsive, open, and trusting people. Such people have a great deal of self-knowledge, including an awareness of their roles or "games," manipulations, and double messages. Trustworthy people tend to be more authentic and more aware than others. Their integrity prevents them from exploiting others or using them as objects. They are experienced at listening intensely and being totally available to others. They do *not* give advice, criticize, or attempt to change others. They know that all they have to share is themselves as they truly are and allow those to whom they are relating to be all they can be at that moment in time.

In a trusting situation, two individuals can explore each other and involve themselves in mutual growth, in a fully sharing process, a moment-to-moment transaction. And, just as one does not learn to swim by watching others swim, in a growing relationship people are willing to risk, respond, and get involved. They bring trust, courage, openness, the ability to tolerate ambiguity, and, above all, a personal commitment to becoming all that they can become. They must struggle with the desire to know and be known to be responsibly involved in the relationship. The intensely personal fulfillment of such trust and risk can be immeasurable. Yet the values of self-disclosure, trust, and risk must be personally and individually chosen. It all depends on the situation and the relationship—which are constantly changing.

Values in Transition

Value formation, value conflict, and value change give rise to many human difficulties—problems of identity and maturation; racial, sexual, or religious conflicts; family disputes; the struggle between freedom and responsibility; and the opposition of rational thinking and emotional expression. The values of young people confronted for the first time with the problems of the adult world often conflict with the demands of adults. These clashes of values can be very painful for all those concerned and usually result in experiences that change our pictures of ourselves and our society.

Although much has been written about the trauma or pain of adolescents in coming to terms with their own values in conflict with social values, little attention has been paid to the problems of values in adults. *Just as young people are constantly changing values, so are most adults.* Adults often are not aware of this confrontation as adolescents are. Adults usually consider their own guiding principles as relatively stable. Yet as the culture changes, each of us continually changes also. Often the painful transition in the adult goes unrecognized as a value change.

Pain springs from our resistance to change and from the tensions between old beliefs and new realizations. Looking at sources of difficulty in determining values can help us. *External conflicts* are those between our personal values and the culturally derived values. *Internal conflicts* often occur when values are not internally consistent, but values need not be internally consistent. *Constant changes* in values cause pain when we view values as static. *Disparity* between verbalized values and behavior causes tension. Yet there is often a natural disparity between verbalizing values and acting them out. When we become more aware of these sources of difficulty, we can be more accepting of ourselves and others.

Each of us can benefit by becoming more conscious of change and conflict in values as a necessary condition for growth.

- Write down your values and find any conflicts between the values you have listed. If you value marriage and family, for example, and you also value freedom, visualize the requirements of a family of individuals who join together on a path through life. How might that value limit your options to be free, to go anywhere you want to go, to do anything you want to do, any time you want to do it?

    Order your values according to priorities: most important to least important. Remember that values can be lived at different times in life. Freedom first and family later, for example, or family first and freedom later.

- Try to remember your values of ten years ago. It may help you to think about where you lived, what relationships you had, what you were doing at that time. With the help of the lists of values on pages 74 and 76, write about several values you have now that are *different* from those you had five years ago. First simply name the values that have changed. Have they

Conflicts in values usually result in experiences that change our pictures of ourselves and our society.

changed in intensity or direction? Or have they been replaced? Then list several values that are relatively the *same* as you had five years ago. How stable are these values? How are these values related to your concept of yourself—your self-identity?

In this chapter, Creating Self-Concept, we have looked inward to examine who we are and what we value. We have explored the forces that have created our self-image and self-esteem. We found that self-esteem depends upon a realistic self-concept which we communicate first with ourselves and then with others in relationship through self-disclosure, trust, and risk. In the process of valuing, we find some degree of personal power. We can assert ourselves as individuals and we can raise our sense of self-worth.

Few things in life are more directly related to happiness and quality of life than liking the self and others. Self-understanding and self-acceptance are the foundations for our interactions with others. When we can function effectively in intrapersonal communication, interpersonal communication improves and relationships become more satisfying.

FOR FURTHER READING

Canfield, Jack, and Wells, Harold C. *100 Ways to Enhance Self-Concept in the Classroom.* Englewood Cliffs, N.J.: Prentice-Hall, 1976.
> These exercises may be used by teachers, parents, or students of any age to enhance self-development.

James, Muriel, and Dorothy Jongeward. *Born to Win.* Reading, Mass.: Addison-Wesley, 1971.
> The authors suggest theories and exercises that will help the reader develop positive self-esteem and self-confidence.

Jourard, Sidney. *The Transparent Self.* New York: Van Nostrand, 1964.
> This study is one of the best-known and most easily read paperback books on self-disclosure.

Powell, John. *Why Am I Afraid to Tell You Who I Am?* Chicago: Argus Communications, 1969.
> The author writes a poetic and personal example of how self-disclosure is a way to find the self.

Rogers, Carl. *On Becoming a Person.* Boston: Houghton Mifflin, 1961.
> Rogers develops his theory of what it is to be a human being, how to grow through self-acceptance, and how to create a positive environment for the growth of others.

Simon, Sidney, et al. *Values Clarification.* New York: Hart, 1972.
> This book offers a clear exposition of the value process with exercises, questions, and activities that can lead to clarifying one's values.

4

Communicating with Others

We have been exploring communication as a process of creating meaning, perception, and self-concept. Intrapersonal communication provides us with methods for getting to know ourselves better and gives us a solid basis for interpersonal communication—particularly as we will be experiencing it in this class. But the theories, principles, and experiences learned here apply to all fields of communication both inside and outside the classroom.

Interpersonal communication *generally concerns itself with speaking transactions involving two or more people in a setting of mutual interest and personal closeness in which the primary content of the communication is each individual in the group.* The messages concentrate on the sharing of the self as a person in a warm, supportive environment. Each person in this situation assumes the roles of both sender and receiver of verbal and nonverbal messages. During these transactions each person shares his or her perceptions, intentions, and values.

There are different types of groups: primary groups, social groups, problem-solving groups, educational groups, and therapy groups. **Primary groups** give us our earliest experiences and begin with the family. They are complex, intimate, and important to personal and social growth. When we go to school our peers and friends are included in our primary groups, the most basic groups to which we belong. In this class we will concentrate on the kinds of interactions and communication transactions that occur in primary groups, since they form the foundation for the other types. Other courses are designed for problem-solving, education, or therapy. This book stresses personal transactions in which the content of the communication message deals with the individual person in relationship.

INTERACTING WITH OTHERS

Although we need other people in order to communicate, the mere presence of others in our field of consciousness does not necessarily result in interpersonal communication. Although you are aware of other people in an elevator, you usually do not respond to them nor they to you. In fact, in our culture we often pretend no one else is present, which provides us with a way of dealing with more people in our environment than we can possibly relate to. In certain social situations, we do not look at other people directly or speak to them. Each individual chooses how to react to the many social conventions we have been taught. Our culture suggests that starting a conversation with strangers in an elevator is inappropriate—in fact, it may even be an invasion of another's privacy.

Similarly, a collection of people standing in line at a movie do not make a "group." A group has some cohesive bond other than mere presence. Usually people in a group interact with one another in some verbal or nonverbal manner that has a purpose, defined or not. For example, individuals at a party are there for the purpose of socializing and having fun.

In an interpersonal communication class, members share many of the goals of a social group, a personal interaction group, and a dyadic group. Usually the purpose of socializing and relaxing at a party involves small talk and a casual atmosphere. In contrast, members of this class meet to gain information about themselves and about the theory of interpersonal communication, to practice that theory in small groups, to experience themselves in interaction, to share feedback on the effects they have on others. Ultimately, the class members hope to apply what they learn and experience to their personal relationships outside class.

In the interpersonal communication class, self-disclosure, risk, feedback, emotional involvement, and personal relationships are more or less appropriate depending on the level of intimacy each individual freely chooses. At times we all choose to remain superficial in our relationships. One way we avoid depth in a conversation is by talking about cars, sports, movies, books, current events, politics—any topic except *ourselves*. Sometimes we are unaware of our attempts to avoid self-disclosure. In this class, we can learn how to respect lines of privacy when people are *aware* they have drawn these lines.

We have the opportunity in this class to experience, if we choose, what happens when we risk and share ourselves even when we allow others to choose to risk less or more of themselves. It is difficult to value intimacy and yet respect another's privacy. Here we can practice accepting and acknowledging others with their different backgrounds, diverse characteristics, and different values. We commit ourselves to practice approval and encouragement of others. We can experience our interdependence with others by giving and receiving emotional support without discrimination as to physical appearances or beliefs. We can learn how to initiate and expand relationships as we learn and practice our communication skills.

Becoming aware of social conventions can help us respect others' privacy and deal more smoothly with interactions.

- Discuss situations, as in elevators, where we do not make eye contact or speak to strangers. How do you feel about ignoring others or pretending they are not there? Try starting conversations with people in elevators or in lines while waiting, and record their verbal and nonverbal responses. How do they react?

- The limits of intimacy and privacy are situational. How do they differ in large groups, small groups, and two-person communication? Give specific examples.

- How easily do you start conversations at a social gathering? Do you initiate or do you wait until someone comes over to talk to you?

- How do you define intimacy and privacy? Discuss a situation in which you felt someone violated your limits.

- Discuss social situations in which you have experienced discomfort.

- Discuss social situations in which you have felt stimulated or successful in communicating. What do such situations have in common for you?

In this class you may have many experiences in small, unstructured groups designed for practicing the theories of interpersonal communication. Some people initially experience some anxiety or defensiveness. As masks and roles are cautiously given up, the real persons begin to emerge. As a climate of safety is created, individuals start to express real feelings, both positive and negative. People begin to hear each other as they form relationships and begin to care about each other. With caring comes the ability to risk giving and receiving honest feedback. These group experiences tend to carry over into communicating and relating outside the group.

The interpersonal communication class offers experiences not afforded in work, in the church, in other classes, or in modern

A small group practices interpersonal communication.

family life. It provides a place where emotions and thoughts can be spontaneously expressed without first being carefully censored or bottled up for fear of hurting someone, being disliked, or losing a relationship. These small groups can be used to experience and share disappointments and joys, anxieties and values, fears and hopes. Such humanizing elements often result in developing patterns of communicating and relating that are more fulfilling than those of the past.

Jack and Lorraine Gibb write that growth is a feeling of the inner self—"an emergence and fulfillment of an unguessed inner potential, emerging, and becoming." They say: "In our experience this optimal growth occurs most frequently in groups that have no professional leader . . . in which . . . emergent and interdependent strength is maximized." They believe that human growth is essentially a social and interdependent process.

There are a number of guidelines that may help your group relate more openly. This checklist can also be used to evaluate your group participation after each meeting. Discuss each of the following guidelines:

1. Use the "I" point of view (in place of "people . . . they," or "one . . . oneself," or "you").

2. Avoid judgment words ("good/bad," "right/wrong," "should/ should not").

3. Avoid giving advice ("If I were you . . .").

4. Avoid superficial conversations and small talk (cars, sports, movies, clothes).

5. Take responsibility for your decisions and actions (avoid blaming others or rationalizing).

6. Listen to others—not only to their words but to the tone and feelings behind the words. Watch for nonverbal cues.

7. Listen to yourself—try to find ways in which you are deceiving yourself (saying what you do *not* mean, professing feelings you do *not* feel, denying feelings you *do* feel). Express thoughts or feelings as honestly as you can.

8. When you listen, ask questions. Try to clarify what the other person is saying. Give feedback about how the other person is

coming across (to you), but be open to his or her rejection of your perceptions.

9. Avoid trying to get others to talk; it's *their* choice.

You will get out of a group what you put in. You can choose to contribute little, but if you do you are likely to receive little. And everyone has something to contribute, for we are all unique.

Two-Person Communication

During a single day, most of us interact with many people. Sometimes we simply ask for directions; at other times we become involved in complex transactions with individuals we have known for a long time. To *simulate* these natural interactions in an interpersonal communication course, we sometimes function as a whole class, sometimes in small groups, and sometimes in pairs or **dyads.**

Because our most common form of everyday interaction is the dyad, we need to develop skills in **two-person transactions.** Such competence is the basis for developing meaningful relationships as well as being the model for functioning in larger groups. We can begin by sharing with others in the class what we have learned about ourselves, for this information is the subject matter of interpersonal communication.

Sharing ourselves fully can best be accomplished with one other person. Friends, spouses, business acquaintances, family members, classmates—*two persons communicating at any time constitutes a dyad*. The dyad is the fundamental unit from which we originally learn about communication. Although similar to all small groups, the dyad is also different in that each participant can experience more involvement, more satisfaction, more frustration, and more participation than in larger groups. In experiencing two-person communication, keep in mind that it is in many ways a microcosm of the larger group.

In studying dyadic communication, we soon become aware that many of our daily transactions seem to be unstructured— talking to someone in a line at a store or theater, at a park or an athletic event, at a party or library. However, these interactions only *appear* unstructured; in reality, they follow established social agreements and roles. Each encounter has a hidden set of rules for socially acceptable communication.

Two-person communication is our most common form of interaction.

Communication between two people often stems from needs and is therefore goal-oriented. The purpose of communicating with others may be to express affection, to share ideas and information about each other, to accomplish some task, to persuade the other person to think or act as we want, to express feelings, to come to agreement about conflicting needs, or simply to enjoy the company of other human beings. Most of these goals overlap, interact, and operate in multidimensional or even contradictory ways.

In dyadic communication, my perceptions of myself, of you, and of how you perceive me influence what I choose to say to you. Your perceptions of yourself, of me, and of how I perceive you influence what you say to me. A dyad begins when two people become aware of each other. First we notice one another and make some kind of verbal or nonverbal contact. When we perceive each other's presence and begin to give meaning to each other's behavior, the dyad develops. We exchange greetings with another person on the street, we share a secret with a friend, we discuss a problem with a confidant; we hope for understanding, sympathy, and support.

On rare occasions, each of us has experienced meeting a new person with whom we quickly developed openness and understanding. Our conversations, at these times, seem to flow freely, without effort or pretense. In these moments, each of us confirms the other person as he or she is, supports the other person's uniqueness, and empathizes with the other's feelings. When we listen attentively and without making judgments, a sense of trust and safety develops. Thoughtful, sincere questions further indicate attention and interest. Such rapport between individuals is the ideal most of us strive for.

But we cannot always be attentive with each other. We cannot always be caring, especially if something in our own lives is disturbing us. Physical appearance, spontaneous attraction, and personality can start a relationship off like a rocket, yet that initial experience can rarely be maintained. The quality of a *sustained* relationship involving intimacy, affection, and love lasting over a period of time differs from a short, one-time meeting. Long-term dyadic relationships, which are usually the most satisfying in our lives, require tolerance, patience, and mutual commitment. These subjects will be developed in greater depth in Chapter 10, Communicating in Relationships.

The following activities provide structured experiences of two-person communication.

- Divide into pairs and take turns asking the following questions:
  1. What makes you happy?
  2. What do you consider to be your strengths?
  3. What do you regard as your weaknesses?
  4. Do you find it easy to make friends?
  5. What difficulties are you experiencing in your life now?

- Tell your partner about an interpersonal conflict you experienced. Describe the behavior, conversation, and persons involved in the conflict.

- Tell your partner about a time when your reaction was:
  1. "Why did I say that?"
  2. "I wish I hadn't done that!"
- Tell how you feel when:
  1. Someone criticizes you (give an example).
  2. Someone compliments you (give an example).
  3. You are initiating a conversation with a stranger.
  4. You ask for a favor.
  5. You ask for, or accept, or refuse a date.
- After sharing, thank each other, and say good-bye.

Even neutral or negative group meetings can be a learning experience. We can look at our own responses and get to know ourselves and others better. We can transfer what we learn in this class to the outside world, and often we find that our experiences of ourselves and other people change in remarkable ways.

Interaction Styles

Interaction styles are both situational and personal. There are as many ways to interact as there are people. We have no definitive list of rules governing interaction; and we never will have one because there are too many rules and they are too complex. They vary too much and change too rapidly. Yet we can describe some aspects of interaction—such as beginning, ending, and interrupting communication—and discuss some guidelines.

First, the interaction must start. *Beginnings* of conversations are affected by the situation, the nonverbal communication, as well as by the individuals involved in the conversation. We not only have certain rules for classroom situations, for example, but also different rules from one class to the next. In the conventional classroom, students raise their hands to speak; but in an interpersonal communication class, we interact more as we do in our one-to-one relationships in small groups. Each student decides when he or she will initiate a conversation, what contribution to make, how to get that response into the conversation, when to share, when not to share, and even when to change the topic.

In most interpersonal communication classes, the subject of being "interrupted" comes up. Some students intensely dislike being interrupted. In fact, they are offended by it. They believe that being polite involves letting people finish speaking. Responders (people who have comments to make about almost everything) suffer great discomfort if they must wait their turn. Listeners who have responses to make but are afraid to interrupt often lose their thoughts while waiting for their turn to talk. Other people who feel they must have their "speeches" prepared before they speak find that the whole topic of conversation has changed by the time they are ready to comment.

Once a class gets to know the individuals in it, we begin to make "space" or time for slow responders. We often accept interrupters and recognize that they frequently make an effort to hold back their responses. We watch each other for nonverbal cues. We ask shy or silent students if they mind someone asking them questions. We often find that they actually appreciate being invited into the conversation because it is so difficult for them to make an entry. We can even have agreements about signals—for example, we can signal people that they are repeating something they have said before.

The tremendous need to interact in a communication class sometimes causes discomfort. We therefore discuss taking turns, alternating messages, and sharing time. Sometimes two people talk at the same time. The rules on equal time that work for television do not work for groups. We cannot measure how much time each person spends talking and listening, but we can notice rhythms. Our relationships in the class take on different pacing and alternating rates. We can learn to give each other cues about taking turns. We can talk about silences—we can ask: "Who finds silence uncomfortable? Who breaks a silence first in the class or group?" These coordination problems usually occur on an unconscious level. One purpose of this class is to become aware of them so that we can be conscious of how we communicate with others.

Most of us have difficulty with *endings*. Different situations and different individuals have different styles for endings. Ending a conversation can be well coordinated whether it be a letter, a phone call, or a face-to-face encounter. In a class, the clock determines when the class is over. But in most situations we do not have such well-defined endings, and we all have to learn ways to handle them: the end of a meeting, the end of a day with someone, the end of a vacation, the end of a relationship.

The following questions can guide a discussion of the individual styles used by each group member in interacting.

- Notice how you and how others *initiate* conversations. What options are open in each situation?

- What response styles do you have? Are you more of a responder or a listener? Do you often feel guilty for talking too much or not enough? How do you adjust to differences in pacing?

- How do you feel about sharing time equally when talking? Do you know a person who talks too much yet whom you like? Do you know a person who talks too little yet whom you enjoy?

- How do you take turns or interject your comments into a conversation?

- What conversational phase presents the most problems for you: initiating, keeping a conversation going, taking turns, choosing topics, changing topics, endings?

- How do you feel about people who talk too much, talk too little, interrupt, finish the other person's sentence, or abruptly switch topics or endings? How might people develop these styles?

Class discussions on how people feel about endings provide the opportunity to develop skill at completing a communication.

- In class, discuss the following topics. How do you end a telephone conversation? Do you have friends who are too abrupt for you, who simply say good-bye and hang up? Do you have friends you don't seem to be able to get away from because you don't know how to end the conversation? We all use typical expressions: "I'll call you tomorrow," "I'll see you when I get back from my vacation," "We'll all get together next week." These are promises of some future contact. What expressions do you rely on? A goodnight kiss, a parting joke, a loving comment depend on the situation and the individuals in the relationship. In a class, a teacher may save a few minutes at the end of the period to summarize what he or she wants the students to remember. How will you bring your interpersonal groups to an end?

In this class, we are learning to become more aware of all the dynamics of interacting with others in different situations. As a result, we will become more aware of our own personal styles and the ways that others interact. *Interacting styles are an intricate part of the communication process.*

Group Norms and Goals

Whenever people gather in groups of two or more, they develop group norms and goals specific to their particular interaction. For example, we can study our own interpersonal communication class as it develops its own norms, rules, and goals. Some campus regulations, such as no smoking in classrooms, come from outside the class itself. Attendance rules, test and grade requirements, credit units, and degrees are part of the academic structure. In addition, each college defines the course content and sets up certain guidelines for the curriculum. Then each teacher defines

Groups develop norms and goals which are specific to their particular interaction.

and interprets more concretely what he or she considers important. The individual student decides what to participate in. As a result of all these interactions, no two classes are ever the same.

Group norms often develop without being verbalized. If one student uses a swear word and sees another student flinch or look embarrassed, he or she may or may not accept that discomfort as a guide for choosing language. The student who is uncomfortable has the option to remain silent or to tell the class, "I feel uncomfortable with swear words." Then the other members of the class must choose whether or not they will be more selective with their language. Similarly, each student, verbally or nonverbally, will let others know what he or she believes is appropriate content for discussion. One class may discuss sex more freely than another. One class will choose to be social; another will choose to be intimate. The language and topics, the emotional tone of the class, the norms, the goals—all are affected by the interactions among instructor and students in class, in groups, and outside of class.

Each individual has some responsibility for what occurs in this class. One student may ask questions of a shy student who does not want to be the center of attention. Another student might ignore the silent one. Whatever others do, the shy student then will have some choices: to speak, to say "I pass," "I don't know," or "I don't want to talk." After a week or two, the class settles into some established guidelines that they themselves have often unconsciously created. Each individual in the class has made some contribution to the group's social controls and direction. These norms may include dress and hair style, as well as language and content. Each person consciously or unconsciously makes his or her contributions, verbal and nonverbal.

Sometimes group norms, if left unexamined, get in the way of achieving group and individual goals. If members accept a norm of continual politeness, for example, they may not experiment. In your interpersonal communication group, you can experiment with different ways of communicating and relating:

If you usually agree with others, try disagreeing.

If you usually say yes, try saying no.

If you often rebel or resist others, try going along with the group.

If you smile even when angry, try talking without smiling.

If you usually wait until someone else talks, try initiating.

If you usually start conversations, try waiting.

If you usually try to be polite, see how it feels to express annoyance.

If you usually defend yourself, try saying "I hear you."

If you usually need a lot of approval, ask for critical feedback.

If you usually control your feelings, try expressing them.

If you are ordinarily a secretive person, try sharing a secret.

If you ordinarily compliment others, give critical feedback.

If you have difficulty accepting a compliment, try saying "Thank you."

If you have difficulty giving compliments, try saying "I appreciate you."

If you recognize some difficulty in the way you respond to others, tell your group. For example, you might say, "I have difficulty saying 'Thank you.' I want to learn to acknowledge others." As you experiment with new ways of communicating, focus on examining how they feel. When we become aware that we are manipulating, protecting or attacking, describing or judging, we broaden our options. The Joker can become more serious, The Mother Hen can let others stand up and protect themselves, The Attacker can learn to describe rather than judge.

The tone and quality of each group will differ not only from each other but also from meeting to meeting. Certain kinds of behavior strengthen a group. Acceptance, self-disclosure, trust, caring, expressing feelings—all can provide the members with comfortable, positive experiences. But people also grow through uncomfortable experiences, through becoming aware of their own self-deceptions and the ways that they irritate others. We can learn how to confront others with our feelings in positive ways. For example:

"Bob, sometimes you have a tendency to horse around in our group and I feel uncomfortable with that."

"Jane, I feel as if you talk a lot about yourself, and I want to talk about me too."

"Curt, I notice you often get off on tangents and I have a difficult time following you. I would like to let you know when you are losing me; would that be all right with you?"

"John, sometimes I feel as if you are daydreaming. You keep looking out the window and I wonder if you are with us."

Confronting someone with your feelings means expressing those feelings without hostility or manipulation. Many people want to hear what another person finds difficult to deal with in addition to what people like about them. For example, Jan, the mother of five children, has worked all her life as well as kept house and raised children. Because of her busy schedule, she finds little time for small talk or social amenities such as "Hello," "How are you today?" "I'm fine, and how are you?" Jan starts right out with what she has to say. Some people find her abruptness difficult to handle. When they tell her and she explains how crowded her time schedule is, most people can then accept her abruptness. And Jan also has the option of being more sensitive to those people who prefer to get to the essence of a conversation gradually.

Increasing our sensitivity to communication patterns and relationships is our goal. It is impossible to understand human relationships without understanding something of how we as communicators relate to each other. When we define our relationships, we place boundaries on the ways we communicate. And our interactions are often simply attempts to clarify or redefine our relationships. *Interpersonal communication and relationships are inseparable.*

INTERPERSONAL VALUES IN COMMUNICATING

In the last chapter we explored personal values. Whenever we imply that we can become better communicators, we imply that some ways are better than others—therefore, we want to explore **interpersonal values** in communicating. We begin here only as a foundation upon which to build throughout this course. In Chapter 1, for example, we discussed *awareness*. We assume that being

*Kindness in words creates
confidence.
Kindness in thinking
creates profoundness.
Kindness in feeling creates
love.*

Lao Tzu

aware of what is being communicated is better than being un-aware. In Chapter 2, we found that *empathizing* with others is one way to overcome communication breakdowns, particularly when they are caused by conflicting perceptions. In Chapter 3, we suggested that *self-disclosure* and *trust* can be valuable assets in communicating and relating. In this chapter, we will learn some ways to communicate *acceptance*—to confirm, validate, and support others. Then we will explore what it means to become more authentic and real in communicating.

Communicating Acceptance

How can we communicate acceptance to others and nurture self-acceptance in ourselves? Thomas A. Harris, M.D., author of *I'm O.K., You're O.K.*, says that children who have had a lot of approval generally trust others, have self-confidence, and feel they are "O.K."

Harris points out four basic life positions: (*1*) I'm not O.K.—you're O.K., (*2*) I'm not O.K.—you're not O.K., (*3*) I'm O.K.—you're not O.K., and (*4*) I'm O.K.—you're O.K. In the *first* position, we feel at the mercy of others. We need support and recognition from those we perceive as being O.K. We worry about what others think, and we communicate to others that we are self-rejecting and need their support. In the *second* position, we show rejection of both self and others. In the *third* position, we reject all others, want to be alone, are ultraindependent, and do not want to get involved. In the *last* position, we accept both ourselves and others, and we communicate appreciation of all human beings. This last position facilitates the development of close, meaningful relationships and open communication with others.

Considerable research indicates that self-acceptance and the acceptance of others are related. If you think well of yourself, you are likely to think well of others. Self-acceptance can set up self-fulfilling prophecies where expectations concerning the self and others are confirmed as a result of behavior.

Each of us at times needs the support of others. In certain situations, most of us experience moments of depression, cynicism, or self-doubt. And most of us at times may be neutral or indifferent to others. To increase your self-acceptance, you need to let other people know you and experience you. Self-assurance can be learned.

Children who receive a lot of approval generally feel they are "O.K."

Harris uses Eric Berne's concept of The Parent, The Adult, and The Child voices within us. He says The Parent is life as it was taught; The Child is life as it was felt; and The Adult is life as it is. Harris suggests that the goal is to "plug in" The Adult and turn off the frightened Child. He says The Adult knows that if being smarter (or best) were essential to happiness, few people would be happy. We cannot change the past, but we can recognize the "tapes"—all those Parent and Child recordings of our past: those archaic fears. We can learn to replace the critical Parent voice with self-acceptance. The goal is to explore the possibilities of change, to establish self-esteem, to develop self-direction, to discover freedom of choice, and to accept responsibility for actions and growth.

Most of us need practice and suggestions about communicating acceptance. We can learn, for example, that praising and reassuring can be as threatening as criticism. The mother who says "good boy" implies that her son is good only as long as he behaves the way she wants him to behave. Accepting communication simply says: "I am listening." "I understand." "I am interested." "Tell me more about it." "I am here with you."

Culturally we have learned certain stock responses, certain role-related dialogue that usually communicates judgment, criticism, obligation, or advice. These role responses in the left-hand column below relate to an identity that can be changed. As you read about The Judge, The Lecturer, The Commander, The Preacher, and others, see if you recognize any of these responses in yourself. Ironically, criticizers are usually their own worst enemies because they often use these negative responses on themselves as well as others. Responses in the right-hand column simply list some expressions that communicate acceptance. If overused, they too can be stock responses. But as examples of acceptance they can be used as a starting point.

Role	Communicating Acceptance
The Judge—evaluates/judges: "That's stupid." "You're lazy." "You're wrong."	"What can be done about that?" "Let's see if something else might work."
The Lecturer—argues/instructs: "That's not the way." "It's true that . . ." "These are the facts." "Do it this way."	"What would happen if . . .?" "Which way seems better?"
The Commander—orders/directs: "Don't do that," "Do what you are told." "No! You can't." "You must." "You have to . . ."	"Are you aware that . . .?" "Let's discuss your options." "You appear disappointed."

The Preacher—moralizes/obligates:

"It's your duty." "You should (not)." "You ought (not)."   "Which do you think would be best?" "What do you feel might work?"

The Threatener—warns/admonishes:

"You'd better." "If you don't . . ." "Listen to me . . . or else!"   "I want to understand why you don't want to do it." "What did I say that turned you off?"

The Avoider—withdraws/diverts:

"Let's discuss it later." "I forget . . ." "Let's change the subject."   "Let's look at this further." "Can you tell me how you're feeling?"

The Questioner—examines/interrogates:

"Why . . ." "Where have you been?" "What's the *real* reason?"   "I've missed you." "You don't need to explain if you don't want to."

The Analyzer—interprets:

"What you need is . . ." "What's wrong with you is . . ." "Your problem is . . ."   "What are your choices?" "What would you like to do?" "Give me some examples."

The Joker—is sarcastic/"kids":

"Just like all men (women)!" "Where did you get your degree in wisdom?" "Burn the school down."   "I care about you." "I appreciate your understanding." "Your interpretation is different."

The Helper—offers solution/advises:

"Why don't you . . ." "If I were you . . ." "Let me suggest . . ." "It would be best if . . ."   "I hear what you are saying." "What would you suggest?"

The Praiser—approves/gives positive judgment:

"You are right." "You are so nice." "I approve."   "I'll listen." "You sound happy."

The Sympathizer—reassures:

"Don't worry." "Don't feel bad." "You'll feel better tomorrow." "It's not that bad . . . everybody feels that way."   "What worries you about that?" "This is a difficult time for you."

Confirming Others

Martin Buber said that "a society may be termed human in the measure to which its members confirm one another." It is much easier to write about and to know than to practice positive, supporting communication. When we respond to people, we either confirm the speaker's messages or deny them. How can we convey agreement or disagreement with a message without invalidating the individual?

Be gentle with yourself. You are a child of the universe, no less than the trees and the stars: you have a right to be here.

Desiderata

Some people make others feel more whole, more worthwhile, more valuable than other people do. These nurturing people are warm, empathetic listeners as well as dynamic, energetic, positive people with strong ethical or value systems. They inspire hope, imagination, and optimism in others. They create good feelings in others, an aliveness that is contagious. In the presence of such people growth, self-awareness, and humanness can be experienced.

We are disconfirmed when treated as if we did not exist, as if our behavior and feelings were stripped of their meaning or consequences, and when our self-definitions are invalidated. Many studies indicate that it is worse to be ignored than to be criticized or punished. In a study of grammar school students, those who were commended or complimented for their good work improved. Those who were punished with bad marks or negative comments also improved, although not as much as those who were rewarded with positive feedback. The students who were ignored, given no grades and no feedback of any kind, declined in performance. This experiment has been repeated at different times with different groups. The most devastating experience for human beings is to be treated as if they did not exist. Even negative recognition is better than none.

In our culture, we have learned certain stock responses that are nonsupportive messages. When we feel uncomfortable about another person's feelings we may say: "You shouldn't feel that way!" "You don't really mean that. You're only saying that because you're angry. You'll get over it." "Forget it. You'll feel better tomorrow." "Everybody feels that way sometime." Even answering the small child who says, "Nobody loves me" with "*I* do" tells the child he or she is wrong. Most of these messages deny the feelings of the other person. *When we cannot handle other people's feelings, we cannot really listen to them.* It is better to say: "I hear what you're saying, and I don't know what to say to make those feelings go away. I wish I knew what to do. All I can do is be here with you. And I do care about you." To the small child you can say: "I know how it feels to feel as if no one loves you. At times in my life I have felt as if no one loved me. It doesn't feel good to feel that way."

We need to become aware of ritualistic replies that are not really personal or supportive but are roles that we play— affirming mother, good-guy boss, supportive teacher. *In genuine support, every time we communicate we create a personal, new response.* Never before have we responded to this human being in this situation with these feelings. It requires energy and time to respond to another individual in such a personal way. It also takes a great deal of self-esteem and personal identity to have the energy to give to others without feeling that their problems might engulf us. When we do not feel this strength, it is more genuine to say: "I can hear you are suffering and you want to work that out. At the moment I find it very difficult to give you my energy because I have used so much of it today to work out some personal problems of my own. I am with you at a time when I have very little to give. I just wanted to share that with you."

Confirming others in a relationship involves giving them supporting messages, both nonverbal and verbal, that recognize their ideas and feelings as valid. Supportive messages also communicate that we are interested in others as unique individuals, that we are willing to become involved with them as people. Such nonverbal gestures as finding them a chair, standing up and moving toward them with a smile, being prompt for an appointment, sitting near them, or touching them all show caring. Verbally, we can communicate that we understand others and can hear what they are saying, that we feel empathy for their point of view, and that we are concerned about them and recognize their needs and goals. In all these ways we communicate our regard for others as special, unique human beings.

Many of us are reluctant to give support unless we are *agreed with,* which makes us feel another person is confirming us. So the important confirming relationships are not those in which people simply agree with each other, but those moments when we are listening and sense the deep differences between ourselves and

Confirming others involves giving them both verbal and nonverbal support.

others and yet can trust others with their differences. Unless we can risk the effects of these differences, the deepest level of support will not be experienced. *The test of relationship is its ability to survive stress—to risk knowing and sharing the deepest experiences of difference with others. The ultimate risk is confirming others who are not like us.* This kind of risk takes great personal strength and results in self-confirmation for our own values. For it is in our differences that we find the wonder of caring and loving each other. It is our uniqueness, rather than our likeness, that needs support and validation. These are the gifts we can give to each other.

Confirming another person does not mean agreeing or giving positive reinforcement simply to make others feel better. Support includes the intention to understand others, to find out how they feel and think, to encourage open communication. You create trust by showing appreciation of others as people, by expressing yourself in return with such expressions as "I'm glad you are sharing your feelings with me. It makes me feel close to you when you trust me and are yourself with me." In the process of giving support, we gain as well as give personal growth, self-awareness, and humanness. People who make others feel more whole, more worthwhile, and more valuable create these same feelings for themselves.

Learning how to confirm others begins with becoming aware of one's present style of communicating.

- Place yourself on the following continuum. Where do you operate much of the time in your relationships?

Confirming————————————————— Disconfirming

Confirming	Disconfirming
enhances self-evaluation	fails to enhance self-image
direct, open, clear messages	responses are absent, off the subject, unclear
congruent	incongruent
relevant to prior message	irrelevant, ambiguous, inadequate
immediate response	delayed response
expressed understanding	confused, dissatisfying, disinterested
personal	alienating, impersonal

- Choose one person in your group and say: "What I value about you is . . . ." Complete the sentence for every person in your group.

- Write down the name of every person in your family. Then complete this sentence for each person: "What I appreciate about _____ is _____."

- Notice a waitress, bus driver, police officer, or salesperson who acts friendly or serves people with a smile, and tell his or her boss how you appreciate that person and that you hope the boss will communicate that appreciation to the employee.

- Write a note of appreciation to someone: friend, relative, teacher, author, politician.

Being Authentic

The most beautiful gift we can give each other is the truth.

Anonymous

Honesty in communicating comes from being authentic and real. The body, for example, communicates nonverbal messages that are sometimes more honest than words; and when verbal and nonverbal messages are congruent, our body language reflects that unity. The body is much less subject to conscious deception than thoughts and language. Honestly expressing feelings becomes possible when we allow our feelings into consciousness. There are always new thoughts and feelings coming to the surface; therefore *awareness is a lifelong expanding process.* With more awareness, being authentic becomes a conscious choice.

In *The Search for Authenticity*, J. F. Bugental says that authentic concern seems to be a matter of "being willing to make commitments, to let things matter, and yet to retain sufficient perspective so that one is not catastrophically imperiled or overcome by reverses." Authenticity involves a selective commitment of energies with less concern about how others see us. Authentic people say no to many possibilities and to many people because they are selective in their use of time and energy.

In his book *The Transparent Self*, Sidney Jourard writes about inauthenticity as the "tendency to treat oneself as an object, a tool to be manipulated . . . to bring about popularity, vocational success, power, and similar goals. When one treats oneself as a tool or as a thing, one treats others in the same way. This repression of what is real results in self-concealment and a loss of touch with the self."

In Martin Buber's model of communication, I (sender) and Thou (receiver) exchange a message that acknowledges the free identity of each person. The very basis of authenticity depends upon acknowledging the receiver *as a person* rather than a thing to be manipulated. When in conflict (personal or social), we sometimes send ambiguous or contradictory messages. We exhibit qualities we may label artificial, insincere, or hypocritical. Hypocrisy is the act of pretending to have a character, beliefs, or principles that one does not possess. Simply wanting to be more honest may result in perceiving the self as more honest than another person considers us. Pretending, being silent, or trying not to hurt someone can also result in feeling unauthentic.

Other conflicts in communication include cutting people off before they have made a point, changing the subject when you do not want to listen, or distracting another person with gestures and expressions. Perhaps there can be no *absolute* interpersonal value system; yet each of us must draw personal lines somewhere. Carl Rogers suggests the following values in communication:

Moving away from facades, defensiveness, "oughts," pleasing others, meeting the expectations of others.

Moving toward goals and potentialities; being real, being one's self, being one's real feelings, being what one is.

Positive values: being self-directed, valuing oneself and one's own feelings, being in process; sensitivity to others, acceptance of others; deep, intimate, complete relationships; openness to all inner and outer experience; sensitivity to inner feelings in oneself and others and to the realities of the objective world.

These values have a common thread. Each individual with such values can move toward his or her own survival and growth and also give others room for actualization and socialization. A climate of respect and freedom in which each human being is valued as a person crosses all cultures and time, thus contributing to the ongoing process of human evolution.

Merely defining and discussing values in the abstract is less effective than giving specific examples from your experiences.

- We all occasionally pretend to be what we are not. Discuss a time when you were unauthentic with another person. How did you feel? What alternatives were there to pretending?

- Describe a time when someone was unauthentic with you. How did you feel? How would you have preferred that person to behave?

- Recall a time when you chose to be honest and in the process hurt someone's feelings. How did you feel? Do you think you might have handled the situation differently?

- Discuss some specific experiences you have had with value conflicts.

Once you have thought out a value system, it might be worthwhile to look at those values as *goals*—directions toward which you would like to move. Empathy, warmth, respect,

Every man alone is sincere. At the entrance of a second person, hypocrisy begins.

Ralph Waldo Emerson

genuineness, self-disclosure, and trust are qualities to develop. To deal openly and directly with others in the immediate moment, to let them know where they stand with you, and to acknowledge where you stand with them takes a great deal of practice. *To become more conscious of language, thoughts, body, emotions, and behavior requires intention and commitment to the communication process.*

FOR FURTHER READING

Harris, Thomas. *I'm O.K., You're O.K.* New York: Harper & Row, 1967.
    Harris presents a practical way to use Berne's theory of transactional analysis (Parent, Adult, and Child) to communicate acceptance of self and others.

Luft, Joseph. *Of Human Interaction.* Palo Alto: National Press Books, 1969.
    The author presents "The Johari Window"—a model that illustrates how being open or closed affects understanding of self and others in relationships.

Rogers, Carl. *On Encounter Groups.* New York: Harper & Row, 1970.
    Rogers describes the evolutionary process of group interaction and suggests ways for individuals to interact in leaderless groups to produce personal growth.

Stevens, Barry, and Carl Rogers. *Person to Person: The Problem of Being Human.* Lafayette, Calif.: Real People Press, 1967.
    Stevens writes personal material which illustrates the process of self-disclosure and also connects three of Rogers' key papers.

Stewart, John (ed.) *Bridges Not Walls.* Reading, Mass.: Addison-Wesley, 1973.
    This collection of essays by communication experts stresses ways to develop relationships and avoid communication barriers.

Wilmot, William. *Dyadic Communication: A Transitional Perspective.* Reading, Mass.: Addison-Wesley, 1975.
    Wilmot has produced an excellent book on the two-person communication process.

Part Two

Aspects of Communication

In Part One, The Basis of Interpersonal Communication, we explored the processes of creating meaning and expanding consciousness. We talked about how reality and perception affect us, and we examined how self-concepts are formed. We worked with both personal and interpersonal values.

As we move into the second part of the book, Aspects of Communication, we will discover the network of forces involved in interpersonal communication. If you experience the feeling that you have covered this material before, search deeply for some variation. Behavior does not change simply because something is said. If a concept appears repetitive to you, look for some fresh relationship between the old concepts and the new material. An insight must be repeated again and again until it is truly experienced.

If some question sounds as if it has been asked before, try to find a new answer in this new context. You may find that your thoughts and feelings are different this time or that you have moved deeper into the subject. When you have grown in some small way, an underlying truth will come to light for you as you connect the web of ideas presented here. As your consciousness expands, allow yourself to ponder anew. Enlightenment comes with the experience of new insights—a fresh synthesis of what you may already know.

Language is a machine for making falsehoods.

Iris Murdoch

5

Talking: How Language Communicates

LANGUAGE AND CULTURE

We are trapped in two communication "prisons," both of them invisible. The first of these is the structure of language itself. The second is the effect of culture on language. All cultures have characteristic ways of dividing up space and time. Space rules teach us the distance to stand from other people and the distance at which to build one house from another. Time rules are equally important. Some cultures stress punctuality; others do not. Even within the United States, certain subcultures respect promptness, while others do not. These unspoken, unconscious rules are programmed into us as children.

Benjamin Lee Whorf says that if we think in one language, we think one way; in another language, another way. This concept helps to explain why our thought is a prisoner of our language. Eskimos have seven different words for snow—they can actually see seven kinds, whereas most of us can only see powdery snow or hard-packed snow. But whereas Eskimos see only a "horse," we can see a "mare," a "stallion," a "pony," a "bay," a "paint," a "chestnut," and so on. Yet vocabulary is a relatively *minor* distinction made by different languages.

*The limits of my language
are the limits of my world.*

Ludwig Wittgenstein

Language sets limits on our perceptions, influences our behavior, and categorizes our experiences. For Hopi Indians, time is not plural. They can see five people, but not five days. They do not think in terms of past, present, or future. For us, time is a commodity that is measurable and occurs between fixed points. Time can be "wasted" or "saved." We can buy time to make decisions and sell time to advertisers. We keep records, diaries, accounts, histories. We plan the future with schedules, programs, and budgets. We pay wages for time worked, rent for time occupied, interest for time that money is loaned, depreciation for time used, and premiums for fixed times of insurance. Hopi culture has none of these beliefs about time. The sequence of events is important to the Hopi but not how "soon." They build their houses brick by brick over a period of many years.

Einstein said, "Our language is compelled to work with words which are inseparably connected with primitive concepts." Einstein joined light to time and time to space; energy to matter, matter to space, and space to gravitation. He transcended the ordinary limits that language sets on perception to find a unity among the forces of gravity, electricity, and magnetism. Every great scientific breakthrough involves transcending the limits of language, perception, and experience.

Language shapes not only our self-images but also our whole lives. We cannot think about or talk about ourselves without language. Language enables us to label our emotions and thoughts; with words we can distinguish one feeling from another and one idea from another. In this sense, language helps us to discover and create ourselves; to establish our relationships to places and people; to sustain our relationships with others; and to identify, shape, and give meaning to our world. This interpretation of language and experience helps explain why language is so personal. Although our cultural language limits our perceptions of our world, each of us also has a personal language that strongly influences our self-images, how we project those images to others, and how others see us.

If you begin to think of language as an extension of yourself, as a medium through which you relate to the world and give meaning to your experiences, you will become more aware of the centrality of language in your life. Words can change our lives. *Language is powerful: It shapes and records your perceptions of reality; it shapes everything you are and all that you are becoming.* James Miller, in *Word, Self, Reality*, says:

Words do not simply accompany experience; more frequently, they *are* the experience, or are its primary content. We live surrounded by language, inside and outside us. It can strangle and suffocate us, or it can connect and link, strengthen and renew us. . . . With it we make our world and ourselves . . . we proclaim our identities, shape our lives . . . and leave our impress on the world.

We possess our language at the same time it possesses us. In this dual process of possessing and being possessed, we use language as a personal, symbolic, and social tool. Anything we say is true only in some situations, not in others; only for some people, not for others. If we are aware of the shortcomings of language, we will gain more control over the way we communicate.

The term *language* includes both verbal and nonverbal symbols. Nonverbal symbols—posture, gesture, vocal inflection, facial expression—are not separable from verbal language. It is impossible to utter a word without some vocal inflection or body involvement. This same interdependence between the verbal and nonverbal subsystems is found even in the act of silent reading. *Language, verbal and nonverbal, is a process.*

WORDS

To linguists, the basic elements of language are sounds. To students of human communication, the basic elements of language are *words*. If words referred only to objects, our communication problems would be eased considerably. But words also refer to events, properties of things, actions, feelings, relationships, and so on. And when our purpose is to translate our experiences so that they can be communicated, then we have difficulties. We cannot communicate the experience itself; we can only communicate a symbolic representation of the experience. Saying "I have a toothache" does not communicate the experience of pain. *Communicating involves sending verbal symbols which create a meaning similar to the one in the mind of the sender.*

Our language is made of individual words put together in certain patterns. Most words have more meanings than dictionaries can keep track of. And when we consider further that each of us has different experiences, memories, likes, and dislikes, it becomes clear that *all* words evoke different responses in each individual. In order to know more about how we use language, we need to look at individual words. *Words are symbols that stand for other things.* Often we confuse those symbols with the things they

"When I use a word," Humpty Dumpty said, in a rather scornful tone, "it means just what I choose it to mean—neither more nor less."

Lewis Carroll

style (stīl) *n.* [ME.<L. *stilus* (sp. infl. by unrelated Gr. *stylos*, pillar)] **1.** manner, fashion **2.** a particular mode or form of skilled construction, execution, or production; the manner in which a work of art is executed *a)* often used for: beauty or loftiness of style *b)* a definite type of architecture *c)* a manner of executing a task or performing an action **3.** manner or mode of expression in language, as distinct from the ideas expressed; way of using words to express thoughts **4.** distinction, excellence, originality, and character in any form of artistic or literary expression **5.** the way in which anything is made or done; manner **6.** *a)* the current, fashionable way of dressing, speaking, acting, etc. *b)* something stylish; esp., a garment of current, smart design *c)* a fashionable, luxurious existence [to live in *style*] **7.** distinction and elegance of manner and bearing.

Figure 5–1 Words are symbols that stand for other things.

represent. The words are *not* the objects or the original events experienced.

The infinite images symbolized by words create great language difficulties for us. Exploring one word can show us how much its meanings vary. The whole class can use the same word.

- Choose one word for a concrete, physical object such as *chair.*
- Develop a detailed mental image of the object that word stands for and describe the chair in writing.
- Share your descriptions.

A better understanding of abstract and concrete words, general and specific words, denotative and connotative words will help us control our use of language, learn more about ourselves, relate better to others, as well as become more clear and precise in our thinking. *Clarity* and *precision* help us say what we really intend to say. It is like being in the driver's seat—in control of the car. As Mark Twain said: "The difference between the right word and the *almost* right word is the difference between lightning and the lightning bug."

Figure 5–2 Language words and grammar.

Abstract/Concrete

Symbols vary in definiteness of meaning. As children learn a language, they begin by learning words that refer to persons or things, such as *doll, ball, momma, daddy, shoe, door.* It is easy to learn such words because they refer to specific objects or people;

their meaning is relatively clear and definite. Many words have less definite referents. Our words vary greatly, from things we can see, feel, touch, and hear (concrete) to words that name feelings, ideas, or actions (abstract). Abstract words refer to things that cannot be seen, touched, or heard, such as *happiness, envy, intelligence,* and *communication.*

Abstract words and ideas cause us a great deal of difficulty in communicating because they conjure up so many different images and experiences. We can point to the referent of such concrete words as *apple, spoon,* or *dog;* but we cannot point to the referent of such abstract words as *love, courage,* or *cheating.* The word *cheating* can be used for copying someone else's answers on a test, accepting too much change at the store, charging too much for work, or hiding an ace in a game of cards. There is no single meaning of the word; moreover, what one person considers dishonest may not be what another person considers dishonest. Complex words, such as *democracy, culture, evil,* and *justice,* have different meanings to each person who uses them, as well as to each person who hears them. It is difficult to use such words in a way that makes clear exactly what is meant.

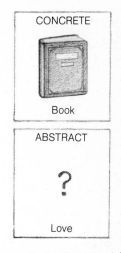

Figure 5–3 Concrete/abstract.

General/Specific

Words run on a continuum from general to specific. The word *chair* is a general (concrete) word that symbolizes a whole class of objects. The phrase "red leather rocker" is more specific because it does not include as many objects. "My red leather rocker" is as specific as I can get because it implies one particular chair within the entire category. The figure below shows how these words can be placed on a continuum.

Figure 5–4 Words can be placed on a continuum from general to specific.

If you say "I have a pet," that sentence has less meaning to me than if you say "I have a full-grown, gray Siamese cat as a pet." Your intention to share with me an image of your *specific* pet makes it more real for both of us—you have created a much clearer image. If you say "I have a car," you may simply mean "I have transportation." If you choose to say "I have a red '68 classic Mercedes-Benz," you are sharing something very different. The listener not only gets a clearer image of the object but also gets more information about the speaker.

Denotation/Connotation

Words have **denotative** and **connotative** meanings. The denotation of a word is its exact, literal meaning. Its connotation is the added meaning the use of the word suggests. A word's denotation identifies its referent. It is a definition as given in a dictionary. A word's connotation gives a secondary or implied meaning. It carries additional meaning, which is often emotional or judgmental.

At the end of the day, when a man says to his secretary, "I am going *home*," he means he is going to the place where he lives. When a soldier in a foreign land tells his comrade "I am going home," he connotes that he is going to his homeland, a place of comfort, safety, and peace. We have many culturally induced emotional responses to words. The words *childish* and *childlike*

"I'm going home."

"I'm going home."

Connotation/denotation.

have the same denotation (characteristics of a child), but their connotations differ. The word *childish* suggests an undesirable quality such as immaturity or silliness; *childlike* suggests desirable qualities such as trustfulness, simplicity, freshness, innocence. Words such as *democracy, children,* and *education* may elicit more favorable social attitudes than *communism, propaganda,* or *anarchist.*

Although dictionaries give some information about the shades of difference among words, context tells more. The situation, the prevailing social attitude, and the people who use it all contribute to the public connotations of a word. Beyond that are the private connotations that stem from each of us, from past personal experiences, age, sex, and value systems. For one person *school* connotes confinement; for another it means intellectual excitement; for still another it signifies sociability. *In choosing your words, you show something of yourself and your value system.* You may often show something of your intentions even when you are not conscious about what you *intend:* to flatter, to hurt, or to describe.

In addition to choice of words, the structure of a language specifies rules of grammar for combining words. A message of four words—*you, her, dislike, only*—can be ordered in several ways so that each arrangement carries a different meaning. For example:

You only dislike her.   Only her you dislike.

Her only you dislike.   Only you dislike her.

You dislike only her.

How others interpret your language depends on the arrangement of words. Different orders result in different meanings; but because we learned the order and structure of words as children, the process is so automatic that we give it little thought. As a result, we often fail to communicate the messages we intend.

In addition to choice and arrangement of words, voice *inflection* affects meaning. For example:

You only *dislike* her.   *You* only dislike her.

You only dislike *her.*   You *only* dislike her.

In these four examples, the words and their order are identical. Yet voice inflection changes the meaning. And the emphasis placed on different words becomes so automatic that we are usually unaware of this aspect of communication. The rules for combining sounds into words and words into phrases, clauses, and sentences make up the *grammar* of a language. As we become more conscious of the different dimensions of language, we can improve the accuracy of the messages we send to others.

THE LANGUAGE PROCESS: SENDING AND RECEIVING

Interpersonal communication as a language process includes many variables:

The **sender**—a person who creates and sends a message.

The **message**—a combination of language and nonverbal communication.

The **channel**—the environment through which the message is transmitted and the context of the communication event.

The **receiver**—a person who hears the message.

Feedback—responses and reactions, verbal and nonverbal.

All these variables operate continually in an ongoing transaction between sender and receiver.

The Sender: Language and Personality

What you are stands over you the while, and thunders so that I cannot hear what you say to the contrary.

Ralph Waldo Emerson

Do the words we use determine our personalities? Or are our personalities reflected in the words we use? Like the question "Which came first—the chicken or the egg?" these unanswerable questions are worth asking because they make us more aware of the connections between words, speech patterns, and the uniqueness of each individual. **Psycholinguistics** is the study of the interaction between linguistic behavior and personality.

A "linguistic personality"—a set of language behavior patterns—is a substantial part of a person's identity. The sense of self is generated, sustained, and preserved in language. Translated into language, the experiences and thoughts that make up a

The speaker sends the message.

person's life can become self-definition. Because verbal behavior reveals personality, simply developing skill in the observation and use of words can change how we relate to ourselves and others.

If we can objectively listen to the patterns of our own speech, we can see into the relationship between the words we use and the way we view the world. Sometimes simply changing the words and patterns will change our view.

- Go through one of your past written assignments and circle words that denote the *absolutes:*

all	everyone	everything
none	everybody	nothing
always	nobody	everywhere
never	no one	nowhere
forever	every	only

- Go through your writing and circle *judgmental* words. For example:

  good/bad   stupid/smart

  right/wrong   lazy/industrious

  should/shouldn't   silly/sensible

- Find your *generalizations.* For example:

  People . . . never change.   Parents . . .

  Nothing ever changes.   Teachers . . .

  Women/men . . .   Teenagers . . .

- Find *unqualified* expressions. For example:

  It is a fact that . . .   I'm sure that . . .

  It is true that . . .   I know that . . .

  I am certain that . . .   There's no doubt that . . .

When we make absolute statements, we forget that most judgments are relative to the situation and person. What is "bad" to you may not be bad to another person. What is "good" to you depends on your judgment system. Success and failure are relative to one's value system and goals. Using words such as *many* or *most* people, rather than *everyone,* reminds us that seldom does "everyone" feel, think, or do the same things.

Statements derived from particular instances are called **generalizations.** We need to generalize, just as we need to stereotype people, to create order. But hasty or unsound generalizations blur our perceptions. Generalizations are often used by politicians and advertisers to get people to act in certain ways. Sometimes children use generalizations to manipulate parents: "Everyone's going, so I have to go, too." To say "all people with money are snobs" or "foreign languages are of no value to high school students" is misleading. When you learn to avoid generalizations, you will become equally aware when someone else tries to manipulate you with careless language.

Our speech habits are at least partly determined by cultural influences. We often adopt such habits from our parents; we pass them on to the next generation; and thus the habits become self-perpetuating. Yet when we become aware of them we are free to choose whether to continue to use them. One example is **oversimplification.** In our culture many people ask *why* others think, feel, and act as they do. The "why" questions lead us to function as if there were only one answer. But there is no single answer. Causation is multiple. Statements that begin with *because* often oversimplify the situation.

In place of why, see if you can get more information by asking *what* is happening. *What* are the meanings behind what is going on here? *How* can we make what we are saying more clear? Meanings are also multiple—there is no single "meaning." Ask: "What can be done about it?" There are many alternative courses of action in any situation. Ask: "What are my options?" "What are your options?" "What are our options in this situation?" Asking *what, how, when,* and *where* helps us avoid the tendency to search for *the cause, the meaning, the answer.*

In addition to oversimplification, we can become aware of excessive use of inflexible words such as *everybody, all, no one, never.* These words restrict options. Conversely, excessive use of vague terms—*perhaps, maybe, seems*—may indicate an inability to make decisions or take a stand.

Linguistic personality also includes voice quality, voice dynamics, pronunciation, vocabulary, and style. We often recognize voices over the phone without being told who is calling. **Voice dynamics** include intonation, rhythm, relative continuity, and speed. Some people habitually use a wider range of pitch than others who speak in a monotone. A person's voice may indicate personality—or one of many personalities that person has available. We all change our voice patterns occasionally, depending on the role we are playing.

The following structured experiences offer an opportunity to identify your speech habits.

- Choose a partner. Talk to each other using only sentences that begin with the words *why* or *because.* Every sentence must be either a question beginning with *why* or an answer beginning with *because.* Then discuss this experience.
- Talk with your partner for five minutes. Begin every sentence with "you should . . . ." Share your feelings about this experience with the rest of the class.

Another personality-linked speech habit is **oververbalization** (talking too much), which may be used to cover up inexact thinking or nervousness or to find meaning in life while actually running away from looking. The opposite tendency, **underverbalization,** may accompany rigid thinking, stereotyping, prejudice, anxiety, need for approval, or perfectionism in speaking or thinking. Each of us differs in *pacing* or timing in our thinking and talking. If these differences are too great, people may not be comfortable in spending much time together. Becoming sensitive to these differences can lead us to find a better balance depending on the situation, the purpose of the communication, and the relationship.

Another speech habit is **interrupting** others. It takes energy to hold back a response until a speaker is finished—then the response may no longer be appropriate. And listeners who hold back much of what they want to say out of politeness often have difficulty sharing their ideas. Cultural rules such as "Don't interrupt!" are so strong that many people are unable to carry on an active conversation. Discussing oververbalizing, interrupting, underverbalizing, and other speech habits can help create better relationships.

Autosuggestions *are suggestions we give ourselves through our use of language.* Autosuggestion, like self-fulfilling prophecies, can influence behavior. When you put your beliefs and expectations into words, the words affect your behavior either positively or negatively. For example, we may say:

"If I stop smoking, I'll gain weight."

"I always get a headache when I don't eat."

"I always get sick when I stay too long in the sun."

"If I eat at night, I can't sleep."

All these statements give us suggestions about behavior and its results.

Autosuggestion can also be used to achieve positive results. Instead of saying "I've always been a poor speller," you can say "My spelling is better than it used to be." Similarly, words can be used to influence others. Telling a child "You seem to be reading better" can be an encouragement that produces further growth in reading.

Many of our language habits are unconscious. By not looking at the ways we use words, we often give up power over ourselves.

Words can be used to avoid responsibility and to hypnotize ourselves. *But words can also be used to create new patterns of behavior in ourselves and in others.*

Our behavior is affected by the statements we make to ourselves.

- Write down some *autosuggestions* that describe behavior you
  want to develop. For example:

  "I'm aware that . . ."

  "I am more sensitive now about . . ."

  "I will remember my dream when I wake up in the morning."

  "I am becoming more specific in my use of words."

  "I can hear myself now when I make generalizations."

  "I am becoming less judgmental about myself."

  "I am beginning to like myself better each day."

- Notice when other members of this class unconsciously give
  themselves suggestions or verbalize self-fulfilling prophecies,
  either positive or negative. Share these observations with each
  other.

- Notice words that indicate regret, self-pity, or self-blame.
  Finish writing the following sentences:

  "If only I had [done something] . . ."

  "What if I had [done something] . . ."

  Now rephrase the sentences to give yourself *positive* suggestions: "Next time . . ."

- Choose a partner and finish the following pairs of sentences.
  Notice the changes in meaning and attitude:

  I have to . . . / I choose to . . .   I need . . . / I want . . .

  I'm afraid to . . . / I'd like to . . .   I can't . . . / I won't . . .

Expressions such as "I need" instead of "I want," or "I can't,"
instead of "I won't," result in our giving up personal responsibility. Our language is so powerful it quite literally shapes what we
see of the world.

*The structure of our language leads us to identify things, ascribe
qualities to them, and then react to those things on the basis of our
labels.* The verb *is* implies something that exists independently of

our personal experience of it. For example, the statement "I am lazy" implies laziness is *all* that I am. But I could describe the same behavior without judging myself: "I prefer to sleep later in the morning" or "I prefer going to the beach to cleaning the house, so I go to the beach."

Labels and judgments restrict us and our self-images. For example, "I am conservative" or "I am intuitive" are in a sense deceptive statements; nobody is simply conservative or intuitive—we are much more than that. Becoming aware of labeling and the "is" of identification can result in better communication by making us more conscious of what limits we set on our minds and experiences.

One way of correcting this labeling process is to "own" such expressions—for example, "*I believe* he is lazy" or "*I perceive* her to be lazy." Such qualifiers show that you recognize that the perception is yours instead of inside the other person. This modification can also help you qualify self-statements: "*I feel* I am lazy" is less absolute than "I am lazy." In addition to qualifiers, you can *disidentify* by avoiding the word *is*. What remains is a human being with the power of originating action and moving toward its potential.

If you discover the identification games you play with words, you can learn to disidentify.

- Go through some of your writing and circle all the *am* and *is* words. For example, use the "Who Am I?" exercise from Chapter 3 (pp. 58–59) and circle the *to be* verbs. Disidentify by rephrasing what you wrote without using *am* or *is*.

- Instead of "Who Am I?" ask the question "Where Am I?" Write an imaginative description of where you are in your life or where you are in relation to friends or family.

- Share your description with your group.

If our semantic habits are related to our behavior, will changing our language result in changing our behavior? This question is worth exploring. If a person stops using such words as *all*, *always*, *never*, and *forever*, will the change in language also change the way he or she thinks? If you change dogmatic language, will you stereotype less? Will you become more flexible? Will becoming more specific tighten up your thinking processes? Will being more concrete help you clarify decisions? Will cutting down on the pure quantity of words improve the thinking of those people who ververbalize? How might more verbalizing change the behavior of people who underverbalize? These questions have no answers. Clearly speech patterns can be changed, but the effect of such changes on your personality cannot be measured scientifically. Only you yourself can experience the connection between language and personality—through your awareness of it in your own life.

Differences in perception and self-concept have a major influence on how we communicate. Whatever the subject of the conversation, we all inevitably talk about ourselves, striving to symbolize and share ourselves as people. Language, in this sense, is self-projection; we filter reality through our own personalities. Since no two people ever perceive "reality" in exactly the same way, we must keep perceptual differences in mind when we discuss how we use language.

Language is also affected by the **context** *of a relationship:* parent/child, sales clerk/customer, lawyer/client, doctor/patient, teacher/student, friend/friend. Beliefs, moods, and values change in the context of a relationship. What a person decides to share depends on the relationship. And our communication is often distorted by differences in sender/receiver backgrounds, personalities, and expectations.

Moreover, language changes over time, so that words have different meanings to people of different ages. New patterns in language arise to describe changes in behavior and values. The term *rip off* may mean "tear off" to an older person, but it may mean "steal" to a younger one, or even "kill," depending on geographic region. Age, sex, race, cultural background, social status, intelligence, education, economic status, marital situation—all affect perception in ways that make communication difficult.

The Message: Meaning-Centered Communication

Interpersonal communication classes are *meaning-centered* rather than message-centered. Although the words are important, the feeling state of the group is also significant. *Meaning-centered communication emphasizes personal involvement, which requires the development of special sending and receiving skills.* As a sender moves toward self-disclosure in a safe environment, by agreement the receiver applies nonevaluative listening.

If we value one another as individuals and want to continue a relationship, we must learn to construct messages that will support the relationship at the same time we send our messages. Most of us have learned to send **indirect messages.** We have learned how to avoid taking responsibility for our own feelings by creating negative messages. One way we avoid responsibility is to use the words *you* or *we* rather than *I*. When people are late and you are angry, you may want to blame them, accuse them of being thoughtless, or punish them so that in the future they will behave as you want them to behave. If these are your *intentions,* you may say "*You* really make me feel angry when you're late" or "*You* shouldn't be late" or "If *you* were more considerate, *you* wouldn't be late."

You may also ask questions that do not really request information. Your voice intonation may give part of the message—"Do you know what time it is?" or "What were you doing that made you so late?" or "Why can't you ever be on time?" or "Why were you late?" Such questions are asked not for information but to put the other person in the wrong through the use of blame-loaded words, voice intonation, and avoidance of personal responsibility for feelings.

Another source of communication breakdown is suppressing our real feelings. Some people do not believe a "nice" person should get angry, or they fear conflict. Such an individual might remark pointedly, "I used to get very angry at people who were late." The unstated implication may be "I'm a bigger person than you are, so I can handle your inability to keep agreements." This statement may also be used to deny needs or dissatisfaction, or it may be used as a manipulative technique to avoid confrontation.

To take responsibility for one's own feelings is often difficult. A **direct message** would be "I'm angry because you are late." This message not only reports my feelings—which is risky—but also involves admitting that the anger is in me rather than in you. We have been told that using the word *I* is self-conscious or narcissistic. But these terms are often used as excuses to avoid confronting others with real feelings.

Another aspect of direct messages is dealing with feelings when they occur—not later. Accumulating bad feelings toward another person usually results in communication problems later. Dealing with feelings *when* they occur helps us avoid "stock-piling"—saving up grudges until they all explode inappropriately at some other time. If you store up anger, it may leak out when the other person hasn't done anything.

When we take responsibility for our own frustration without blaming the other person, we both have an increased possibility of a cooperative effort in solving our problem. Even if the other person's behavior does not change, we will have expressed our feelings rather than let them boil inside us for a future explosion. Moreover, keeping feelings inside us can eventually make us physically ill.

In contrast, the "I" message is used to accomplish several goals:

To state honest feelings.

To take personal responsibility for feelings.

To avoid manipulating the other person.

To avoid denying my own needs.

To avoid attacking the other person.

To avoid "blame games" and accusations.

The "I" message can help us construct messages that will do minimal damage to the relationship—we become sensitive to the other person's reaction; we learn skills that will help the other person to accept our message; and we risk sharing true feelings. The "I" message contains no direct suggestions. Its purpose is not to change another person's behavior. Together we can talk about the options for creating a more satisfactory situation. Although an "I" message may create some emotional reaction in the other person, it will usually be far less accusing than the "you" blaming statement. We must work together, sensitively listening, each responding from his or her own understanding of the relationship at any given moment.

The "I" message also helps us avoid trying to take responsibility for anyone else's feelings. If, when leaving a party, you say *"we* had a very good time," you are speaking for another person's feelings. But if you say "*I* had a very good time," you are allowing the other person to take responsibility for his or her own feelings in the relationship with a third person. Often spouses and parents speak for their mates or children. We can learn to avoid inappropriate "we" statements that deny others the opportunity to speak for themselves—and we can also insist that others allow us the same opportunity.

"I" messages give another person a clear idea of our real feelings. We can also give nonblameful concrete descriptions of the specific behavior that bothers us. Here are some examples of "you" statements changed to "I" statements:

1. A father sees his teenage son working with electricity and says:

   You message—"You shouldn't do that; you'll foul up and get shocked."

   I message—"I get scared when you work with electricity. I'm afraid you'll get hurt."

2. A woman whose husband watches baseball every Sunday afternoon says:

   You message—"You waste every Sunday on that darn TV set and you never talk to me or do anything."

   I message—"I look forward to Sundays when you're off work. I want to spend time with you, talk with you, and do things with you."

3. A woman who wants a date to take her to the movies says:

   You message—"You always want to sit around and watch TV. You never take me anywhere."

   I message—"I enjoy movies. I would like you to go with me so that we might share this movie together."

4. A parent says to a child who doesn't want to go to bed:

   You message—"You always cause me trouble at night. You know it's past your bedtime and you need your sleep."

   I message—"I am concerned that you won't get enough sleep and that you won't be able to wake up in time to go to school tomorrow."

"I" messages can give the listener an understanding of what behavior he or she is engaging in that causes the speaker problems. The more specific the speaker is in describing the behavior, feelings, and effects, the clearer the communication.

We have learned many ways to defend ourselves verbally against the knowledge that we control our own feelings and are responsible for them. The following statements are paired to show how we can communicate our *responsibility:*

1. "You hurt my feelings."
   "I feel hurt because of the things I tell myself about your behavior and your reactions to me."

2. "You make me feel bad."
   "I feel bad because I have learned to pretend that this behavior makes me feel bad."

3. "I can't help my feelings."
   "I *can* help the way I feel. And at times I choose to be upset."

4. "You make me angry."
   "I've decided to be angry. I can often manipulate others with my anger and make them do what I want."

5. "He makes me sick."
   "I make myself sick."

6. "Deep water like oceans and lakes scares me."
   "I scare myself about deep water."

7. "You are embarrassing me."
   "I allow myself to feel embarrassed."

8. "You really turn me on."
   "I allow myself to feel good whenever I'm with you."

9. "You make a fool of me."
   "I make myself feel foolish by taking others' opinions of me more seriously than my own."

10. "You make me happy."
    "I feel happy—I allow myself to feel happy."

Messages such as "You make me . . ." are culturally learned self-suggestions. The language pattern of "you" messages suggests that the causes of your feelings are external. But without your cooperation, no one can make you feel anything. You can choose direct messages using "I" if you wish to take responsibility for your feelings and invite further communication. Direct messages elicit responses rather than closing off the other person in a right/wrong issue. Usually they allow for listening, for reflecting what has been heard, and for returning expressions of feelings. We cannot read each other's feelings. We need to communicate them.

Written messages can be signs or symbols.

Messages can be verbal or nonverbal, oral or written. Written messages can be signs or symbols. We can also send messages with photographs and art. Interpersonal communication, then, includes a *source or sender*, a *meaning-centered message*, a *channel* through which the message is sent, and a *receiver* who listens and responds. Now we are ready to explore the channels through which we send our messages.

The Channel and Context

A children's game called "Telephone" illustrates how messages get distorted. A group of children stand in a line. The first child makes up a sentence and whispers it to the second child who in

Communication channels include telephone, television, radio, film, printed materials, and air.

turn passes the message to the third child. Each child passes the message to the next one. When the message gets to the end of the line, the last child says the sentence out loud. The final product rarely bears much resemblance to the original message. A somewhat similar distortion occurs in most of our interpersonal communication. *Beginning with the assumption that communication gets distorted, we can become more sensitive to how breakdowns occur in sending and receiving messages.*

The source of a message you send is in your mind. Then you alter the picture in your mind by attempting to translate it into symbols/words that you believe will be understood by the receiver/listener. Therefore, it is extremely important to select words that represent thoughts and feelings which are recognized by others in the same culture. Using *specific* words helps the listener to recreate a picture similar to the one in the sender's mind. Once words are uttered, they are no longer pictures in the mind of the sender. Then, as the words pass through the channel (air/environment), such variables as poor acoustics and external noise (traffic, coughing, electric motors) can result in distraction. If the speaker talks too rapidly, indistinctly, or softly, the message will not get transmitted through the channel. And if it does get transmitted despite all this interference, the message must then be translated by the listener. The listener must hear the words and then transform them into a picture in his or her mind. From all the words we receive, we select only what we want to hear— what fits our reality—and reject what does not make a coherent picture in our minds.

Alterations, omissions, and additions occur when the receiver reproduces the message to fit his or her own assumptions and experiences. Reception can also be affected by missing a word or phrase, by poor hearing, lack of attention, or a wandering mind. All of us at times have experienced hearing without listening. The act or response of listening can be distinguished from the physiological function of hearing. We hear many sounds but *listen* to only a few.

Communication channels include such systems as telephone, television, radio, films, books, newspapers, and letters. When you talk, face to face, air is the channel. When you write a letter, paper and pencil provide a channel for communicating.

Communication takes place in a **context.** Variables in the context are time of day, location, distractions, surroundings, weather and season of the year, the subject of conversation, clothes, the persons communicating, and the presence of other people. Sights, smells, sounds, and all the sensory input of the moment affect our communicating. In communicating, both sender and receiver are affected by the channel and the context. Whether a message is clear or distorted may well depend upon either the channel or the context.

Background sounds affect our moods and our ability to concentrate or relax. Notice the sounds in a classroom (an air conditioner, the buzzing of electric light fixtures, scratching on the blackboard, a student clicking a pen, the instructor tapping a finger or foot). Settings and situations vary for each individual. And individuals differ in their ability to screen out background noise.

• This activity illustrates how selective our listening really is. Stop reading for a moment and listen carefully to all the sounds around you. Can you hear a television or radio? Voices? Anyone moving around in the building? Can you hear the hum of a machine or a dripping faucet? Can you hear any

sounds from outside: a car, crickets, birds, something dropping on the roof, the creaking of the house? List all the sounds
you hear.

- To illustrate how language changes from context to context,
  discuss the following questions. How does your language
  change when you talk to a parent or a friend? How does your
  mother's/father's language change when they talk to you or to
  an employer? *Context includes where, when, with whom, and
  under what circumstances the communication occurs.*

The Receiver: Listening and Hearing

By becoming more aware of the differences between hearing and
listening, we can be more conscious of those times when we are
not receiving the message. *To hear* is to perceive by means of the
auditory sense. *To listen* is to give attention in order to hear and
understand the meaning of a sound. Listening involves fixing
attention on the other person—posture, lips, eyes, head tilt, finger
movement, voice tone, pauses, silences. Listening also includes
attending to our own reactions as we process the total message,
including the sender and the situation. The importance of the
spoken word is that it does not remain with the speaker. It
reaches out to the listener, converting him or her into a speaker
even when silent, for we all respond inside.

Listening takes energy. A listener must adjust to the pace of
the speaker. The average, uninhibited speaker can vocalize at a
rate of only 125 to 150 words per minute. But a listener with no
auditory problems can hear and understand from 300 to 700
words per minute. In one research study, groups of students were
equally divided on the basis of academic ability and exposed to
the same recording of a lecture. One group listened to the recording at the regular speed. The second group listened to the recording at a speed increased by 25%. The group listening to the
speeded-up recording retained more information when tested
afterward. This experiment illustrates an important difficulty
with listening to a speaker.

*The gap between listening speed and speaking speed may
create an emotional barrier between speaker and listener.* The
resulting impatience, indifference, and boredom are emotional
blocks to listening. Few of us wait for each word to be uttered. We

stop listening and our minds wander off to other thoughts. Our attention span is short and, unless we have an important reason to listen, we tend to drift away. We must have a strong need to listen. It is possible, however, to practice and develop a genuine listening intensity.

Another speech convention that needs to be examined is the taboo against interrupting, as we have discussed before. If you are not sure what has been said, the sender may appreciate your interest if you interrupt to say "Will you repeat that?" or "That's not clear to me" or "I'm not sure what you mean" or "Can you give me an example?" Feeling free to interrupt *occasionally* can help us stay in touch with the speaker. It is interruption which disregards the speaker that we want to avoid.

Learning to listen attentively *can help us communicate and relate better.*

- Describe a situation when you were aware that you were listening attentively. Who were you listening to? How were you feeling?

- Describe a situation when you became aware that you were *not* listening. Who was talking? How did you feel about the situation?

- Describe a time when you were talking to someone and felt that person was not listening. How did you feel? What did you do? Did you continue to talk? Did you stop or change the topic? Did you ask, "Hey, have I lost you?" What other options do you have when you've "lost" someone?

- Discuss your options when you are aware that you've lost the trend of a conversation. How do your options depend on the situation? How do you feel when you realize that others are aware they have "lost" you?

- Discuss ways you "tune out" people. When do you do this? Do you have different patterns with different people?

Listening skills, however important, are not often stressed in school. Our educational system concentrates on reading and neglects listening. A survey of listening taken from written answers in school shows that in first grade children get 90% of their information through listening, in the second grade 80%, in the eighth grade 45%, and in the twelfth grade 28%. A successful college student who is a good reader may be a poor listener. Tests show little correlation between a high IQ score and listening; yet there is a high correlation between IQ scores and reading skills.

Most of us enjoy talking. We usually listen to ourselves as we talk. It often feels good to talk to someone else who will listen to us. Each of us has a strong desire to be heard—to be listened to silently and objectively by an interested person. We need sounding boards to reflect our words. In this class, we can practice both listening silently and listening actively. **Silent listening** involves giving positive reinforcement through nonverbal cues or positive sounds. **Active listening** involves restating either the content or the feelings of the speaker to indicate we have received the message.

I know you believe you understand what you think I said, but I'm not sure you realize that what you heard is not what I meant.

Anonymous

The following activities can help us learn basic listening skills.

- Work in pairs—one person is the speaker, the other the listener. The speaker talks for five minutes about a communication experience in which another person didn't listen. The speaker describes the situation, the person, and the feelings. The listener has the following options: (1) Simply listen attentively, nodding his head when he understands. (2) Make sounds like "uh-huh" to indicate that he understands. (3) Verbally make short statements, such as "I see" or "I understand." (4) Restate what has been said—for example, "You felt like . . ." If at any time the listener does not understand what is said, he or she can say "That's not clear to me. Will you restate that, please?" Do not probe for additional facts. Do not evaluate what has been said. Do not offer advice, even if it is requested. Keep yourself and your values out of this situation. Simply listen.

- After each person has had a chance to be speaker and listener, discuss this experience. Was it difficult to listen without offering advice? Was it difficult to listen without judging? What nonverbal cues did the listener give? Was there a difference in your ability to listen with a time limit of five minutes (compared to the normal conversational exchange of comment for comment)?

We sometimes listen to obtain information.

Purposes of Listening   People listen to enjoy, to evaluate, and to understand. These different purposes usually overlap. To obtain information, we must be able to evaluate the accuracy of information, to separate facts from inferences. *To enjoy* music, sounds, and people, we share feelings and experiences through conversation. *To evaluate* our world, to find out what we value and how we wish to live our lives, we listen to others as well as to ourselves. *Yet one of the most important reasons for listening to each other is to understand other people and how they perceive their world.*

Empathic listening—listening for understanding—requires seeing the other person's world and experiencing his or her viewpoint without making value judgments. When we listen empathically, others feel more secure and express themselves more freely. People develop trusting relationships, which lead to more self-disclosure and shared knowledge in nonthreatening situations without judgment. Judging others increases their defensiveness and diminishes our own understanding. Empathic listening *confirms* the speaker as a person. Judgment *disconfirms* the speaker and blocks communication. When we listen for understanding, we get to know how other people feel about what they are saying, what they are sharing, what they are experiencing.

In *intrapersonal* listening, speaker and listener are one and the same person—sending and receiving is a process of actively responding to the self. We have the capacity, not always developed, to be conscious of our own thoughts and reactions. We can develop our own great potential for awareness and personal consciousness.

Interpersonal listening is much more complex. A message can be heard and interpreted in as many ways as there are receivers. The variables include setting, relationship, different perceptions of two people, different interpretations of words/symbols, conflicts in intention and purpose, and attraction/repulsion between the sender and the receiver—to name just a few.

Some people believe that thinking interferes with listening to and experiencing another person. As we think, we evaluate, judge, and anticipate the other person. These activities interfere with listening. Instead of listening, we think about, think for, and think ahead of the speaker.

In our culture, it is difficult to listen without *thinking about* the other person and what he or she is saying. But if you have the habit of thinking about what the other person is saying, you are speculating about his or her motives, wondering about the person's "true" intentions, or judging what is being said—for example, you may be thinking, "How insecure he seems!" "What does she really mean by that?" "I like what he's saying." or "That's stupid!"

Another habit is *thinking for*—mentally directing what the other person should be doing, thinking, or feeling. It is as if you wish to solve problems for the person. You may think, for example, "You shouldn't feel that way." "You should make up your mind and act." "It would be better if . . ." "The best thing to do in that circumstance is . . ." "If only you would stop, reconsider, and think positively, then . . . ." We often try to give advice instead of listening. Thinking for the speaker prevents listening.

Another habit is *thinking ahead*—completing other people's thoughts before they have had a chance to finish what they are saying. Because we all think, listen, and speak at different rates, differences in speed of sending and receiving cause us a good deal of discomfort. And, because we can think so much faster than we can talk or listen, thinking ahead prevents listening.

One habit we can develop that contributes to better listening is *thinking with* other people. We can simply try to understand what others mean by what they are saying. Our goal is to comprehend the gist of their expressions, how things look from their point of view, how they are feeling about the issue. Developing the habit of empathic listening helps us understand others.

The technique of thinking with *another person can help us listen more effectively.*

- Work in pairs. Sit opposite your partner and listen to him talk about how he feels about a friend. Concentrate on his face in a posture of attention. Think only of your partner's thoughts. Allow yourself to *experience* your partner. What are his feelings? Emotions? Words? What is he saying?

- Now formulate in your own words the message you have received. For example: "You feel . . ." "You are saying . . ." "You think . . . ." When your partner agrees that you have received his or her feelings *and* thoughts and has acknowledged your understanding, the communication has been completed.

Active listening involves concentrating on what the speaker has to say.

If we can acknowledge the different kinds of listening and their different purposes, we can use the listening abilities most appropriate for each situation. Listen *analytically* when it is important to understand the structure of a message, when you need to analyze the logic of statements supporting main ideas, and when you need to make a decision based on the information given you. Listen *objectively* if your own preconceived ideas on the topic will interfere with your ability to develop a neutral point of view or comprehend what is being said.

Active listening involves concentrating on what each speaker has to say. It helps to sit up straight and look directly at the speaker. Try to listen from the speaker's point of view, which requires that you listen empathically, as if you were in his or her place. Try to place yourself on the same wavelength so you can understand feelings as well as words.

When we are listening to enjoy, whether it be music or the company of another person, we can simply experience enjoyment. In most interpersonal communication, the primary purpose of listening is to understand other people and experience them as unique individuals. Tuning in requires *being with* people. Suspending judgment may be difficult, but it can be learned. And it can create more productive relationships—relationships built on understanding rather than judgments.

We can practice listening with accuracy.

- Form groups of three.
- Assign letters: *A*—speaker, *B*—listener, *C*—observer.
- *A* will have three to five minutes to describe himself in terms which would help another person understand how and why he communicates the way he does.
- *B*, the listener, will then summarize the important points given by *A*.
- *C*, the observer, will give *B* feedback about the accuracy of his or her listening and summarizing. *A* will evaluate both *B* and *C*.
- When all three people are satisfied that they have communicated, that they understand what *A* presented, they can switch roles.
- Each person gets to be a speaker, listener, and observer.

- The process may be repeated by forming new groups of three.
- In a class discussion tell what new insights you gained.

Active Listening   Listening involves caring—feeling concern for the opinions, desires, and feelings of others. Listeners have far more to assimilate and far more to work with when they care. They can give more of themselves. Because we think much faster than we can talk, we have time to anticipate what the speaker is going to say. As someone speaks, we weigh the verbal information to see if it supports the points being made. We can also listen "between the lines" in search of meaning not necessarily put into spoken words. If our intention is to listen with the "third ear" for broader meanings behind the words, we can develop not only our skills of listening but also those of relating.

Listeners who participate in the communication process with an intent to understand others are far more than passive receivers. They are "understanders"—people who use their eyes and mind to go beyond listening. Tuning in to other people creates energy that flows back to the speakers. Even as they speak they are receiving the attention the receivers are sending. To tune into the self as receiver while being tuned into the other as sender requires a level of consciousness that all of us can develop. One method that leads in this direction is called **active listening**.

Active listening involves a restatement of either the message or the feelings of the speaker without giving advice, analyzing, or probing. We cannot always be actively listening to others for none of us can be loving human beings *all* the time. I cannot listen when I am blinded by my own emotions, problems, or needs. I cannot listen to people who I feel are trying to manipulate me. I have difficulty listening to someone who is a problem to me. I have difficulty listening to people I am trying to persuade against their own wishes. Moreover, there are times that simply do not call for listening, as when a child needs to go to the bathroom. And there are some individuals I may simply choose not to listen to.

Listening does not necessarily solve problems. But some relief occurs when we can get a problem out into the open by expressing it verbally. I can actively listen when other people have problems they want to talk about or feelings they wish to express. When I feel accepting of others and want to take the time to listen, when I feel trusting and believe that others can solve their own problems without interference or advice, then I can stay outside the problem and listen actively. At such times I am more apt to pick up "double" messages—confusing or conflicting messages, such as a verbal message that contradicts a nonverbal message. I may hear a "highly coded" message the other person is hiding from himself or herself. To listen actively I simply reflect back what I hear so that the other person can see how it sounds when I restate it.

To be a valuable listener, I must remind myself that the meanings of the messages are not in the words but in the sender. I must remind myself not to project my own values into the feedback I give. It takes time to learn to communicate, and we must be patient with ourselves and with others.

Active listening is simply restating either the content or the feelings of the speaker. The following activity provides an opportunity to practice active listening.

- Choose a partner.
- Briefly write down a problem you are having with another person.
- Take turns. Decide who will be the first to share his or her problem.
- Outline the problem, the person, the situation, and how you feel about it.
- The listener restates the problem and feelings as accurately as possible. (Each person can speak only after having restated the ideas and feelings of the previous speaker to that person's satisfaction.)
- Discuss this experience.
- Use active listening with the people you live with or your friends. Write about the experience.

Feedback: Responding and Acknowledging

Just as there are different kinds of listening, there are different kinds of responding. Carl Rogers conducted a series of studies on communicating face to face. He found that the *responses* fell into five main categories: evaluative, interpretive, supportive, probing, and understanding. He found that most of us evaluate more than any other response. Interpretive responses were next, supportive third, probing fourth, and understanding the least common response. Rogers found that when a person used one kind of response 40% of the time, other people stereotyped that person as that kind of responder.

If we recognize our responses and begin to use the response most appropriate for each situation and relationship, our communicating and relating will improve. In your small groups, note how each person responds. Give each other feedback about what responses might be most appropriate for the discussion of the moment. It may be best to set aside evaluative responses at first and begin with *understanding* responses so that you can check out with new acquaintances whether or not you really understand what they are saying. A *supportive* response is appropriate when the other person is feeling insecure. Each of us experiences moments of feeling low, and at these times we welcome support. When we wish to tell senders what their problems mean or what they really feel, we use an *interpretive* response with the intent to teach. A *probing* response is used to seek further information, to continue the discussion, or to discuss a point more fully. The *evaluative* response makes a judgment about rightness, appropriateness, or effectiveness. *When we reach a certain level of trust in a relationship, we can accept another's comments about our behavior.*

All of us can become more aware of the ways in which we respond to others. We can learn how to use a variety of responses and become more familiar with which responses fit which situations and relationships. Read the following messages and write a response for each category:

- "I'm really worried. I haven't been able to find a job and I'm getting into debt. I hate to ask my parents to help. My dad won't believe that I'm really trying to find work anyway."

  Evaluative response: Probing response:

  Interpretive response: Understanding response:

  Supportive response:

- "I really feel so depressed now that Tom and I have broken up. I have a hard time getting to know men. I just don't understand men anyway. It seems as if I can't keep a relationship going even if I do get one started. I wonder if there's something wrong with me."

  Evaluative response: Probing response:

  Interpretive response: Understanding response:

  Supportive response:

- "I'm having a lot of trouble with my teenage son. He's into drugs and dropped out of school. I don't like the kinds of friends he hangs around with either. But he's bigger than I am now and I don't know what to do about him. It seems as if I don't have any control over him. At times it seems as if he doesn't have any control over his own life either. I don't know what to do."

  Evaluative response: Probing response:

  Interpretive response: Understanding response:

  Supportive response:

Some people develop the habit of responding by asking questions. Many of us get defensive when we are asked questions. As children, when our parents asked "Why did you do that?" "Why are you late?" "Why didn't you do your homework?" 'Why don't you ever pay attention to me?" we seldom knew the answers. Usually "why" questions have many answers, but, as children, we reached out for the first acceptable response. We also learned we could satisfy people with answers they wanted to hear. Then we learned how to ask questions that did not ask for information but put *others* on the spot.

In an interpersonal communication class, we can become aware of questions that are not really asking for information. These questions can be translated into statements. For example:

Question: "Why do you keep picking on Jane?"
Statement: "I feel that you pick on Jane."

Question: "Why are you late?"
Statement: "I get upset when you are late."

Question: "Why don't you like me?"
Statement: "I get negative vibes from you."

When a sincere question is asked, it is a request for information. Notice how you and others ask questions.

- Choose a partner. Ask each other any questions you wish, but do not answer any. Every sentence must be a question. Keep doing this for about five minutes.
- Now discuss your experience—your feelings about asking and being asked questions.
- Change every question into an "I" statement. For example; "Why are you wearing a sweater today?" "I notice you are wearing a sweater." "I like/dislike your sweater."
- Now discuss your feelings about making statements and receiving statements.

Feedback is an especially useful response in many situations. In small groups and dyadic relationships, feedback can help us see ourselves as others see us. You may want to find out how you are coming across to others in your group by asking for feedback. Thanking others for feedback, rather than becoming defensive, can reassure the group that the request for feedback is sincere. If people ask for feedback and then become upset by what they receive, others will be less likely to risk making comments in the future.

Feedback—verbal or nonverbal—can provide us with constructive information that may help us become more aware of ourselves. Feedback can also give us an indication of how accurately others receive our messages. In addition, feedback can let us know how we are doing in relationships.

Since growth takes place best in a nonthreatening atmosphere, it is helpful to avoid defining people and to concentrate on *describing* behavior. Instead of saying "Karen is too quiet," we can say "Karen only talked once in our group interaction today." We can avoid giving advice. We can share ideas and information without suggesting that anyone take a particular action. We can spend time exploring alternatives and leave the final decisions to the person who has the problem. And, finally, we can give feedback that is appropriate to the time, place, and persons involved.

If you want feedback, you can ask for it. For example: "Do I frown when I speak?" or "Do you understand how I feel?" or "Do you know what I mean?" If you want to give feedback to another person, you can say: "Can I tell you how I am hearing you?" "I would like to tell you how I feel about what you are doing." *Feedback can be positive or negative.* Most of us prefer to be supported in what we say and do; but if we are annoying someone, we may want to become aware of it.

When giving feedback, be as specific as possible and give examples like these:

"When you say 'good' or 'bad,' I hear you judging."

"I hear you as being supportive of Jim when you tell him you understand how he feels in that situation."

"I hear you giving advice when you say 'ought' to do something."

"Were you aware that you didn't let him finish what he was saying?"

"Are you aware that you smile a lot?"

"Are you aware that your voice has a sarcastic tone?"

You may feel that certain feedback you receive is relatively accurate or inaccurate. If someone gives you feedback, you can answer by saying:

"Yes, I agree with you."

"That's the way I see myself."

"That's what I mean."

"I don't see myself that way."

"I didn't feel that."

"It's interesting that you interpreted my feelings that way."

"Thank you. I'll look into that and check it out in the future."

Feedback used in small groups answers the questions "How are we doing as a group? Are we understanding each other? Are we enjoying each other's company? Are we learning about each other and ourselves?" Sometimes learning can be uncomfortable. If all the feedback is positive, it may be comfortable but boring. Although we all need to be appreciated, we also need to know if we are contributing, disinterested, or confused. As we observe conflicts between verbal and nonverbal communication, we can make that known and clear up the discrepancies. For example: Mary thinks that smiling is "phony." John sees Mary as solemn. Richard thinks she's unhappy. And Alice thinks Mary's angry. Given this kind of feedback, Mary can discuss her values about smiling and what it means to her.

Feedback serves many different purposes. For example:

Confirmation: "Yes, I hear what you are saying." "I can hear what you are feeling."

Content: "What I hear you saying is . . ." "You said . . ."

Feeling: "You feel depressed." "You feel anxious."

Action: "You want to run away." "You want to hit someone."

Clarification: "Can you repeat that?" "That's not clear to me." "Can you give me an example?" "I don't quite understand what you mean."

Noting ambivalence: "I hear what you're saying and your hands are clenched." "I hear you saying you don't care and your voice sounds high and tight."

The actual words used in giving feedback are not as important as the trusting atmosphere that can be created. When we receive a message, verbal or nonverbal, we can question our own interpretation to see if it is accurate. For example, we can say:

"Is this what you feel?"   "You think . . ."

"Is this what you intend?"   "You sound puzzled."

"You sound upset."   "I hear . . ."

"I think I hear you saying . . ." "Is this what you mean?"

"You wish . . ."

Feedback helps sender and receiver reflect each other's messages in order to modify any distortions in what is heard or expressed. *Sending clear messages and receiving accurate mes-*

sages are essential for effective communication. Feedback can help us send and receive messages that honestly and directly communicate what we feel.

Effective feedback, both positive and negative, can be used for personal growth. By describing rather than evaluating, the sender gives the receiver the option to use the feedback or not. Immediate feedback is usually more effective than delayed feedback and can be interpreted more accurately by paraphrasing what has been said. Specific feedback is more useful than vague comments; and feedback that suggests behavior that can be changed is more productive than comments about personality. *Above all, feedback should be given with the intention of enhancing communication and improving relationships.*

Feedback helps us keep in touch with each other as we communicate.

- In small groups of five or six, practice *asking* for feedback. For example: "What is your impression of me?" "How do you feel about what I do in class?" "What have you noticed about me?" "What do you want to know about me?" (When others give you feedback, thank them.)

- Practice *giving* feedback to other members of your group. When you make a comment, form it as an "I" statement. Notice what kinds of feedback you have difficulty giving. If you find it difficult to give certain members feedback, discuss that with them and ask the group to give both of you feedback on the discussion.

An **acknowledgement** *is something we say or do to show others that we have received and understood their statements or actions.* The most commonly used acknowledgements are "All right," "OK," "Fine," "Thank you," and "Good." An acknowledgement is ordinarily perceived as encouragement—a communication of approval, concern, and attention. When people have no indication that something they said was heard and understood, they may feel angry, puzzled, hopeless, or lonely. It feels like giving someone a gift and not receiving a thank you or even a smile. It feels like writing a letter and not getting an answer. *The communication cycle is not complete until the speaker has been acknowledged in some way.*

Thank you cards and letters provide feedback communicating appreciation.

When people continually do a job without acknowledgement, they may lose incentive. They feel that it does not matter whether they do a good job or not. We acknowledge people with a raise in pay or status to validate their ability. Children whose communications are not acknowledged can become "obnoxious" because of their need for attention.

People who feel frustrated may talk more, interrupt, or become silent with hopelessness. Because their communication has not been acknowledged, they may give the same message over and over. Husbands and wives, employers and employees, react in the same way when they are not acknowledged. The message tends to persist because it is never received. Understanding and acknowledgement, either verbal ("I hear you" or "I got it") or nonverbal, let the speaker know that the message has been received. *Acknowledging the gift of communication is an essential element of interpersonal communication and enhances human relationships.*

We can learn to acknowledge the statements of others with whom we are communicating. Such acknowledgement increases the quality and clarity of interpersonal relationships.

- Choose a partner and discuss a specific issue in a personal relationship outside of class that is giving you trouble. The listener is simply to acknowledge the speaker whenever the listener feels that he or she fully understands what the speaker is trying to convey.
- Then the listener becomes the speaker. (Switch roles.)
- At the end of the discussion, thank your partner for sharing. "Thank you" is an acknowledgement.

Language, then, is made up of meanings that are learned and culturally derived. It is composed of words, symbols, or referents that can have many different meanings—meanings which are in people, not in the words. Then these words are put together (consciously or unconsciously) into some kind of structure according to certain rules.

The language process includes the sending and receiving of messages which are unavoidably connected with how we think. Some linguists believe that all thought is subvocal speech. Language aids thinking in such a way that we can try out ideas in the mind without acting them out. Language can also make thinking concrete by putting it into words that can be shared. *We speak as we think, we think as we speak, and both processes can be studied to improve interpersonal communication.*

BEYOND LANGUAGE: FEEDFORWARD

Feedback is useful when we perceive that our words are not sending our message. From the facial expressions or body movements of my listener, for example, I may get nonverbal feedback that my meaning is not received. Feedback is also useful if the person who is sending the message is *unaware* that he or she is not communicating. The listener can then choose to give verbal feedback, such as "I'm not sure what you mean" or "Will you repeat that?" or "It's not clear to me what you are saying." In both cases, feedback, nonverbal or verbal, implies a built-in system for change. It is useful when the boundaries of language are understood. Yet feedback works on conscious or unconscious assumptions of redundancy—the belief that we can repeat the message in some form so that we can be understood. *Such feedback is static because we are limited to the use of verbal or nonverbal language.*

Feedback gives us a direction, but when something beyond language is needed, we want to find new ways of expressing certain needs. I. A. Richards describes such expression of needs as **feedforward.** In our attempts to go beyond words, to get to what feedback cannot reach, Richards suggests that art, music, and poetry can transcend language. He says that feedforward is a process like pulling the end of a ball of twine and then allowing the ball to unravel itself. If you set the action going by "pulling the end of the twine," the unraveling process itself takes over.

Suppose a person has an intense experience one bright sunny day and wants to write a poem about it. The principle of feedback says: "Let's write a poem about the bright sunny day." Feedforward assumes at the outset that the poem might not be about the sunny day at all, but rather some *feeling* the sunny day has evoked. Feedforward urges the person to let the poem write itself. The process of feedforward is more difficult in the beginning because there is no direction or content. Yet feedforward doesn't deny structure, whether it be in a poem, a painting, or communication with another person. It is hard to say "That's not what I'm feeling" and begin again. Feedforward is an act of risk and uncertainty. It requires self-trust, self-esteem, and courage.

It is not only artists and poets who can experience these mysteries of creating. We are all the creators of our own feedforward systems. All of us can explore our unique inner sources. There is a desire in each of us to *transcend* language in order to get closer to the creative source within. Connecting with this center gives our lives meaning and vitality.

There are means of making contact with this center and keeping the channels open. Dreams, for example, illustrate the relationship between the personal, cultural, and deeper levels of experience. Imagery and fantasy as modes of exploring feedforward have also led to insightful experiences. Attention to paradox can assist us in making more use of intuition and altering our perceptions of reality.

Myths and symbols illuminate new directions and give us new meanings. Dance, movement, and music also provide us with recreative experiences. Innovative experiments with light and song, film and photography, enhance sensory awareness and evoke significant symbols. Meditation and consciousness expansion, poetry and literature—all these paths offer visionary possibilities for our pilgrimage to find ways of transcending language.

FOR FURTHER READING

Barker, Larry. *Listening Behavior.* Englewood Cliffs, N.J.: Prentice-Hall, 1971.
> The author describes problems people have in listening.

Chase, Stuart. *Power of Words.* New York: Harcourt Brace, 1953.
> Chase discusses semantics, meaning, and communication with practical application to better listening and understanding.

Condon, John C., Jr. *Semantics and Communication.* 2nd ed. New York: Macmillan, 1975.
> This widely used textbook presents ways to improve our uses of language.

Gordon, Thomas. *Parent Effectiveness Training.* New York: Peter Wyden, 1970.
> Gordon offers an excellent discussion of active listening and feedback which can apply to any two-person communication event.

Hayakawa, S. I. *Symbol, Status, and Personality.* New York: Harcourt Brace, 1953.
> The author, a linguistics expert, connects language and its effects on individual personality.

Reik, Theodor. *Listening with the Third Ear.* New York: Farrar, Strauss, 1948.
> This book presents an intimate and revealing account of how the author has learned to use an "extra sense" in listening and hearing in order to find the hidden meanings in what is said and not said.

THE MIND: OBJECTIVITY AND SUBJECTIVITY
MIND PROCESSES
    Abstracting, Generalizing, Stereotyping
    Classifying Facts, Assumptions, Judgments
    Forming Beliefs and Attitudes

EXPECTATIONS
CONSISTENCY AND DECEPTION
MIND POTENTIAL
    Imagery and Visualization
    Creativity

6

Thinking: How the Mind Communicates

THE MIND: OBJECTIVITY AND SUBJECTIVITY

The processes of the mind include all the conscious and unconscious activities of a human being. One definition of the mind is "that which thinks, feels, and wills, exercises perception, judgment, reflection, etc." The brain can be studied scientifically, but the mind can only be observed indirectly—it is an abstraction. We cannot feel it, observe it, or measure it in any satisfactory way. The mind uses the tools of logic for verbal abstracting and results in our using words to classify things. *The mind and language cannot be separated.*

When we try to understand something logically, we classify. We strip away what is unique and leave that which is universal. Abstract knowledge, unlike experience, is not vivid or firsthand. Although it is useful to label human beings, we miss varieties of emotions and attitudes in the individual. When we want to study humanity and our history, we deal with universal human qualities—the qualities that make us a species. The basic emotions of love and fear are universal, for example, but we all experience unique varieties and nuances of love and fear. As soon as we use verbal symbols—words—our knowledge becomes indirect and less sensitive to individuality.

When we think logically, our tools are concepts and words rather than experiences. *We place a distance between ourselves as subjects and other persons as objects.* In order to communicate the verbal, the logical, the analytical, we become less emotional and more "rational." Carl Jung believed that people can be classified as predominantly thinking or feeling types in terms of their personal ways of making judgments about their world.

To achieve the balance between thought and feeling that is most comfortable for you, begin by becoming aware of how you habitually deal with your world.

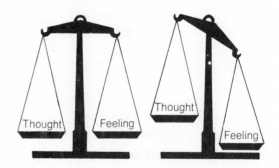

- Imagine that the scale shown above can tip one way or the other. Where would you place yourself most of the time?

- Although your answers to these questions may be very subjective, they may stimulate some thinking: Are you comfortable with the balance between your thinking and feeling responses to your world? Would you want to move in one direction or the other?

- Ask others who are close to you (family or friends) how they see you or where they would place you on this scale. Remember that the answers of others are also subjective—you may learn more about *them* than you learn about yourself. Where would you place your friends?

Purely intellectual perception is neither possible nor desirable. But in many important areas of life—law, education, science, business—"rational" decisions must be made to guide large groups of people. *Decision-makers need to judge objectively.* We need to develop those processes of the mind that help us verify information. Abstracting, generalizing, and stereotyping may help our decisions or hinder them. We also want to know the differences between fact, assumption, and judgment. And finally, since our beliefs and attitudes are affected by emotions and experience, we want to be aware of their influences.

We are often told to be "objective," to think objectively rather than subjectively. Objective thinking seeks to define external causes, visible actions, public events, that can be verified. *Subjectivity* is based on inner experience and involves the expression of feelings and the satisfaction of personal needs. But can thinking ever be completely objective? Can a thought be completely free from feeling? *Completely unemotional thinking seems to be a contradiction in terms.* If the mind could be completely divorced from feeling, the individual would become a programmed computer, operating only on the basis of information fed into it. As long as we are alive, our bodies and emotions will affect our thoughts.

Thinking cannot be divorced from feeling. Although desire, fear, pleasure, and pain all influence thinking, we can be *more* or *less* objective. The way we solve a geometry problem may resemble the operation of a computer, but our self-image, attitude toward geometry, and interest in the subject all affect our ability to solve the problem. To increase our objectivity, we must recognize and declare our personal feelings. Good scientists recognize their own biases and emotional involvement so that their work can be more objective.

Sometimes the desire to be objective leads us astray into psuedo-objectivity. The psychological term for pseudo-objectivity is **rationalizing.** We rationalize when we deny the subjective basis for our actions and pretend that a thought or action can be justified by a reason. In so doing we are placing the responsibility for our behavior on some outside force. Generally, rationalizing encourages the denial of feelings and desires, and it does not promote the taking of personal responsibility for our communication.

It is important that we develop skills at being objective and rational. We can simply look around us and see the power of our objective culture. But we can also see difficulties that have arisen in this same culture. At the same time we develop our rational skills, we will see in later chapters that we need to develop attunement to physical, emotional, and behavioral aspects of our realities.

MIND PROCESSES

Knowledge is Power.

Francis Bacon

Knowledge about how the mind works can lead to better interpersonal communication. Such thinking processes as abstracting, generalizing, and stereotyping are often performed unconsciously. We can control these ways of thinking. In addition, we need to know whether we are dealing with facts, assumptions, or judgments when we are reading, listening, and speaking.

Most of us experience thinking as something natural—an automatic function that simply happens. As a result we develop careless habits in processing and communicating information. As we grow up, we accept certain beliefs from the culture in which we live. If we are willing to question the attitudes of our culture, we can think with greater precision and accuracy; more important, we can choose our own beliefs.

Abstracting, Generalizing, Stereotyping

The world is full of "stuff"—objects, people, actions, sounds, smells, and sights. Since we cannot possibly process them all, we select from the stimuli out there. Things go on whether we tune into them or not. Yet we decide to pay attention to some things and not to others. We *abstract* only some of the stimuli. Then we apply labels (words) to our experiences. These labels are **generalizations** from previous observations (previous abstractions) and experiences. Some of these labels are more specific (car) than others (transportation). Even at a very low level of abstraction (car), we are classifying. We need to organize the confusing multitude of experiences into similarities and differences. Cars vary a great deal, yet we can classify them all as cars, ignoring the differences. When we classify, we focus on similarities. We cannot think without classifying.

In assigning labels to experiences, we constantly run the risk of **overgeneralizing.** Suppose I drive down the street and see a drunken man. A few blocks further on, I see another. I think: "Nothing but drunks in this town." Then I turn onto the freeway and accelerate to 55 miles per hour. A car passes me on the left. A minute later, one passes me on the right. I think: "All drivers in this state are crazy." I just made two generalizations, each built on only two examples. But reasoning on the basis of too few examples is dangerous. If you listen for this fallacy in conversation, you will begin to hear such generalizing more often. Perhaps then you will avoid this pitfall in your own thinking.

One form of classifying, **stereotyping,** is a generalization about a class of people, objects, or events that is widely held by a given culture. Stereotypes are unbending. Moreover, they are unlikely to be either modified or discarded, because they are based on distorted perception. When we stereotype, we do not really *see* because we have already made up our minds. Stereotyping, like prejudice, shifts responsibility from the judge to the judged. The pattern is to ascribe certain traits to certain groups with little evidence.

Those who stereotype are themselves injured because they are cut off from reality. Some negative stereotypes concern the poor (scheming welfare cheats, lazy, irresponsible, stupid), Jews, Blacks, the police, Indians, Asians, Irish, Catholics, Latins, and so on. We stereotype according to race, religion, ethnic group, sex, age, social class, physical attributes, and personality type. *Once we stereotype, we lose the ability to perceive people as unique individuals.* And the hazard of stereotyping extends to the self. When we classify ourselves as *types,* we lose sight of many other qualities that make us unique.

Classifying Facts, Assumptions, Judgments

We use facts, assumptions, and judgments in our thinking to serve a number of purposes. One is to convey information; another is to communicate emotional experience; another is to shore up an argument. And, like so many aspects of communication, these different functions cannot be completely separated.

A **fact** is a publicly observed agreement. If I observe that there are five men in this room and you agree, we call it a fact based on our concept of the words *five* and *men.* If I say a week is seven days and you agree, we call that a fact. Yet other cultures do not have the concept of a week. Therefore, to identify a "fact," we must accept the same measuring system and the same definitions of the words used. Words are arbitrary agreements on how to define and classify things.

A factual statement describes only certain aspects of "reality," which differs for different individuals as well as for different cultures. Facts mean nothing in themselves; they only take on significance in the context of other facts. Yet if we did not have agreements about meanings and words, we could not communicate at all. We can only exchange information if we agree on the words and measurements used to verify those "facts."

If we see a man wearing glasses and we say "He bought the glasses," then we have made an **assumption.** We assume that he did not steal them and that the glasses were not a gift. *An assumption is a guess about the unknown based on what is known.* Assumptions range from the highly probable to wild fantasy.

As students of communication, we need to become conscious of our assumptions as part of the thinking process. Before we can check the validity of our assumptions, we must be aware that we are making them.

- Choose a partner. Make an observation: "Right now it is obvious to me that . . . (the walls are green, your eyes are blue)."
- Now your partner does the same. "Right now it is obvious that . . . ."
- Next, take turns completing this sentence: "Right now I assume that . . . (you're tired, you're hungry)." (Do not explain your assumption.)
- Then take turns completing this sentence: "Right now it is obvious to me that . . . and therefore I assume that . . . ." (Give a reason for your assumption.)
- Discuss the assumptions you made. Were there any assumptions on which you could not reach agreement?

Whenever we do anything, say anything, or think anything, our behavior is a product of a complicated system of assumptions (guesses). We assume that the ceiling will not cave in, that there will not be an earthquake, that lightning will not strike us. We assume that if we enroll in a communication class, we will gain credits, improve our communication, and meet a requirement.

From generation to generation, we pass down mistaken assumptions and faulty speech patterns that block communication. For example:

1. Assuming that characteristics of things or people are part of them (misusing "is" identifications).

2. Assuming that simple explanations can provide answers for complex questions (oversimplifying with "why" and "because").

3. Assuming that all people feel, think, or respond alike (universality.)

4. Assuming that others feel, think, or respond as we do (projecting our responses onto others).

5. Assuming that our perceptions and evaluations are complete (as if we knew everything).

6. Assuming that what we perceive will not change (assumptions of sameness).

7. Assuming that there are only two possible alternatives (making an either/or dichotomy).

8. Assuming that we know what others are talking about.

9. Assuming that others know what we are talking about.

These general assumptions are easier to list than they are to change. Yet we can, in fact, change these speech/mind patterns. We can begin to use the language of emotions and perceptions rather than of "facts." For example, we can say "I feel that . . ." or "Right now it seems to me that . . . ." We can ask questions: "What do you mean?" "That's not clear to me." "Would you expand on that?" We can ask: "Who?" "What?" "When?" "How?" We can restate, clarify, ask questions, and give each other feedback—all of which will improve communication by modifying assumptions.

A **judgment** *is a conclusion made after thinking.* It may be carefully formed or hastily formed. We reach conclusions through reasoning. An assumption, on the other hand, is an idea we have in our minds without having given it thought. It is arrived at not by reasoning but by merely taking it for granted. Every day we make hundreds of assumptions. Without them, we would have to think about every word we utter, every move, every single moment of every day. We don't have either the time or the energy so we make assumptions. What makes an assumption *unwarranted* is taking too much for granted. Unfortunately, it is very easy to take too much for granted—to assume something with little or no experience.

For decades, many Americans *assumed* that China was a backward country. They made the assumption that Chinese medicine was a conglomeration of herbs and primitive theories. Since the early 1970s, visitors' reports have suggested that China's health care is advanced and that in general it may be better for the average person than what is available in the United States. Similarly, assumptions about American Indian medicine men as "quacks" have recently been found unwarranted. The National Institute of Mental Health is contributing funds to help Navajo Indians study under tribal medicine men.

If you are unaware of your assumptions, you tend to be controlled by them. Unwarranted assumptions can block new understanding and insights. Careful thinkers try to recognize their assumptions so that they can improve their ability to communicate.

We assume that since we have been communicating all our lives, we know how to "do it." We assume that we all communicate in similar ways, see the same things, and agree about experiences. We assume that we have common perceptions and interpretations about experience. Although we will spend most of this course talking about our differences, in practice we continually fall back to these assumptions of sameness. Based on all these faulty assumptions, we make judgments and arrive at conclusions about ourselves and others in the process of interpersonal communication. But the fact that judgments are usually assumed to be the product of thinking does not guarantee their worth. Errors are easy to make. If people are unaware of certain aspects of their conditioning, they are likely to be controlled by those aspects. *We need to reexamine our assumptions and judgments continually.*

Write F *(fact),* A *(assumption), or* J *(judgment) before each of the following sentences. On what did you base your assessment of these sentences?*

- The building you are in is architecturally beautiful.
- Cancer is an excessive growth of certain cells at the expense of others.
- I am catching a cold.
- You will have a good crop this year.
- The play was a tremendous success.
- Women are unsafe drivers.
- Some telescopes can reach out over two billion light years.
- The food in this restaurant is terrible.
- Tomorrow will be a sunny day.
- Henry VIII died in 1547.
- Man is basically evil.
- The author of the book *Lord of the Flies* says: "Man is basically evil."

Nothing is either good or bad but thinking makes it so.

Shakespeare

We form opinions, evaluate something, and then give it a label. Judgmental words in the form of labels often tell more about the person using the words than they tell about the person being described. Yet they affect our thinking and our relating both to ourselves and to others. We need to remind ourselves that judgmental statements are related to the experience of the judge. What is "perseverence" to me may be "stubbornness" to you. What I hear as an "articulate" boy with a mind of his own may be judged by his mother as "sassy." What one person sees as "bravery" appears to be "foolishness" to another. If you can remember to say, "That action seems foolish *to me,*" then you will be reminding yourself that your statement is a judgment, not a fact.

Positive statements or "compliments" are also judgments. When we tell children they are "good" or tell teenagers they are "mature," we are simply saying, "I want you to continue to behave like that because I approve of that kind of behavior." The implication is that the opposite kind of behavior is "bad" or "immature." The statement "I like the way you acted toward your friend" is not a judgmental label tacked on to behavior but an expression of what someone *likes.*

"That picture is ugly." "He is selfish." "She is hostile." These statements assume that these qualities are part of a person or thing. We are labeling them when in fact these are actually responses inside us. We can change judgmental communication by saying, "That picture looks ugly *to me*" or "*I feel* that he acts selfishly." By phrasing our statements as responses inside us rather than in the object, we make it clear that the "ugliness" or the "selfishness" is not a quality in the picture or person but simply in our perceptions.

Forming Beliefs and Attitudes

Communicating can be significantly improved if you learn to send your thoughts more accurately. The starting point in accurate message-sending is recognizing whether you are communicating on the basis of facts or assumptions. Based on a whole complex system of assumptions, we go through life fortifying our beliefs about life, death, God, our relations to others, organized religion—until they become unstated parts of our symbolic world. These become our **belief systems.**

A **belief** *can be defined as confidence in an alleged fact without positive proof.* We all have inside us such systems of beliefs. People tend to behave in a manner somewhat consistent with what they *believe* to be true.

Many experiments have been conducted to show how belief affects behavior. For example, a large lecture class, divided into two groups, was given some information about the lecturer. Half the group was told he was a "very warm" person. The other half was told he was a "rather cold" person. Then the two groups went into the lecture hall together to hear the same lecture by the same man. After hearing him speak, those students who *believed* the man "warm" rated him more considerate, more sociable, and more humorous than those who believed he was "cold." Of those who believed he was "warm," 56% participated in class discussion. Only 32% of those who believed he was "cold" took part.

Our beliefs influence our perceptions and restrict our options in life. The belief system is the organization of everything that a person believes. According to the psychologist Milton Rokeach, our belief systems are composed of all the things we "know" that we *agree* with—all the information, biases, and beliefs we have accumulated since birth. He also says we have inside of us *disbelief systems* composed of all the things we *disagree* with. These two systems affect our openness to information.

To be open-minded is to be receptive to information about one's belief and disbelief systems. If you are willing to listen to views different from your own, your mind is open to new information. It is not easy for us to know about our own beliefs. And it is difficult to evaluate ourselves as being open-minded or closed-minded. Small groups can give useful feedback about how others perceive us. You might ask people you trust how they perceive you—as *relatively* open- or closed-minded.

Some people who describe themselves as skeptics or as having a "scientific mind" may have a belief system that closes out all information that cannot be scientifically validated. Those of us who fear vulnerability to persuasion often put on the shield of the scientific mind. One possible response to all information that you instantly disbelieve is simply not to make any judgment at all about that information.

Are you open or closed minded?

In one class where I was very skeptical about some information a teacher was giving me, I raised my hand and said: "Are you trying to tell me that I should believe what you are saying is true?" (Note that I was not really asking a question. My tone of voice implied disbelief.) The instructor simply said, "Could you take this information I have shared with you and set it aside like a brick, not believing or disbelieving it, but just setting it aside for the moment? At another time you may wish to pick it up again and examine it."

Since then I have often caught myself, the skeptic, saying "that's stupid" or some other judgmental word reflecting my inability to listen to information that threatened a personal belief. Now, sometimes, I am able to hear myself getting ready to close my mind; instead, I simply pick up the information and set it aside for the moment without believing or disbelieving. It feels good to know that I do not have to accept or reject, believe or disbelieve, anything. I can simply set it aside.

Becoming aware of our belief systems can help us respond to the world more flexibly.

- Choose a partner. Take turns completing this sentence: "I believe . . . ." Have your partner write down your beliefs.

- Go back and review what you "believe." Then discuss how your beliefs affect how you listen to contrary information. How do your beliefs affect what you do?

- Take turns completing the sentence "I don't believe in . . . (astrology, ESP, God, etc.)." How do your disbeliefs affect your openness and your actions?

- Write about this statement: "I don't need to change my beliefs. I simply need to become aware of them and how they influence my perceptions and behavior."

- Choose a belief you hold and write about what you think would happen if you believed the opposite.

We can replace "believing" or "not believing" with experience. If some parts of your life are not "working" for you, you may not be experiencing enough aliveness or satisfaction—you may be living mechanically by a belief system. Relearning is getting in touch with those parts of you that may be mechanical.

We were not born with belief systems. And we keep losing parts of ourselves through assumptions, false notions, and belief systems.

Most of us develop certain cognitive styles that affect our interpersonal communication. The psychologist Milton Rokeach, in his book *The Open and Closed Mind*, explores how this dimension of our mind affects our relationships. Rokeach defines **dogmatism** (closed-mindedness) as "(1) a relatively closed cognitive organization of beliefs and disbeliefs about reality (2) organized around a central set of beliefs about absolute authority which, in turn, (3) provides a framework for patterns of intolerance toward others." **Authoritarianism** has many dimensions: rigid adherence to conventional values, a submissive attitude toward idealized authority, a tendency to condemn and punish people who violate the rules, opposition to tenderness and imagination, preoccupation with dominance/submission, identification with power figures, exaggerated assertions of strength and toughness, generalized hostility, and exaggerated concern for punitiveness toward violators of sex mores.

According to Rokeach, open-minded people evaluate messages more objectively and differentiate between shades of gray (rather than thinking in black/white right/wrong terms). They rely more on content than on the source of a message. They seek information from a wide range of sources other than their own belief systems. They are more provisional and more willing to modify beliefs. They seek to comprehend inconsistencies rather than to reject, distort, or ignore messages inconsistent with their own belief system. Each of us, depending on the situation, fits somewhere on this continuum between open and closed-mindedness.

The ways of tradition inevitably lead to mediocrity, and a mind caught in tradition cannot perceive what is true.

J. Krishnamurti

The following activities can help you evaluate how open or closed you are to new ideas.

- Discuss where you usually operate on the following scale, as illustrated by various statements.

Open _____ Closed

The world is relatively safe if you use your head.	The world is threatening and hostile.
Some agreements can be made between people about how to act.	Rules must be adhered to.

Most behavior falls on a continuum of many shades of gray.	Most behavior is either right or wrong.
Rules are designed as guidelines and can be modified.	Rules are important and must be adhered to.
Crime is a social problem that can be handled in many different ways.	People who break the law must be punished.
Few statements are either absolutely true or false.	Most statements are either true or false.
Authorities in different fields differ widely in their beliefs and theories.	People who are authorities in their fields can be depended on to give us the right.

- Write about a situation in which you were extremely closed-minded (rejecting all conflicting beliefs).

Our beliefs affect our attitudes. *An **attitude** is an enduring system of positive or negative evaluations, feelings, and tendencies toward certain actions or behavior.* Attitudes influence what we learn and remember, what we perceive, and what we do. Attitudes determine how we vote, whether or not we go to church, how we handle money, and how we feel about marriage, family, and sex. We develop favorable attitudes toward whatever satisfies our needs and unfavorable attitudes toward whatever thwarts or punishes us. Attitudes influence the kinds of people we associate with, whom we choose as friends, and what kinds of activities we engage in.

To some degree you can select your own attitudes and direct your own behavior. You can say "I have some free choices about my thoughts, my attitudes, and my actions. I feel free to make decisions about what I want to do." Experiment with different thoughts and actions. Examine your feelings in response to your different attitudes. How do you feel after behaving in a certain pattern? Positive attitudes radiate energy and success; negative attitudes breed unhappiness and fatigue. Much of the time, we can have more control of our own life than we now choose.

Attitudes toward learning influence our behavior.

Attitudes are human responses that are negative or positive, favorable or unfavorable. A person may be either attracted or repulsed by an object, person, or action. An attitude, moreover, has a degree of intensity that determines what behavior might be elicited in response to an object, person, or action. Although attitudes are difficult to change, with intention and commitment they can be modified.

Other people can help us recognize what attitudes we hold.

- What are your attitudes toward different races? Religions? Political parties? What are your attitudes toward marriage, family, sex, and money?

- How do these attitudes affect your behavior? Are you resistant to information that would change your attitude? Are you open to change?

- One volunteer in each group is to be the receiver of *attitude feedback.* The group chooses several topics such as abortion, drugs, women's liberation, sex, religion, and politics. Using a separate scale for each topic, group members write down how they would predict the volunteer's attitudes:

Extremely
Favorable _____ Topic _____ Extremely
Unfavorable

After all members have given feedback, the volunteer compares his or her answers with those of the other members. Discuss how accurate each person was in predicting the volunteer's attitudes. How does the volunteer feel about the feedback given?

• List three attitudes you would like to change. In your groups, ask others about ways to change those attitudes.

EXPECTATIONS

An **expectation** *is a confidence that an event will occur.* Expectations can make our lives less complicated when they are based on evidence which can help us anticipate the future. But if we expect too much of life or too little, if we have unrealistic expectations of ourselves or of others, we set ourselves up for disappointment. Catastrophic expectations can make us perpetually anxious. Many expectations are unrealistic and cannot be met. We may become cynical if we find that our best efforts fall short of our expectations. And if we expect very little, we may not put forth effort to reach worthwhile goals. The results of unrealistic expectations may be trying to get ahead at any cost, pretending to appear different from our real selves, trying to please others without developing honest feelings of our own, or failing to put forth any effort to reach goals. *Exploring our expectations can help us know ourselves better, which will affect our communicating with others.*

• Write about a time when you experienced intense disappointment because something you *expected* did not happen.

• What are some of your expectations for yourself?

- How do you respond to unmet expectations? How do you feel? What do you do? What other feelings or actions could you choose?

- Share your experiences of expectation and disappointment with others.

Much unhappiness occurs in our lives when we expect others to fulfill our needs. We often use expectations as a standard or as a control of others' behavior. If others act in accord with our expectations, we feel those people are "good"; if they do not, they are "bad," "wrong," or "unacceptable." Ironically, people who judge others often turn the same judgments against themselves. When they do not fulfill their own expectations, they feel they are "bad." The difference is that we can be responsible for our own behavior and decide to change it. But we cannot force others to change, and we cannot be responsible for meeting others' expectations of us.

Expectations about the behavior of others can kill relationships. As Fritz Perls said: "I am not in this world to live up to your expectations. And you are not in this world to live up to mine."

Expectations offer hope for future achievement.

People who expect perfection in friendships, in male-female relationships, in relationships with teachers, bosses, parents, and children often become very unhappy.

We all have illusions about ourselves, others, and society. We sometimes expect more out of life than is realistic to expect. Most advertising campaigns and much mass entertainment present highly idealized people and relationships. But we are *not* all young and beautiful, successful and secure, loving and loved. Not all our relationships are completely satisfying with "happy ever after" endings. When we expect friends, teachers, and employers to behave in certain ways and let them know our expectations, the relationships often suffer. And if our disappointment in others leads us to prefer no relationship at all, we may end up being very lonely.

Examining our expectations of others can help us avoid disappointment and resentment in our relationships.

- Write about some expectations you have had of others that have caused you unhappiness. Do you expect more from others than you give? Are you confused about what you want from others?

- We often expect other people to know what we want. List several people and what you expect from them. Do any of these expectations need to be modified?

The most important step is to recognize the expectations that give us trouble. One common yet unreal wish is the desire to be loved unconditionally. This ideal may be something that all of us experience at some time. But in reality no one gets this kind of love. We may behave in the worst possible way to test those who love us. Or, at the other extreme, we may play the role of totally accepting parent in our attempt to give that "unconditional love" we desire but do not receive.

An **expectation trap** is the anticipation of totally incompatible behaviors. Parents or teachers who expect children to be obedient, respectful, and loyal at the same time they expect these children to be curious, questioning, and independent are setting up a **double bind.** People often set up wholly incompatible expectations for both themselves and others.

One of our great expectations may be to live in a perfect society—a utopia. We want people in our society to be consistent in what they say, what they feel, and what they do. But in reality our society is pluralistic with much diversity because of the uniqueness of all the individuals in it. Some of our highest expectations have to do with attitudes and behavior connected with sex, pleasure, duty, honesty, the value of hard work, success, sacrifice, loyalty, and many other values that are in conflict and cannot be fulfilled in our society except in the fantasies presented by movies and television.

We often expect too much of our institutions. We complain: "The schools don't teach." "The postal system is terrible." "The government doesn't work." "The courts are unjust." But institutions cannot function independently of human judgments, abilities, and integrity. We often ask our institutions to do more than is possible and in the end we may damage their capacity to do anything effectively. We expect them to improve *everyone's life* simultaneously—to the disadvantage of no one. But what is relevant to one group in our society may be irrelevant to another. The vocal supporters of each side of an issue (the nuclear safeguards initiative, for example) seem unable to believe that those opposed to them could possibly be honest, intelligent, or reasonably informed.

On the other hand, if our expectations are too low or if we expect the future world to be a terrible place as if predetermined, those expectations can be so powerful as to freeze our ability to act in the present. If you believe the worst will happen, you may say "Why bother to do anything? Nothing will change anyway." Expectations can immobilize a person who believes that actions won't change anything. Anticipating negative responses from others can shut down communication if it tends to disallow another person's freedom to respond differently from the expectation. If we expect too little, of course, we often end up with exactly that. *Expectations offer hope and the will to achieve goals when they are constructed from experience, reason, and a true understanding of emotional needs.*

Many of our expectations are based on the assumption that other people know what we want. Communication breaks down when others do *not* know what we want. Much disappointment can be avoided if we clearly state what we expect and then discuss ways to modify expectations so that they are reasonable.

We have many options about ways to communicate disappointment. We can express feelings, hide them, or find some kind of compromise. We can communicate explosively or covertly, now or later. We can blow up or work out our feelings inside ourselves. In each case, we must take responsibility for the methods we use to handle what we are experiencing.

Some people work out expectations in writing; others think them through, define and refine them, revise and adjust them. In relationships we can try to see the other person's viewpoint in order to readjust expectations. When we turn our attention to the other person, we sometimes get a better perspective on our own expectations and feelings.

- List the major expectations you have of yourself, others, relationships, and institutions.

- List things you have managed to do this year: accomplishments, travel, new friends, good times, good parts of relationships. Notice how many expectations are *fulfilled.*

- List unrealized fantasies you enjoy that do *not* need to be managed—fantasies that clearly belong to your imagination.

Hopes not only make us human but can make us feel healthy, determined, and vital. Our plans and goals for tomorrow are part of our identity and tell us who we are and who we are becoming. Therefore, how we communicate these expectations *is* important.

CONSISTENCY AND DECEPTION

A foolish consistency is the hobgoblin of little minds.

Ralph Waldo Emerson

Most people prefer a state of security, consistency, balance, or freedom from anxiety. When we do not experience this state of equilibrium, we feel tension. As a result of this tension, we attempt to restore equilibrium. *When we experience new information that conflicts with old information, we suffer* **cognitive dissonance** *or inconsistency between the established cognition and the new.* If you believe you are doing well on the job and your boss tells you that you must improve, this discrepancy can create cognitive dissonance. For significant dissonance to result, the new information must conflict with beliefs that are relevant to your dominant needs—needs for job security, social approval, or self-esteem.

We seek to reduce the tension generated by dissonance in several ways. If you smoke and read statistics that lung cancer and heart disease are highly correlated with smoking, you may rationalize—give reasons why you should continue smoking. Or you may belittle the source of the statistics ("they don't know what they're talking about"), accuse the report of bias ("that's just propaganda"), find new information which fits the belief you don't want to change ("my grandfather smoked a pack a day and lived to be a hundred"), or simply escape by not listening to the opposition.

Reduction of dissonance does not always involve these defense strategies. It is possible that when you find out smoking is dangerous to your health you will stop smoking; many people have. However, behavior is sometimes difficult to change. Most of us feel comfortable with our belief systems, and we are not very receptive to information that would require us to change—we fear what we do not know. It takes overwhelming evidence to persuade us to change our beliefs or our behavior, especially in areas such as religion.

Leon Festinger, a psychologist, studied cognitive dissonance in making decisions. He found that when consumers were trying to make a decision about which item to buy (for example, a car), they might carefully find arguments for both competing items: a Ford versus a Chevrolet, for example. Festinger also found that when consumers had made a decision and bought the car, they would then *justify* the decision by finding many reasons why the car they bought was superior. It appears that when we have two choices of almost equal value, we regard our final choice as the more sensible and superior of the two.

The need for consistency often prompts us to deceive ourselves or others. Everyone at one time or another exaggerates, conceals information, and distorts stories. Sometimes these story-telling exploits entertain, and people experience pleasure as they listen, knowing that the situation is exaggerated. At other times, we simply withhold information that might result in another person's not getting a job or not being recognized socially for some past behavior. Or we pretend we do not hear or understand what someone is saying. Where does evasion end and deception begin?

Most of us have said one thing and thought another or done one thing and said something different. And most of us notice inconsistent behavior in others more readily than in ourselves. One problem is that we live in a culture that values *consistency*. Are we consistent if we say one thing and do another? If we feel one thing and say another? *We must decide for ourselves the degree of consistency that we value.*

Human beings are prone to **self-deception.** Self-deception may be a matter of perceptual distortion, memory distortion, or thought distortion. We find it difficult to let go of our own reality. *We defend ourselves by keeping unwelcome reality out of view, especially trying to suppress self-knowledge that does not fit our values.*

Attempts to meet life's problems and to escape pain, frustration, anxiety, or guilt sometimes take the form of self-deception (lies one tells oneself). In this case the liar and the one lied to are one and the same; therefore, the liar does not *intend* to deceive. Our basic tendency to erect false ideals that can never be reached results in basic human conflict within the self. Dissonance occurs whenever a person simultaneously holds two inconsistent cognitions (ideas, beliefs, opinions). This state of inconsistency is so uncomfortable that people try to reduce the conflict by changing one or both cognitions. To reduce dissonance, we defend our self-image; self-justification can then reach startling extremes. We ignore facts rather than admit that our judgments or decisions are wrong. Before making a decision, people seek information. Afterward they justify themselves with reassurance that they did the right thing.

Sometimes self-deception takes the form of **defense mechanisms.** It is not necessary for us to judge these techniques. We need only be aware of them. Sigmund Freud, the founder of modern psychoanalysis, believed that to escape pain, frustration, anxiety, or guilt we developed certain defense mechanisms, most of them unconsciously. Bringing these defenses out into the open where they can be examined permits us to decide whether we want to use them or not. The following list may help you find stock responses you use when you are feeling the need to defend yourself:

1. **Repression** is the deliberate exclusion from consciousness of an idea, desire, feeling, or experience—a denial of reality. We

If you saw a bullet hit a bird, and he told you he wasn't shot, you might weep at his courtesy, but you would certainly doubt his word.

Emily Dickinson

often avoid disagreeable realities by ignoring them. We turn away from unpleasant sights, we refuse to discuss unpleasant topics, we ignore criticism. A woman may deny a vision problem in order to avoid wearing glasses. A middle-aged man may deny his age by pursuing a younger mate. The phrase "love is blind" illustrates our tendency to see what we want to see—to create people as we wish they were rather than seeing them as they are. Like the ostrich who buries its head in the sand, we create a world that is compatible with our needs by denying reality.

2. **Withdrawal** is escaping reality and pain, responsibility or decisions, by pretending. We not only deny reality—we embellish it, making the world as we would like it to be. Productive fantasy can be used in problem-solving and in creative imagination that results in achieving goals; but when we imagine that we are rich, powerful, respected, popular, or heroic to the extent that our fantasies interfere with reaching our goals, then withdrawal can be a defense and an escape.

Withdrawal can be a defense or an escape.

3. **Compensation** is an attempt to disguise an undesirable trait by emphasizing a positive one. A person with a physical handicap may strive to get high grades in school. A girl who feels unattractive may develop a sparkling personality. A boy who has trouble reading may become an exceptional baseball player. Not all compensatory behavior is desirable. To overcompensate for a perceived weakness, a person may become a bully or a boaster. When compensatory behavior results in superior achievement, it can be helpful; but when it becomes exaggerated or takes antisocial forms, it may be destructive both to the individual and to others.

4. **Projection** is attributing one's faults, thoughts, or desires to others. We blame others for our own mistakes or attribute some unacceptable impulse, thought, or desire to them. If I feel guilty about being stingy, I may blame my father for being "a tightwad." If I feel guilty about wanting sex, I may blame a woman for being a flirt. Fate and bad luck are targets of projection. Placing blame and finding fault in others can be carried to extremes that distort reality in order to protect one's self-image.

5. **Rationalization** requires an individual to make up false reasons to justify actions, feelings, or thoughts. Rationalizing involves devising logical, socially acceptable reasons for our behavior. "It was for his own good." "It hurt me more than it hurt him." "Everyone does it." There are many expressions that justify behavior. The "sour grapes" response—"I didn't want it anyway" or "I didn't really like her anyway"— belittles something or someone and allows us to save face.

6. **Displacement** is shifting an emotion or fantasy from one thing or person toward another. The woman who has a fight with her boss goes home and takes it out on her husband, who spanks their child, who kicks their dog. Such displaced emotion allows the woman to keep her job, but the price may be her relationship with her husband. Usually it is better to express negative feelings in a positive context with the person for whom they are intended.

7. **Regression** is the process of acting out a childhood stage—of going back to a time without responsibility, a retreat in a time of stress. Occasionally an older child will regress to bedwetting, thumbsucking, or other behavior when a new

baby is born. A frustrated adult may throw a temper tantrum or sulk when experiencing great emotional pain. Adults who run home to a parent when life gets difficult may continue to be unable to solve their personal problems.

This brief list may help you find some of your favorite techniques for escaping reality and defending your own self-image. It is difficult to say that defense mechanisms are good or bad. When they result in self-defeating responses, they can compound difficulties. But sometimes they make life tolerable for the moment. Like soldiers who protect themselves in war, children need to survive. But adults may use so much energy defending themselves against an imaginary enemy that they cannot cope realistically with life. Once we become aware of our defenses, we often stop using them. Then we can face unpleasant truths, accept criticism, face real problems, and accept responsibility for our behavior even if we experience pain as the price for giving up self-deception.

Identifying the phrases we use to defend ourselves can help us become aware of self-deception.

- Make a list of self-deceptive expressions. ("He did it first.")
- Make a list of defensive responses often made in answer to praise. ("I really didn't do anything.")
- Give examples of defense mechanisms you have used or observed others using: repression, withdrawal, compensation, projection, rationalization, displacement, regression.

Self-image usually includes the line "I am a decent, moral person." When our behavior does not live up to that line, we find ways to resist recognition of what we have done. Our culture has taught us it is wrong to cheat, lie, and steal. Once we have acted out behavior defined by others as "wrong," we may resort to a defense mechanism. In one experiment, tests designed to encourage cheating were given to a class. Before the test, the students were measured on their attitudes toward cheating. After the test, they were measured again. Those students who cheated became more lenient in their attitudes; those who resisted the temptation to cheat adopted even harsher attitudes than before. *People find internal reasons to justify their behavior and will go to extraordi-*

nary lengths to defend their actions. An experience lied about (or altered) usually becomes a problem. When we tell the truth about it, the problem often disappears. Becoming aware often requires that a person be willing to suffer conflict or tolerate contradiction, inconsistency, or dissonance.

Tracking down our self-deceptions *can liberate us from boring, rigid defense mechanisms.*

- Write about past, present, and future self-deceptions:

  About the past: How have I selectively distorted my past? What do I tell myself to make my parents "wrong"? What do I gain when I blame others?

  About the present: What discrepancies can you see between what you do and what you express?

  About the future: What fictions do you maintain about the future in the form of expectations of yourself and others? What investments in false identities do you defend?

- Write about the following kinds of self-deception (give examples from your experience):

  Distorting perceptions (sensory, emotional, intellectual).

  Distorting memories.

  Distorting thoughts to avoid discrepancies or inconsistencies between what you say and do.

A **double bind** *is a contradictory communication.* One kind of double bind occurs when people are punished for accurate perceptions of themselves, others, or the outside world. If abusive parents demand that their dependent children see them as gentle and loving, even when they come home drunk and hit the children, the children may be forced to perceive reality the way the parents define it. If children are repeatedly exposed to this kind of confusion, they may find it difficult to learn how they "should" see reality. In addition to having a confused reality, they may feel guilty for being unable to feel what they are told they "should" feel to gain their parents' approval. And even that guilt may be labeled as a feeling they "should not" have.

Another example of someone in a double bind is the spouse who occasionally feels sad and is therefore perceived by his or her mate as an example of failure, since marriages are supposed to "make people happy." The mate reacts by saying, "After all I've tried to do for you, you ought to be happy." The spouse's feelings become associated with being bad or ungrateful. Then he or she may pretend to feel happy, which can result in a deeply felt depression. Depression can also occur when people feel they are responsible for something over which they have no control, such as divorce, illness, or death.

Another double bind occurs when a person makes a demand and prohibits certain actions at the same time. Parents who want their children to have "minds of their own" may at the same time want their children to be obedient, get along well with adults, and "not cause any trouble." The father who wants his son to be a daredevil or "one of the boys" and at the same time wants him to be law-abiding puts his son in a double bind. And the mother who wants her child to win at any cost and yet be honest at the same time may be putting the child into an impossible double bind.

When people say "Be spontaneous!" they have just set up a double bind. No matter what the other person does, it cannot be a spontaneous act now. A mother who wants her children to come visit, saying "I wish sometimes you just wanted to come see me," may be unhappy if they do not come and unhappy if they do—because she may think they only visit because she asked them to. Similarly, the wife who asks her husband for a display of affection places both herself and her husband into a double-bind situation—because she may feel "he only did it because I asked, not because he felt affectionate." In any situation where one party has power over another (parent/child, teacher/student, employer/employee, doctor/patient) and then pretends not to have control and claims equality, both the victim and the victimizer are in a double bind.

Becoming aware of contradictory communication can prevent some double-bind situations.

- Make a list of commands or appeals that set up double binds. For example: "Be spontaneous!" "Love me!" "Be independent!" "Grow up!"

- Write about a double-bind situation you have experienced. Describe your feelings and actions. How might it have been avoided?

We have moved from an exploration of language to thought processes. Thinking can be classified as objective or subjective or somewhere on a continuum between the two. Some of the mind processes include abstracting, generalizing, and stereotyping. We can classify our thoughts into such categories as facts, assumptions, judgments, beliefs, and attitudes. We have many misconceptions about thinking and reasoning: One is that logical thinking results in The Truth; another is that a logical person is infallible. But thinking is subject to errors in perception, in the use of language, and in interpretation of information. Thinking and reasoning, moreover, cannot be separated from emotion and feeling. It is possible to feel deeply and still think logically; to feel deeply and think illogically; to be without emotion and think logically; or to be without emotion and think illogically. After our study of language and thinking, we will explore how the body and emotions affect our communicating and relating.

MIND POTENTIAL

Man's mind stretched to a new idea never goes back to its original dimensions.

Oliver Wendell Holmes

The human brain has often been called a biological computer. Actually, it is more like several interconnected computers, each with its own specialized functions, yet each interdependent. Dividing the wrinkled outer structure of the brain in half, from front to back, is a tissue of fibers by which information can be transmitted from one hemisphere to the other. Although on very simple levels each hemisphere is said to perform the same functions as the other in mirror image form, each hemisphere tends to specialize. The degree of independence has been the subject of recent brain research.

Robert Ornstein, in *The Psychology of Consciousness*, claims that each hemisphere shares the potential for many functions, that most activities require the use of both hemispheres, and that most of us tend to specialize using the left or right half. The *left* hemisphere (which controls the right side of the body) specializes in abstractions, logical thinking, temporal and sequential information, verbalization, intellect, analytical science, and mathematics. The *right* hemisphere (which controls the left side of the body) has to do with passion, orientation in space, aesthetics, art, spirituality, music, body image, recognition of faces, fantasy, dreams, intuition, and visualization.

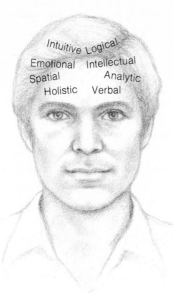

Brain hemispheres.

Most of Western education has dealt with verbal memorizing and analyzing of facts. The heavy emphasis on the "three R's" has left us little time to develop the skills of mental imagery. Today many educators are exploring ways to teach those abilities less developed such as imagery and visualization. Jerome Bruner suggests that the brain can be developed to work like a "symphony orchestra" rather than a computer or printed circuit.

Imagery and Visualization

One theory suggests that images held in the mind contain energy that can transform behavior and produce effects that extend to the world around us. Aristotle believed that images have the power to stimulate our emotions and motivate us to effort. Members of Eastern cultures of all centuries have used imagery and the power of the imagination to change themselves and their environment. In the last fifteen years, interest in imagery and visualization has resulted in research in many different fields. For example, the physiologist Edmund Jacobson found that when we imagine ourselves to be running, we produce muscle contractions in our bodies that give us exercise.

Imagination can operate simultaneously at several levels—sensation, feeling, thinking, and intuition. Various types of imagination include the visual (creation of visual images), auditory (utilization of sounds and music), kinesthetic (muscular sensations of tension and relaxation), olfactory (odors), gustatory (tastes), and tactile (touch sensations).

Evoking images can be one of the most important and spontaneously active functions of a human mind. Because this function operates both in conscious and unconscious spheres, it can be controlled, trained, and used as a method for self-development. Techniques for relaxation which contribute to better imagery are found in Chapter 7, on the body. Although the subject of imagery and visualization is a mental process, it can also be used to change behavior and will be discussed further in Chapters 7 and 9.

Creativity

Some men see things as they are and say, "Why?" I dream things that never were and say, "Why Not?"

George Bernard Shaw

In the early 1960s considerable research on creativity resulted in studies of artists and scientists, the creative process and creative thinking, and the relevance of all this to our lives, individually and socially. Confusion surrounds the word *creativity*. Creativity is defined in the following ways: as the learning of new responses, as advanced problem-solving, as the ability to transfer learning to new problems, and as the process of sensing gaps or disturbing elements, forming ideas about them, and communicating the results.

Not only do we have difficulty defining the word, but we do not know much about the creative process. One psychologist suggests we should use the term *creativity* to refer to "rare and unique talent in a particular field." Yet I believe *every* human being has the capacity to be creative as a result of his or her uniqueness.

Studies of creative people show that certain qualities result in creativity: flexibility, originality, and fluency (quantity of output). Creativity involves intuitive leaps—a synthesis of ideas from widely separate fields of knowledge. According to the biographies of geniuses, insights which suddenly bridge seemingly unrelated subjects come to individuals who have acquired great knowledge and spent long periods of time in concentrated effort. *Thus personality, motivation, and discipline all affect creative output.*

We do not have any *facts* about creativity. People who study creativity do not agree about definitions, processes, or products. Yet we experience creativity all around us: automobiles, airplanes, books, music, art. Glance around you. Almost everything surrounding you was invented and designed by someone. The sum total of all these creative acts makes up the world we live in—not only the physical environment but our mental one too. Our minds are filled almost entirely by symbols originally formed by creative persons.

Although we have not developed reliable tests to measure creativity, most of us have experienced flashes of it. We have been able to relate things or ideas with great insight and intuition. *Creativity may be measured not in terms of* products *but in terms of the exciting processes of the mind.* The brain functions as a communicating machine—processing information, scanning, ordering, selecting all at extraordinary speed. The symbols shown on the screen of the mind flash by so fast that we sometimes don't record them. Yet ultimately the mind feeds back and feeds forward in flows of creativity. Creativity depends upon its own free flow; yet we all need help in acquiring the tools of *communication* before we can translate or share our creativity. *The individual mind has unlimited potential to be creative and to communicate that creativity with others.*

Figure 6–1 An exercise in imagination.

Imagination is related to creativity. List as many shapes as you can see in Figure 6-1. Make your own ink blots using colored inks. Write stories about what you see. Write about how what you see can be "used." Share these writings.

In the last two decades, mind research has involved the study of hypnosis, dreams, mind control, split-brain functioning, imagery, extrasensory perception, and biofeedback. Biofeedback machines measure our control of such physiological processes as brain waves, heart rate, oxygen consumption, galvanic skin response, muscle tension, and temperature. All these studies seek to find patterns in our perceptions of the world, and many of them are specifically directed at expanding our mental abilities. You may wish to explore some of these exciting possibilities.

Creativity is the encounter of the intensively conscious human being with his world.

Rollo May

These studies are based on the idea that the biological functioning of the mind, unique in every individual, can be affected by learning. Beliefs, attitudes, and values are learned. You are not born liberal or conservative, closed or open-minded. You are not born believing in a god, valuing freedom and human dignity, or loving humanity. And because beliefs, attitudes, and values are learned, they can be unlearned—if you are aware of them, if you know what they are, and if you decide to change them. *Our ability to "change our minds" may be our greatest freedom.*

Self-education, stimulating, exercising, and "feeding" your mind takes time, attention, and *intention.* Lack of stimulation, inadequate discipline, and lack of goals can do to the mind what lack of exercise, improper diet, and poor posture do to your body. There is no saturation point in learning. Making your life an ongoing educational experience is largely a matter of perception and attention. When you become aware of mind traps such as overgeneralizations, oversimplifications, unwarranted assumptions, and cognitive dissonance, you can make your mind work more efficiently and with greater precision. With a precise mind, your communication will become more precise.

The philosopher William James said: "The mind is at every stage a theatre of simultaneous possibilities . . . . The transition from a state of puzzle and perplexity to rational comprehension is full of relief and pleasure."

FOR FURTHER READING

Beardsley, Monroe C. *Thinking Straight.* 3rd ed. Englewood Cliffs, N.J.: Prentice-Hall, 1966.
> This is a classic text in logical thinking and its effects on communication.

Chase, Stuart. *The Tyranny of Words.* New York: Harvest Books, 1938.
> Chase stresses how language difficulties originate with unclear, ambiguous, illogical thinking.

Ellis, Albert, and Robert Harper. *A Guide to Rational Living.* Englewood Cliffs, N.J.: Prentice-Hall, 1961.
> This book is designed to help individuals capable of honest self-evaluation to solve common problems through developing a realistic approach to living.

Ornstein, Robert. *The Psychology of Consciousness*. San Francisco:
W. H. Freeman, 1972.
 Ornstein explores the different uses and abilities of the right and
 left hemispheres of the brain and offers suggestions for
 developing abilities unilaterally.

Rokeach, M. *Beliefs, Attitudes and Values*. San Francisco:
Jossey-Bass, 1968.
 The author researches the effects of belief systems, attitudes,
 and value formation as they relate to the thinking process.

Zimbardo, P. G., and E. B. Ebbesen. *Influencing Attitudes and
Changing Behavior*. Reading, Mass.: Addison-Wesley, 1969.
 The authors show how behavior can be changed by changing
 attitudes.

NONVERBAL COMMUNICATION
   Body and Personality
   Sensory Awareness: Touching and Seeing
   Kinesics: Body Movement and Stress
   Proxemics: Space and Environment
MIXED MESSAGES AND SILENCE
THE BODY AS REALITY

A good painter is to paint two main things, namely, man and the working of man's mind.

The first is easy, the second difficult, for it is to be represented through the gestures and movements of the limbs.

Leonardo Da Vinci

7

Being: How the Body Communicates

NONVERBAL COMMUNICATION

Nonverbal (nonword) communication includes gestures, posture, body movements, and touching. Such communication from our environment, from other people, and from our own bodies is very subtle; often we are not aware of these messages, particularly when they are involuntary. Becoming more aware of the nonverbal messages we send and receive can help us communicate more effectively. Some researchers say that nonverbal communication may carry as much as 65% of the social meaning between people. Thus improved nonverbal communication can greatly affect our interrelating with others.

From thousands of experiments, photographs, videotapes, and personal observations, experts agree that certain body gestures, facial expressions, and postures can often be interpreted with some degree of accuracy. Interpreting gestures is not simple—it takes practice and understanding, and even then we can only make *tentative* interpretations. However, gesture-reading can offer clues that you can confirm by asking the sender what they mean. You can also examine your own gestures to see if they confirm the attitudes, emotions, and feelings you consciously hold.

When we feel ourselves getting defensive, our muscles may begin to tighten, especially around the mouth and eyes. We clench fists, fold our arms, or cross our legs. But it is very difficult for us to *see* our own nonverbal gestures. In our culture, we have been taught *not* to look. Therefore we miss many important aspects of human relationships. In other cultures, men may stare at women, looking them up and down. In our culture, we consider such behavior rude. Similarly, when a child stares at a man with a missing leg and asks "Where's his leg?" an embarrassed parent will rush the child away and tell the child to be quiet. In waiting rooms people look at the floor, at the ceiling, straight ahead—anywhere except into the eyes of another person.

Communicators often remain unconscious of their own nonverbal communication. We may communicate hostile, defensive, critical, and suspicious messages without even knowing we are doing so. Sometimes we do not know what we are really feeling. If we become more aware, we can sometimes eliminate nonverbal messages we do not really want to send.

How would you interpret these nonverbal messages?

Sometimes our gestures and facial expressions match our verbal communication; at other times, they are incongruent. A nervous laugh intended to indicate amusement may be a sign that the laugher is unsure or perhaps even frightened. If verbal and nonverbal meanings contradict each other, the nonverbal gestures often prove to be the more expressive of real feelings.

When we do not communicate what we are trying to say, we may be giving double messages unknowingly and confusing the listener. Observing gestures is a first step toward untangling these double messages. Are you aware when you are frowning? What does it mean when you frown while telling someone "Everything's OK"?

Because nonverbal gestures depend on the sender, we must ask the sender what they mean. Tapping feet, drumming fingers, clicking pens—all these mannerisms may indicate boredom or nervousness. Avoiding a look may be interpreted as dishonesty, or shyness. Yet such interpretations could be wrong, so we need to ask. Some people talk with their hands and body. Others talk with their eyes or their facial muscles (smiles, frowns); others talk by shaking their heads (in agreement or disagreement). But we cannot be sure what these nonverbal cues mean unless we ask.

Moreover, often we are not aware of the messages we are sending. One class listed gestures, facial expressions, sounds, and other nonverbal signals. They then made one column for what these signals might mean and another column for how these signals affected their feelings. The list of signals numbered thirty. The list of possible meanings numbered close to three hundred. How they made different individuals feel resulted in as many responses as students. A smile, for example, is enjoyed by some people and thought by others to be insincere. One student said: "I never stopped to notice or think about gestures. Now that I have, I see so much more. But more important than what I notice in others, I can now often see what my own face is doing. I have learned much more about myself."

Just as language is used in a context and means something in relationship to what occurs before or after, so nonverbal messages also mean something only in context. A single gesture cannot tell us what is going on in the other person. Nonverbal cues cannot be translated in isolation. So the message we think we are getting must be confirmed by the sender before we reach conclusions. Although most of us are nonverbally illiterate, we do have the ability to read and use nonverbal language—and, through intention and concentration, we can develop nonverbal skills.

Which items on the following list are you most conscious of? Which items do you not ordinarily notice? What are your personal attitudes, values, and feelings about each of these items? Listen to the responses of others in your group.

- Environmental factors: living space, working space, colors, arrangement of furniture.
- Time and space: personal space, distancing, privacy, territory, seating arrangements, atmosphere, timing.
- Dress, grooming, scent.
- Body structure and physical characteristics: build, bone size, height, weight, gender, skin color, size of nose, color of eyes.
- Body movements: posture, walk (stride, pace, strut), feeling of muscles, tendons, joints.
- Touch: shaking hands, gripping, holding, back-slapping, punching, pulling, caressing.
- Gestures: use of hands, arms, head, legs.
- Facial expressions: mouth (smile, grimace, muscle movements); nose (nostrils flared or pinched); eyes (contact, avoidance, pupil dilation, dullness or brightness); forehead and jaw (tense or relaxed, held forward or back).
- Voice: pitch, tone, rhythm, stress, volume, intensity, expression (angry, humble, sad, happy, alive, dull).
- Physical condition: fatigue, pain, energy, health, somatopsychic effects (fear, anxiety, trust, defensiveness, or joy as expressed by the body).
- Social and cultural influences: class, church, business, family context, large group, small group, dyads.

A discussion can call your attention to these often unconscious factors that affect your communication and relationships. Be tentative about the conclusions you reach. Ask for feedback from others about their nonverbal messages. Check messages you think you are giving or getting. *Nonverbal communication must be verified verbally.* Developing our ability to communicate effectively involves paying attention to nonverbal messages.

- Make a list of gestures that you notice for each person in your group. (For example: nods head to encourage, waves arms, uses hands, drums fingers.) Share this list by having one person at a time listen to what all the others wrote down about him or her.

- In your group share times when you have received and times when you have given mixed messages.

Body and Personality

Many of us have lost awareness of our own bodies. We are often unaware of how we sit, stand, or walk. We can learn a great deal regarding our feelings about ourselves, our personalities, and our character traits simply by observing our bodies. When we are afraid, we may stand with head thrust forward resulting in neck displacement and shoulders and rib cage out of line. If this type of carriage becomes set, we may experience headaches and bursitis from the muscle tension.

Knowing is a translation of external events into bodily processes . . . into states of the nervous system and the brain: we know the world in terms of the body, and in accordance with its structure.

Alan Watts

We have found that body functioning is related to emotional states and that emotional states often indicate personal reaction patterns to events in our lives. People who are sick, weak, or tired reflect their poor physical condition in their muscles and posture. Even the center of gravity differs in different people—chest, stomach, even as low as the hips. We all have habitual ways of holding our shoulders: retracted, raised, squared, rounded, or dropped. The chest may be expanded, rigid, relaxed, puffed up, or soft. People carry their body weight on different parts of the foot: over the heels, on the toes, over the whole foot. Posture can be straight, swaybacked, or hunched forward. Some backbones are rigid and stiff; others seem flexible. Sometimes we sit with crossed legs and folded arms as if protecting ourselves or shutting out attack. Head and neck tension and shallow breathing may accompany unconscious resistance to others.

*The study of **somatopsychic** effects is the study of how body posture and carriage affect emotions and personality.* We carry our bodies in characteristic attitudes or postures. The helpless, pleading body carriage asks for kindness and consideration. The habit of manipulating others by looking like a helpless child involves a muscular arrangement of the body. The body soon takes on this attitude, which then becomes a habit defining and often limiting the individual's growth and stifling personal change. If this muscular set becomes habitual, the muscles shorten and thicken and the emotional attitude may become fixed—the head, for example, may be set on a meekly bending neck.

"Poor me! I need help.
Please be kind!"
'Pay attention
to me!'

Habitual body posture reflects personality, attitudes, and self-image.

Facial expressions can be warm and accepting or cold and rejecting. The jaw may be thrust out aggressively or tucked in humbly. The forehead may be raised or furrowed or blank and expressionless. The nostrils may be retracted or sagging, active or passive. Each individual develops habitual muscular arrangements of expressions, body posture, and movement.

Can we actually become more attractive by becoming aware of somatopsychic effects in our bodies? Can altering posture and expressions modify our personalities? Many people believe that we can change by changing our bodies—that consciousness of our bodies can change our responses to life and our relationships.

Cultures have biases about what they consider physical attractiveness. Because we have a democratic bias in America, we do not generally like to admit that we often judge people on their looks. We like to believe that we judge people on their merits. However, research indicates that people who are regarded as physically attractive are liked more and considered more intelligent, personable, sensitive, warm, responsive, kind, and interesting than people who are not judged physically attractive. Moreover, studies indicate that attractive children get more attention and better grades from teachers and that nurses and doctors pay more attention to mental patients who are attractive than those who are not. Yet, ironically, some of the "beautiful" people feel as if people like them *only* because of their looks. Many "beautiful" young people have difficulty in life *because* they are attractive. They may get used to grade school teachers giving them good grades. When they get to college where research papers, examinations, and other criteria are used, they find it difficult to compete with students who have not had preferential treatment. And they often have an intense fear of getting old.

These and other findings have a number of implications for students of human communication. It can be to our advantage to pay attention to diet and nutrition which keep our body and skin healthy. Dressing appropriately and neatly can be learned. Studying ways to improve our appearance and make ourselves more attractive is *not* vain. We know that appearance can affect our ability to get employment, to make friends, and to experience interactions with other people.

- Close your eyes and ask yourself: "What word best describes my appearance?" Write the first word that comes to mind. Why does it describe you best? What do you dislike most? What do you think others dislike most? How do you know this is true? What do you like best about your appearance? What are your best features? Have you received any compliments recently? Do you believe them? *A positive self-image comes from having a realistic picture of both your strengths and your weaknesses.*

Sensory Awareness: Touching and Seeing

A first step toward becoming more conscious of the body is to get in touch with our sensory equipment: eyes, ears, nose, mouth, and skin. One of the effects of living in a culture that emphasizes cognition (thinking) is that many of us have become physically deadened. Therefore the effort to experience—to become aware —often arouses anxiety. You may notice that you resist following body awareness exercises. If you are resisting, go *with* the resistance. Look at it, experience it, and let go of it. If you decide *not* to let go, you can choose to pass. One way to let go is simply not to fight resistance. Notice anxiety, fatigue, boredom, annoyance. Sense these opposing forces. Become aware of when your mind wanders and your attention lags.

The following activities can help us get in touch with our bodies as well as our feelings.

- Tap and slap different parts of your body to awaken your senses. Stand with your eyes closed and put your hands up to your head. With your fingertips and wrists relaxed, start to tap your head with your fingertips—first light tapping, then a lively, stronger tap. Pause for a moment and notice the effects until they subside.

- Tap your face in the same way. Try one side at a time and see how it feels when you stop. How does the untapped side feel? Pause and experience the effect fully. Then continue.

- Using the whole hand, slap each arm beginning with the opposite hand and tap all the way up and down the arm and across the shoulder as far as you can reach. Pause and feel the effect. Then slap the opposite arm. Fully experience the effects.

- Sit down and, with both hands, start slapping one leg at a time.

- Sit on the floor and massage one foot at a time. Notice when you have finished with one foot how the other foot "asks for" the same stimulation—and the accompanying feeling of aliveness.

Sensory awareness includes more than body awareness. Sensory awareness training develops our sensitivity to the environment through practices designed to call attention to what is "out there." Most people react to the world in set patterns—we walk from house to car, drive from home to work, walk through familiar buildings, all without seeing or hearing. "Mind chatter" may keep us from experiencing what is going on around us. We may even react to new situations in established patterns; we allow past experiences to control visions of new and different experiences. We see the world through our expectations, leaving little possibility for the excitement of the new, the aliveness that is around us.

Through paths of silence the senses can come to life again. We can relearn to taste, touch, see, and hear in new, imaginative ways through mind and body expansion.

- Close your eyes and concentrate on *listening.* Say to yourself: "Now I am aware of the sound of the refrigerator motor, the electric clock, settling sounds in the walls and ceilings. Now I am aware of the sound of my own breathing, of a car outside, of an airplane motor, of a child shouting somewhere, of a footstep overhead."

- Close your eyes and concentrate on *touching.* Move around the room, touching objects. Take a walk through the house touching; put your hand under water. Take a walk through the yard; touch the grass, trees, bushes, flowers, leaves—all with your eyes closed.

- Close your eyes and concentrate on *smelling;* open the refrigerator and the cupboards in both the kitchen and the bathroom. Reach in and pull out bottles and boxes and objects; open them and smell them. With eyes closed, walk into the yard—smell flowers, grass, garbage.

- Close your eyes and concentrate on *tasting* different foods: bite into an apple and taste its juice, bite a raw potato, celery, a carrot. With your eyes closed, chew slowly and taste. Notice and be aware. Expand your consciousness and allow your senses to bring you the world outside your skin.

The longer you spend with your eyes closed, the more acute your other senses become. Helen Keller, who was born blind, deaf, and dumb, asked a friend, who had just returned from a walk in the woods, what he had observed. The friend said: "Nothing." Keller was appalled. When she went for a walk, she touched things; she felt the leaves, "the smooth skin of a silver birch, or the rough, shaggy bark of a pine." She touched the branches of trees, searching for buds in the spring or bareness in winter. "Occasionally," she remarked, "or if I am very fortunate, I place my hand gently on a small tree and feel the happy quiver of a bird in full song." Because she had neither the gift of sight nor hearing, she learned the joy of touch, smell, and taste.

It is the skin, the largest organ of the body, that receives our tactile experiences. The sense of touch develops in the human embryo before any other sense. Since the skin is already highly developed before the embryo has either eyes or ears, an infant becomes accustomed to tactile sensations while still in the womb. The initial order of sensory development is tactile, auditory, and then visual. As a child approaches adolescence, that order is reversed. *What happens to infants by way of tactile experience affects their subsequent personalities and behavioral development.* Tactile experience is as basic a need as breathing, eating, or resting. Without tactile satisfaction, we cannot survive.

Ashley Montague, a famous anthropologist, says in his book *Touching:* "It is not words so much as acts communicating affection and involvement that children, and, indeed, adults require." When affection and involvement are conveyed through touch, security becomes associated with touching. People who are not touched enough may never learn to relate to others in many fundamental human ways.

If we do not receive enough touching at appropriate times during early childhood, we may later search out that satisfaction in unusual or unconscious ways. (Stroking, caressing, or cuddling a person implies love, involvement, concern, responsibility, ten-

Touching communicates caring.

derness, and awareness of the needs and vulnerabilities of another human being. All this is communicated through touching.

Each of us needs to touch and be touched. We have thoughts and feelings so deep and personal that words simply do not communicate them. Our most intense joys need to be shared. Our deepest fears and anxieties are more endurable when shared. Yet we often hide deep feelings from ourselves by repressing them. And we suffer greatly, because we need to share ourselves. But that sharing cannot be accomplished merely on a verbal level; our deepest thoughts and feelings can be communicated best by touch and physical intimacy. If you tell people you care about them, they will hear you. If you touch them, they will believe you. No amount of reassuring talk substitutes for a squeeze and a hug or a pat on the back when saying thank you.

Through touch we communicate with ourselves about our physical world: hot and cold, rough and smooth, wet and dry—all the myriad qualities that exist in the touching of objects make our world real for us. But the most important touch is that which communicates affection between human beings. People need to express caring for each other. Parents need to express affection for each other and for their children through touching. Although we need to touch and be touched so much that many of us are starved for it, often these feelings are either bottled up or unconscious. We may be afraid that the floodgates will burst if we are touched—and they sometimes do. People who have not received enough "touch love" often break down and cry when someone does touch them. *It is not words so much as acts communicating affection and involvement that we require.*

Touching other human beings allows us to experience ourselves as members of the same species.

- Do you initiate touch? Do you ask to be touched or held? Describe your feelings about different kinds of touching.

- Have you ever touched someone and been misunderstood?

- Touch someone this week. Choose an appropriate moment, perhaps just touching an arm or shoulder. Write about the other person's response.

Massage is a way of communicating affection and affirmation. You can learn basic stress-relieving strokes and explore your feelings about touching and being touched in a supportive way.

- Choose a partner. We are going to massage shoulders and necks only. As your partner sits in a chair, stand behind the chair and begin by gently massaging his or her shoulders. Ask your partner to tell you if he or she wants you to increase or decrease the pressure. Spend about five minutes together exploring what feels best. Then change partners. Massage at least three different people. Then, in groups, share how it felt to be massaged and how it felt to give a massage. Would you rather give or receive a massage? Tell your three partners how each did the exercise differently.

We can communicate many things about ourselves simply by touching hands: nervousness, anxiety, embarrassment, comfort, warmth, kindness. We can choose to pass among one another, to touch, to rest an arm on a shoulder, to touch a head, to put an arm around another's neck for a moment—in short, to show caring through touch.

Touching experiences can give you a good deal of information about yourself and others. You can also design your own touching experiences. (Remember that any student has the right to pass up any group activity.)

- Choose a partner. Close your eyes and take turns exploring your partner's face with your fingertips. Be aware of your feelings while touching and being touched. Imagine what your partner is feeling. Discuss this experience with your partner. Then share your experiences with the whole group.
- Exchange partners and repeat the exercise. It is most interesting to touch several members of the class so you can experience the differences. The third time is often much more comfortable than the first. Write about your touching experience in class.

As babies, our initial experiences with touching usually came from parents. In a few months or perhaps a year, we began to explore our own bodies and experienced touching ourselves. We explored the shape and texture of our bodies and thus began to develop our body images. When we began to play with other children, we became curious about the anatomical differences between sexes. Most little boys and girls sense that the mysterious feelings drawing them into the learning adventure of mutual exploration are wrong. They have already absorbed from the adult world the idea that touching the human body is indecent.

In some families, the parents rarely embrace or even hold hands. The father may soon decide that his six-year-old is too old to cuddle or even to hold in his lap or kiss. The mother may decide that the five-year-old should take baths alone. Children soon learn to restrain the impulse to reach out and touch others. They sense when they are no longer welcome to get into bed with their parents in the morning. As they grow older, they express the impulse to touch by teasing, hitting, scuffling, or wrestling.

By adolescence, children begin to experiment with kissing games and necking with the opposite sex. In the past girls were taught that sex was dirty and touching would "get you in trouble." Most girls allowed themselves to be touched long before they would initiate the touching. Boys got the idea that they were supposed to be the aggressors with the responsibility for what happened. These culturally induced roles are less observed today, although they still exist to some extent. Now that sex roles are less sharply defined we may experience even greater anxiety when we don't know how we are supposed to act.

Touching between men, between women, and between men and women arouses culturally induced responses. In some societies, it is the norm for men to kiss each other on the cheek to show warmth and friendship. In this country such action might be considered odd. Although touching often connotes certain cultural and sexual meanings in addition to fulfilling basic human needs for affection, *we can learn to communicate accurately the desire, intent, and emotional content of our touching messages.*

Because our culture too often shuts us off from touch when we attempt to get physically close to each other, our attempts may often appear groping rather than caressing. These fumbling encounters may have been disappointing and threatening in the past. In spite of our confusion about what touching means, we can create warmth and caring through touch.

By recalling our childhood family and religious sex programming, we can become aware of how our first boy/girl attractions influence us and question ourselves about what sex and touching mean to us now.

- What did your parents tell you about sex? How did they tell you? What religious teachings about sex were you given?
- What did others tell you about sex? How did they tell you?
- What memories do you have of girl/boy experiences and other explorations with touching?

In courtship we not only allow but expect touching and intimacy. Moreover, we expect one or two intimate relationships to bear the weight of all our needs to communicate through touch. Often our needs to communicate through touch are too heavy a burden for intimacy with one person. Touching can be part of *all* interpersonal relationships.

Like touch, *eye contact* can be a very intimate form of nonverbal communication. Eyes not only receive messages; they give them as well. The language of the eyes is a subtle and complex way of exchanging feelings. People from different cultures learn different rules about dealing with eye contact. Some cultures view direct eye contact as rude. Americans in foreign countries sometimes complain about people who stare or hold a glance too long. Many of us look away from direct eye contact, especially if the other person is a stranger. Being stared at by an unfamiliar person may make us feel self-conscious. We sneak looks while the other is not looking. If one man looks at another man's wife in a certain way, he may be asking for trouble. If a woman looks at another woman's husband in a certain way, she may invite complications.

Eyes express dominance, involvement, and attitude toward others. Submissive people lower their eyes. Disinterested people do not look at others. Furthermore, we can express approval or disapproval of others with our eyes. Many of us are not conscious of the ways we use our eyes. We flirt with our eyes and invite others to become intimate. We follow unwritten rules dictating how and when we will use our eyes.

We can become more aware of how we communicate with touch and eye contact.

- Choose a partner. Spend about a minute on each of the following exercises:

  1. Face your partner. Don't talk or touch but notice how you make eye contact. Experience how *you* feel when someone looks at you. Notice if you or your partner develops any strategies for eye contact. Stay in contact even when you feel you want to withdraw or lower your eyes. Just be aware of what you are experiencing. Is your partner giving you some nonverbal cues about feelings? What other kinds of communication are occurring?

  2. Now reach out and touch hands at the same time you continue eye contact. Notice anything about your hands or your partner's hands (hot/cold, smooth/rough, wet/dry). Note any movements. Do the hands of the other person express feelings nonverbally? Is the grip strong or weak? Still or active? Be in touch with what you are experiencing. Be *with* your partner.

An exercise in eye contact and touching helps us become more aware of how we communicate.

3. Now continue to hold hands but close your eyes. This time there will be no eye contact. What effects do closed eyes have on the experience of touch? What changes do you experience in your feelings? Do you or your partner do anything different in expressing yourselves through touch with eyes closed? Can you risk moving your fingers and exploring each other's hands? Notice what you say with your hands as you move and explore with them.

4. Go through these same three exercises with a second partner and then with a third. Notice differences between the three people you have communicated with.

5. This entire exercise with three different people takes ten to fifteen minutes. Take at least ten minutes to discuss what you learned about your partners. Share with the class how these people were similar or dissimilar. Did you find differences related to whether your partners were of the opposite sex? Discuss your own feelings with the different partners.

• If you prefer not to talk about experiences, write what you learned through eye contact and touch. Experiment with eye contact outside of class this week. See how other people react to different eye-contact strategies (staring, lowering the eyes).

Kinesics: Body Movement and Stress

Body motion, or **kinesics,** includes voice, gestures, posture, facial expressions, and eye behavior. Some of these nonverbal behaviors may be intended to communicate; others may be intended to be expressive. Some may suggest emotions; others may carry information about personality traits or attitudes. Most of us cannot see ourselves except in the mirror or in photographs, which tell us little about the ways in which we communicate through body movements. Therefore, much of the information we get about body motion as a mode of communication comes from our relationships with others.

You can ask people around you to let you know how you use your body to communicate. Moreover, you can record your voice on a tape recorder. Many classes use videotape. Small-group sessions can be recorded and played back so that students can see and hear how they talk in a group and how they use their faces, hands, and bodies to express themselves. Even without these methods, you can become conscious of when your facial muscles tighten, when you are smiling, when you are frowning. Such nonverbal expressions will be interpreted in terms of their context—that is, in terms of where, when, with whom, and under what circumstances they occur.

Aristotle listed five senses: sight, sound, touch, taste, and smell. But he did not recognize the "kinesthetic sense"—the sensations associated with the movements of muscles, tendons, and joints. Most of us move automatically, without awareness of such everyday movements as lying, sitting, standing, and walking. Yet these movements are integral parts of the way we relate to ourselves and others. And we can become aware of them and even change them. You can, for example, become conscious of how you hold your head, whether you tilt it to the left or right, whether it sits directly above your spine or jutted forward an inch or two.

A number of experts have concentrated on teaching people how to get in touch with their bodies. The **Alexander method** is a system that teaches good use of the body through conscious control. F. M. Alexander, an Australian, was afflicted by periodic loss of voice for which medical treatment gave only temporary relief. Around 1900, he began using a mirror to observe himself while he spoke. He noticed a pattern of malfunction throughout his entire body. He could see in the mirror that his customary use of his body, although it caused his vocal problem, felt "natural," while improved posture habits felt strange. Similarly, for example, if you hold your head slightly to the left, when a person who stands behind you straightens your head it will feel as if you are holding it to the right.

Alexander developed a new approach to physical education and health that involved using the body with ease, grace, flexibility, and freedom from strain. He established a school in London and taught "primary control," a specific relationship of head and neck to achieve good body use. His lessons involved three basic steps:

1. Become conscious of your poor habits of posture and carriage.

2. Learn to inhibit them.

3. Learn to replace them with improved habits.

Most of us need an observer to help us through the three steps proposed by Alexander.

- Choose partners. Stand behind your partner, who *sits* in a chair. See if the seated person is holding his or her head straight. If not, gently move the head into a straight position. If your partner has one shoulder higher than the other, move the shoulders to balance them. Then change places and give the other person feedback.
- Change partners. Look at your partner as he or she *stands.* Tell your partner what you observe about the position of head, neck, shoulders, chest, back, diaphragm, abdomen, legs, knees, and feet. Then change places and give the other person feedback.

You can also practice becoming conscious and inhibiting poor posture and carriage by yourself. For example, put down this book and think to yourself "Stand," but do not move. Did you begin to foreshorten the muscles at the back of your neck? Any involuntary preparation for getting up is part of your "physical set."

Becoming conscious of our habits of posture and carriage is a beginning. If we replace uncomfortable or awkward movements with improved ones, sitting, standing, and walking in the new ways will eventually begin to feel right.

With the increased attention being given today to the connections among body, mind, and emotions, many new methods of attending to body movements have become popular. **Functional integration,** offered by Dr. Moshe Feldenkrais, is a way of altering habitual movement responses by reeducating the central nervous system. Feldenkrais suggests we become aware of what we are doing with our bodies rather than just what we say or think. The main goals are to discover unknown reactions and learn a more congenial way of moving. Our relationship to gravity can be improved by converting tension and resistance into easy, full, effective movement. Feldenkrais works with movement to integrate physical and mental equipment into those new patterns most suitable to our present circumstances in life. He says that "training a body to perfect all the possible forms and configurations of its members changes not only the strength and flexibility of the skeleton and muscles, but makes a profound change in the self-image and the quality of direction of the self."

Another area of body unconsciousness is **breathing.** We breathe fourteen times a minute, twenty thousand times a day. Some specialists believe that breathing can change the structure of the body. When you are uncomfortable with another person, you may find that you are holding your throat tightly and scarcely breathing. If you silently scan your body, your attention can include your physical self as it is relating to this other person. You may notice, for example, that you breathe shallowly or deeply.

By expanding your awareness of your breathing, you can control your body responses to others and train yourself to reopen these unconscious areas. Once you get in touch with your own body processes, you can expand your awareness to notice the breathing and body communications sent to you from others.

We can become more aware of our breathing process.

- Sit quietly. Close your eyes. In your imagination, scan your body beginning with your feet and moving up to your head. Watch the passage of your breath in and out of the lungs without controlling its rate.
- Blow all the air out in short, rapid gushes until your lungs are empty. Then simply wait for the air to come in on its own.
- Repeat several times. Notice the firmness and gentleness with which the air refills your lungs. Notice how breathing moves on its own. When the lungs are full, they begin to empty.
- The conscious discovery of inhalation and exhalation and how they differ can lead to experiments you design for yourself. Notice that you can attend to your breathing without interfering in any way. Notice your natural rhythms and note when those rhythms become disturbed in communicating.

Breathing is intimately connected with emotions. Normally, we breathe automatically. Although you cannot will yourself, for example, to digest or not digest food you have eaten, you *can* will to breathe naturally or hold your breath deliberately. Breathing forms a bridge between the conscious and unconscious nervous systems. By watching it, you can observe more of yourself. Once you notice your own breathing, you can then note when another person changes breathing patterns while communicating with you. Such sensitivity and alertness are valuable tools in interpersonal communication.

People who specialize in "body work"—such as Ida Rolf, who developed the technique called **structural integration,** and Alexander Lowen, who teaches **bioenergetic analysis**—believe that all emotional states and personality traits are manifested in the body's structure and functioning. They believe that by proper training we can change our personalities and observe ourselves and others to find clues to personality, attitudes, and character.

Lowen says the legs and feet are the foundation and support of the ego structure. The legs and feet keep contact with the earth. We speak of certain people as being "earthy" or "up in the air," for example, implying that they are realistic or lack contact with reality. People who keep the weight of their bodies over their heels are described as "pushovers." A rigid backbone may indicate decreased flexibility. Lowen sees the "blown-up chest" as indicating a blown-up ego; yet a soft chest, although related to more feeling, may indicate less positive self-regard. Retracted shoulders may represent repressed anger—a holding back of the impulse to strike. Raised shoulders can indicate fear. Squared shoulders may express the attitude of shouldering one's responsibilities, while bowed shoulders can convey a sense of being burdened.

It is not uncommon to see a broad-shouldered person with narrow hips and thin legs, as if all the energy were concentrated in the upper half of the body leaving the lower half impotent. As the legs strengthen, the shoulders droop, the chest becomes smaller, and the center of gravity drops. When the muscles of the upper half of the body give up the function of supporting or moving the whole body, they become more soft, relaxed, and available for quick, sensitive movements. The head indicates certain qualities too. The long, proud neck and the short, bull-like neck represent familiar attitudes.

Our faces, like the rest of our bodies, express our personalities also. Eyes may be bright and sparkling or dull and vacant; cold and hard or soft and appealing. Conflicting expressions can give double messages. Smile lines around the eyes may contradict a frown, for example. Raised eyebrows, lines of astonishment, or vertical lines of rebellion may be used so often that they become carved permanently on the face.

Some individuals who seem to be responded to negatively by others may not be aware of the sneer caused by the upward retraction of the nostrils. Surprise, disgust, pain, disdain—all these expressions can be indelibly marked on a face.

Denying our repressed feelings can become a vicious circle. Restrained muscles can lead to shoulder bursitis or even arthritis. Most of us fear pain and immobilize our bodies to avoid awareness of pain. When our bodies become sources of pain instead of pleasure, we may refuse to accept them: *We may turn against our bodies by ignoring them.* We develop a tendency to measure bodies in pounds and inches, to compare them to idealized forms, and to ignore how our bodies really feel and what they express. Thus repressed feelings are again trapped in the body in the form of tightened muscles which cause stress. As we slowly get back in touch with our bodies, we can communicate feelings we have shut off for years and can learn to reduce physical stress.

Physical and emotional stress can result in body injury. Researchers have classified hard-driving people who fight to control their environment and their lives as **Type A people.** Their behavior follows a pattern: They are highly competitive, feel pressured for time, react to frustration with hostility, set deadlines or quotas for themselves, bring their work home with them, are achievement-oriented, and push themselves to the limit. When Type A people are hit by one of life's tragedies—death, divorce, a financial setback—they often develop high blood pressure or have heart attacks. Age, overweight, drinking, and smoking may add to their stress.

Most of us have read about the stress of living in today's technological world. Therefore the word *stress* usually has negative connotations for us and we try to order our lives so that we can avoid it. But Hans Selye says: "Stress is the spice of life. Without it, we would be vegetables or dead." Physiological stress is a response to any demand made on the body. Stress can occur if we break natural laws (putting stress on the body with obesity, alcohol, drugs, lack of sleep, poor nutrition, or smoking) or if we break social laws with the accompanying fear of social ostracism, such as failing in school or on the job, Three classic reactions to stress are fight, flight, and compromise.

Hans Selye, in his book *Stress without Distress*, defines stress as "the nonspecific response of the body to any demand made upon it." In other words, *stress can be pleasant or unpleasant.* Enjoying stress comes from meeting a challenge. Under stress, our glands produce hormones that stimulate our bodies. The amount of stimulation each individual can enjoy depends on his or her unique physiological makeup. We can analyze ourselves to find the stress level we find most comfortable.

Exposure to stress over a long time can cause serious physical illness, such as hypertension, cardiovascular disease, or mental breakdown. Stress can actually shorten life. The secret, Selye says, is not to avoid stress but to "do your own thing"—what you like to do, what you are suited to do, at your own rate.

From positive stress we gain friendship, gratitude, goodwill, and love toward ourselves; from negative stress we develop hatred, frustration, revenge, distrust, jealousy, anxiety, and hostility. Positive stress comes from selecting a work environment in line with our innate abilities and preferences—the kind of occupation that is play for us. Successful work and social activity cause stress but little distress. Finding work you really like—work that serves people and fulfills your own needs of self-expression and self-esteem—gives you both purpose and identity.

We must all deal with some stress in our lives. If we try to avoid stress entirely, we may end up repressing feelings and trapping stress in our bodies rather than working it out. In his book *Psychological Stress*, Irving Janis describes a study of three groups of surgical patients. One group displayed stormy, emotional outbursts. The second group displayed little fear; they were calm and felt invulnerable. The third group consisted of people who were moderately fearful before their operations. The first group continued their emotional outbursts following surgery. The second group had denied or minimized the suffering and when the inescapable pain of normal recovery became a reality, they became upset, angry, and resentful, blaming the hospital and staff. The third group had asked for and received realistic information, so the after-effects of surgery did not surprise them. Janis concludes that the "work of worrying" may have positive value. His conclusion confirms the research on student stress: Students with the proper balance of stress pass exams with higher grades than students who experience too much or too little stress.

Recently Hans Selye coined the word *eustress* for the stress that makes people come alive. He thinks a person can convert negative stress into positive experience. He says: "Adopting the right *attitude* can convert a negative stress into a positive one—what I call a 'eustress.' "

Many techniques have been developed for stress reduction. Here are three that can be practiced ten or fifteen minutes a day.

- *Progressive relaxation:* Find a quiet place indoors or out. Also find a quiet mental space. Put aside matters not conducive to relaxation. Now make yourself comfortable and close your eyes. Take a long, slow, deep breath and let it go. Become aware of the difference between tension and relaxation by tensing a muscle and then letting it go. Start with your hands. Make a fist and tighten it. Then tighten your wrists. Hold these muscles tight for a count of twenty and then let them go. They should tremble. Then tighten your forehead, face, and mouth.

Relaxation requires "letting go" of stress.

Hold for ten seconds and then let go. Arch your back, raise your chest, push shoulders back as hard as you can. Hold for a count of ten and then relax. Now tighten your stomach, hold for a count of ten, and relax. Tighten all your leg muscles, starting with toes and working up to your thighs. Hold and relax. Allowing relaxation requires a "letting-go" without effort, will, or plan.

- *Autosuggestion:* Program your biocomputer by giving yourself suggestions. Make yourself comfortable; close your eyes. Take a long, slow, deep breath and let it go. Get rid of all tension. Inhale slowly and deeply. Pause a moment; then exhale slowly and completely. Do this several times. Tell yourself: "I now feel calm, comfortable, and more relaxed than before. My feet feel heavy. My ankles and lower legs are relaxed. My stomach, pelvis, and back are relaxed. My shoulders, neck, jaw, mouth, and eyes are relaxed." Now just rest and allow your whole body to relax. With each breath you let out you will relax a little more. You are now in a calm, relaxed state. You can deepen this state by counting backward. Breathe in. As you exhale slowly, say to yourself: "Ten. I am feeling very relaxed." Inhale and say: "Nine. I am feeling more relaxed. Eight. I am feeling even more relaxed than before. (Continue . . . three . . . two . . . one . . . zero.) I am now at a deep, relaxed, peaceful level. I can stay in this relaxed state as long as I choose. Each time I relax like this I will find it easier and easier to relax more deeply until I will relax deeply just by breathing in and out and allowing myself to let go."

- *Imagery:* In the chapter on the mind, we read about visualization and imagery. Here is one example of how imagery can be used to reduce stress. Find a tranquil place. Get into a comfortable position, close your eyes, and breathe slowly until you feel very relaxed. Take about five minutes to empty your mind and relax all your muscles. Now you are in a calm, relaxed state. Imagine yourself in an elevator. Watch the doors close. Now look at the panel above the door and imagine that number ten is lit up. Feel the motion as the elevator begins to descend. As the elevator slowly passes each floor you will become more and more relaxed. Now see the numbers . . . 9 . . . 8 . . . 7 . . . continue counting as you feel more relaxed . . . 3 . . . 2 . . . 1. You are now in a deep, relaxed state. See the elevator doors open. Walk out into a small, comfortable room that is dimly lit. On the wall in front of you is a large screen. Facing the screen is a chair. Sit comfortably, deeply relaxed. Now allow images to come on the screen. Stay in this relaxed space as long as you wish. When you want to return, enter the elevator and return to the tenth floor feeling rested, strong, and relaxed.

Proxemics: Space and Environment

Edward T. Hall, fascinated by our reactions to the spaces we inhabit, has coined the word **proxemics** to describe how our use of zones or territories affects our communication and relationships. Hall lists four distinct zones: public distance, social distance, personal distance, and intimate distance. **Public distance** measures twelve feet or more. This distance is suited for informal gatherings, public speaking, conferences, teachers in classrooms, politicians at rallies, and similar affairs. **Social distance** measures 4 to 12 feet. Most impersonal business is transacted at this distance. This zone is observed in stores when customers talk to clerks, for example. When we have our cars serviced or houses repaired, we keep this distance from the workers. The third zone, **personal distance,** ranges from 1½ to 2½ feet for "close" personal distance and from 2½ to 4 feet for "far" personal distance. The close range may be comfortable at a cocktail party or in a crowded room, yet uncomfortable in a room with only three or four people. Hall calls the far personal distance zone "the limit of physical domination." Because you cannot comfortably touch another person at this distance, more privacy is experienced and yet there is a degree of closeness in personal discussion. We sometimes use the expression "at arm's length" to keep a pushy person from getting too close. This distance is used when two people meet on the street to talk. **Intimate distance** is observed between loved ones and very close friends—from bodies touching to 18 inches. This closeness can be overwhelming for some people, causing them to lean or move back.

Distance is affected by culture. In Arab countries, men touch and hold hands. In our country, most men feel awkward and uneasy displaying this kind of contact in public; yet women or young girls sometimes find it acceptable. In almost all cultures, touching or holding a child is acceptable and valued.

In addition to distance, we often position ourselves in relation to others according to age, rank, or some other variable. A boss may sit at a desk while the employee stands. Lecturers often stand on a platform *above* their audience. A chairwoman may sit at the *head* of the conference table, a father at the *head* of the dinner table, a professor at the *head* of the class, a judge high *up* on a bench. Most of our rules about space, distance, and position have been socially learned and accepted in childhood. As adults, we have become so accustomed to these unwritten conventions that we are often unaware of them.

Closely related to Hall's concept of space is the concept of territory. In his book *The Territorial Imperative*, Robert Ardrey says: "A territory is an area of space, whether of water or earth, or air, which an animal or group of animals defends as an exclusive preserve. . . . We have an inward compulsion to possess and defend such a space." Ardrey believes that individuals mark off certain territory as their own—scientists claim their laboratories, children claim their bedrooms, professors claim offices. Sitting at a table offers a good example of how we set up territorial borders to protect ourselves. When two people sit at a table, both subconsciously divide the table in two. If you move objects into the other person's "territorial zone," the person may become anxious or uncomfortable. When we reach across the table, we say "excuse me" for invading the other's territory. The same situation occurs when we bump a person on the street or walk between two people in a crowd.

In some families, each person may have an assigned seat around the table. In class, people often keep the same seat and avoid a chair that "belongs" to someone else by virtue of that person's having used it before. People place coats or packages on a theater seat to "save" it as if it were their possession.

We often feel apologetic when invading a person's territory. In a library, cafeteria, theater, or bar, we often ask, "Is this seat taken?" Using body language, you may lower your eyes when you sit down. When invading another's territory in a bus by sitting down, you keep your eyes straight ahead and avoid looking at the person sitting next to you, who usually moves closer to the window to avoid touching you. When you invade other people's territories, you put them in an uncomfortable situation. If you get too close, they may move away, cross their arms, or retreat inwardly—thus communicating nonverbally that they do not like having their zone invaded. Much of this body language is unconscious both in sender and receiver.

Sometimes personal space and territory overlap. For example, it is difficult to put your arm on the chair arm in a theater when the person next to you is already using it. In an airplane, you may resent someone in front of you who tilts a seat back into your space. *Understanding space, position and territory—proxemics—can help us interpret the nonverbal body language of others.* Understanding cultural variations in these areas can be especially helpful in relating to people of other cultures.

The following experiments can help us become more aware of our needs for space and territory.

- When you and a friend share a table at a restaurant, move some of your possessions (purse, book, cigarettes, matches) into his or her "territory" (side of the table) and see if your friend unconsciously begins to communicate discomfort.

- Sit next to someone in a situation where you could have chosen a seat farther away: in an auditorium or theater, on a park bench, or in a classroom or library. Notice that person's reactions. Tell the other person about your experiment and ask how he or she felt about it.

- Explore personal space. Try moving closer to people, standing further away, leaning forward, and so on to see how people react. If you wish to play it safe, do some research on kinesics, proxemics, and territory *before* you experiment.

- Automobiles are also used as territory. How close will you allow a stranger to get to your car? When you are in a car, how does it feel to have someone cut in front of you? How much of the road do you "own" in traffic? In a parking lot?

Some of the most important yet unconscious elements that affect nonverbal communication are environmental—furniture, architectural style, interior decorating, lighting conditions, smells, colors, temperature, noises, music, and variations in arrangements of materials, shapes, and surfaces of objects. These factors can be extremely influential on the outcome of our relationships. Rugs, flowers, dirty clothes, paintings, and radio announcements all form impressions that can influence relationships. An intimate conversation can become a tragedy or a comedy if carried on near an airport or in a garbage dump; or it can flourish in an elegant restaurant or a beautiful living room. Where you live, the amount of traffic in front of your house, all the intentional and nonintentional material things, implements, machines, and objects around you affect your life. *Choosing the "right" time and the "right" place for a communication event indicates that the speaker is sensitive to nonverbal aspects of communicating and relating.*

For the next week, take the time to notice what in your environment is affecting you and how it communicates nonverbally to you.

- Write about the objects around you and how you feel they affect you (color, lighting, order/disorder).
- How do odors, colors, and temperature affect you?
- What does your environment tell others about you and your values?

Another aspect of environmental nonverbal communication is appearance. We often interpret appearances—dress and grooming—unconsciously. Clothes can suggest a casual life-style, in which comfort is a primary concern, or a nonconforming life-style, in which the primary concern is to telegraph a message of difference. Colors, as well as design, can signify mood or reflect feelings. Every color and mode of dress can influence contact with others regardless of whether we know about it or not.

Most people dress to please their own self-images—to fit the pictures they have of themselves. Some individuals do not want to be noticed, so they dress inconspicuously. Others broadcast themselves as sports enthusiasts, sex symbols, business executives, playboys/playgirls, or bikers. Most of us also occasionally dress to play roles that may or may not be natural to us. Society is changing rapidly, and the varieties of roles and clothes communicate many different messages. Most of us share ourselves with others through the attention we give our appearance.

Attention to what is in style is more valued by some individuals than others. Cosmetics and hairstyles change constantly. At one time, for example, only women wore perfume. Today men also wear scents. Our response to odor depends on the values of our culture. Some cultures value natural body odors; others find them offensive. In the United States, we have become slowly conditioned through television advertising and mass media to dislike body odors. As a result we have a vast industry making and selling deodorants, special soaps, perfumes, lotions, mouthwashes, toothpastes, and other spray-on fragrances that have become part of our nonverbal language.

Noting how dress, grooming, and appearance communicate can help us to develop control over such messages as well as to pick up information about what others are communicating either consciously or unconsciously.

- What do clothes say to you? How important is dress? What personal values do you attach to the way you dress? What judgments do you make about others on the basis of what they wear (shoes, jewelry, colors)?

- What do you notice about grooming (hair, cosmetics, shaving of legs or face)? What attracts you? What do you find unattractive?

- What sprays, deodorants, or perfumes do you use? When? What do you notice about scents?

We have been exploring proxemics (space and environment, distance and territory), objects and furniture, and dress and appearance as aspects of nonverbal communication. What these aspects communicate is information about your values and your likes and dislikes, as well as your personality and who you are. All these nonverbal messages are connected to your feelings about yourself and are expressed in your behavior.

MIXED MESSAGES AND SILENCE

Knowledge and information are often expressed through verbal communication. Feelings and emotions can be expressed either verbally or nonverbally. *When the messages we receive through language do not agree with nonverbal messages, most of us get confused.* Often the sender is not aware of the conflict. When we lose touch with our feelings, we may unconsciously express one message in words and another with our body. As we receive these mixed messages, we tend to pay more attention to the nonverbal message and feel that the sender is in some sense pretending or confused. If we become aware of the discrepancies, we can tell the sender about the mixed message and verify his or her intentions. When a person is sending us mixed or multiple messages (saying one thing with words and contradicting that message with expressions), we need to translate the multiple messages.

Two or more mixed messages, all nonverbal and occurring simultaneously, are most often unconscious to the sender. For example, a wife may want to be kissed; yet when her husband approaches her she stiffens. If he interprets the stiffening as rejection, he may in turn reject his wife. Or he may force the issue and kiss her anyway. If he is sensitive to her, he may remember that when other people are around she feels uncomfortable about a display of affection. Yet she wants others to know her husband loves her. Remembering this, he may then choose whatever action, in this particular situation and at this particular time, seems most appropriate. He translates the mixed message: "My wife wants to be kissed but feels uncomfortable when I kiss her in front of others." It might also be appropriate here, as in many situations, to ask for clarification.

In this example, we have the sender (the wife), the mixed message (desire yet stiffening), the receiver (the husband), and the situation (people present, time, environment). This is an example of a mixed message *without* words—two *nonverbal* cues each giving opposing messages. The infinite variety of complicated verbal and nonverbal multiple messages and mixed messages most often occur unconsciously. *If we are aware of mixed messages, we become more conscious of the conflicts within ourselves and better express our own true feelings.*

Family members often develop characteristic ways of responding to each other. These stock responses (or "games" as Eric Berne describes them) save us from the discomfort of being sensitive and perceptive and of taking the risk of misinterpreting mixed feelings. The degree to which individuals are willing to risk getting intimate with others, truly knowing and understanding others, depends on their unique personalities, their capacity for taking risks, and their need to relate deeply to others. People who fear others may play games that they themselves are unaware of. If they develop trust in themselves and others, they can learn to risk and therefore experience intimate or "game-free" relationships in which mixed messages can be checked out openly. Being aware of them is a prerequisite to communicating about them.

We communicate on several different levels at the same time, but we are usually unaware of the many ways we are communicating. For example, **silence** communicates. Talking or listening fills our time so much that we are often uncomfortable

You talk when you cease to be at peace with your thoughts; and when you can no longer dwell in the solitude of your heart, you live in your lips.

Kahlil Gibran

Silence and closeness often communicate intimacy.

with silence. Even when we are alone, we talk and listen to ourselves; one part of the brain speaks while another part listens. Keeping our own minds silent is difficult. Those who practice meditation can, for brief periods, empty the mind of language. Those who practice visual imagery can also empty the mind of language, but they fill it with images.

If we are uncomfortable being silent with ourselves, no wonder we feel uncomfortable being silent with another person. We are often afraid of silence because we do not know what it means. We may fear the other person is bored or disapproves of us. We tend to believe that as long as we both keep talking we will know what each is thinking.

In reality, silence serves several functions. *Depending on the context, silence can be positive or negative.* It can bind us together, or it can separate us. Silence can make us feel isolated, or we may deliberately insulate ourselves with silence as a protective wall. For example, you may not talk to a neighbor for fear she will come over all the time and intrude on your privacy. Yet silence can warmly and clearly communicate mutual affection. With those we know best and love, we often do not need to talk. Sometimes a person's mere presence is comforting. To increase our sensitivity enough to know when silence is appropriate between two people can result in very intimate feelings.

Silence by one person always affects another person. Silence can hurt or it can heal. Not lashing out in anger can save a relationship. In anger, we may exaggerate and thus wound someone we love. Or, after having said something that hurts someone, silence and the passing of time may help the healing process more than continuing the debate. Silence can also be interpreted as manipulating or punishing. The "silent treatment" can be interpreted as hostility, anger, coldness, rebellion, or hate. Instead of allowing the issue to cool off, silence may freeze the issue so that it never gets resolved.

Silence can be used as a wall to hide behind. Children may not tell parents about problem behavior at school if they fear revealing this information. If people do not tell us they are troubled, we may drift out of touch with their problems. If students do not know the answer to a question, they can remain silent. But silence in this case can be interpreted as lack of knowledge or as fear of saying something foolish and exposing one's self to criticism.

In some individuals, silence can be interpreted as serenity and self-composure. People with the kind of personality that communicates inner harmony seem to us to be whole in a way that does not require constant verbalizing. With this kind of person, some of us are comfortable and others are not.

Some people speak slowly and pause between thoughts. We assume they are pausing to think about choosing their words. The care with which they think about words indicates that they need to think through a whole thought before risking verbalizing it. At other times, silence can indicate the absence of thinking: daydreaming. *With its many meanings, silence is a significant element in communicating and relating.*

The gaps or silences in communication can be as significant as speech.

- Who is silent in class? Who is silent in your small groups? Who seldom talks? What do you interpret their silences to mean? How do you view these "nontalkers"?

- If you are a nontalker, what does this mean to you? What are you feeling? How do you think others see you? If you are a nontalker, do you want to be brought into the discussion? Do you mind if people ask you questions? If you have difficulty breaking into a conversation, would you be willing to practice "breaking in" without having a carefully prepared speech? Would you be willing to risk not having thought out in advance what you say?

- Often students are silent in groups yet very verbal with friends. What feelings might such people be expressing by silence in a group?

- Sometimes silence is a way of getting attention in a group. If there is a silence in your small group, who speaks first? Are you afraid of silence? Do you try to avoid it? When you are bored or angry, do you tend to withdraw? Do you use silence to shut out others? Can you mention some other ways in which you use silence?

Body language and spoken language depend on each other. Spoken language alone will not give us a full meaning of what a person is saying. If we listen only to the words, we may miss what is being said. *Verbal and nonverbal behaviors can reinforce, contradict, accent, or even substitute for each other.* We must be careful not to stereotype on the basis of first impressions, which may be largely nonverbal. As we get to know another person, we may err in the opposite direction—we may assume that "we know" how this person feels and thus we may miss cues because of our faulty assumptions. Nonverbal cues need to be confirmed verbally with the sender before the receiver can assume that the communication is completed.

People differ in their ability to recognize nonverbal messages and communicate emotional meanings to others. Sensitivity to nonverbal communication is an important means of improving our ability to understand others, to develop relationships, and to communicate what we *intend* to communicate. We can avoid verbal communication, but nonverbal communication cannot be avoided; therefore, we cannot *not* communicate. Freud said: "No mortal can keep a secret. If his lips are silent, he chatters with his fingertips; betrayal oozes out of him at every pore."

Nonverbal communication occurs continuously. Our bodies, space, environment, and even our silences communicate. Nonverbal communication expresses our feelings, attitudes, and values. When we verbalize we send semantic information, but our voice expresses our feelings and judgments about what we are saying. It is not only what we say but the way we say it that carries our real meanings.

THE BODY AS REALITY

The body, the senses, must conspire with the mind. . . . The intellect is powerless to express thought without the aid of the heart and the liver.

Henry David Thoreau

The records of the modern Olympics began in 1896. No one at that time could believe that humans would ever have the speed and endurance that exist now. The improvement of racehorses since that time has been very slight and achieved through breeding. But today there are forty and fifty-year-old people who have broken past world records. Such achievement is due to more than simple evolution. The proponents of body-mind-spirit unity call it **transformation.**

Historically the spiritual quest has demanded transcendence over the body. Today experts are suggesting that *the body is reality*—that the body can manifest the glories of the human spirit. Those who separate the body from the mind and spirit see the body as an *object* to be used. During the Victorian period, the body was looked upon as an instrument, a fortress always on guard against a hostile outside world, using the five senses as sentinels. They assigned the "lower" desires to the body and the "finer" things to the mind and spirit.

But a new valuation of the body's genius for expressing human potential is being suggested by great athletes—runners, swimmers, skiers—who have pushed the boundaries beyond those limits the world had previously defined. Doctors are telling us that our attitudes toward life, our life-style, and our state of mind can create or correct bleeding ulcers, high blood pressure, heart disease, and even cancer. The medical movement toward *wholeness* suggests a body-mind unity.

This *transformation in body reality* is creating new disciplines. Spiritual healers from Mary Baker Eddy to Ruth Carter Stapleton have been offering equal care for body, mind, and spirit. Researchers in sensory perception tell us we have not yet fully developed our sensory abilities. Work with blind people indicates that the blind have "ambient vision"—the ability to sense objects they cannot see. Many blind people learn to move about strange rooms and sense where the walls are. Few of us are aware that we possess such sensory abilities, however, which suggests that our sensory potentials lie far beyond where we perceive them today.

Thinking is conceptualizing *about* what we are experiencing. Awareness is experiencing reality *directly*. Overall awareness includes a clear sense of the reality of the body. Many methods for expanding body consciousness offer us possibilities of change through direct experience. Yoga, t'ai chi, massage, meditation, bioenergetics, rolfing, body patterning, Alexander technique, functional integration, biofeedback—all are ways of directly experiencing body-mind-spirit unity. *Surpassing our physical limits and pushing out the boundaries can bring us in touch with our bodies as instruments of communication.*

FOR FURTHER READING

Ardrey, Robert. *The Territorial Imperative.* New York: Atheneum, 1966.
> This book summarizes the major theory and research on human and animal territories.

Birdwhistell, R. L. *Kinesics and Context.* Philadelphia: University of Pennsylvania Press, 1970.
> The author shows the relationships between nonverbal communication and describes how body language affects and is affected by context.

Brown, Barbara. *New Mind, New Body; Biofeedback: New Directions for the Mind.* New York: Harper & Row, 1974.
> Brown explores ways an individual communicates with the self via the skin, muscles, heart, brain, and other body components.

Gunther, Bernard. *Sense Relaxation: Below Your Mind.* New York: Macmillan, 1968.
> Along with the text on ways to expand sensory awareness, this book includes many beautiful photographs to illustrate sensory awareness exercises.

Hall, Edward T. *The Silent Language.* New York: Doubleday, 1959.
> Hall shows how various cultures use time, space, and other message systems differently.

Knapp, Mark. *Nonverbal Communication in Human Interaction.* New York: Holt, 1972.
> This book presents a thorough survey of the field to date.

Lowen, Alexander. *The Betrayal of the Body.* New York: Macmillan, 1967.
> Lowen describes exercises for his bioenergetic therapy, which relates personality to muscle tension and impaired breathing.

Weitz, Shirley (ed.). *Nonverbal Communication: Readings and Commentary.* New York: Oxford University Press, 1974.
> This collection of nonverbal communication studies covers facial expressions, body language, spatial behavior, and other nonverbal messages.

THE ROLE OF "NEGATIVE EMOTIONS" IN GROWTH
    Anger
    Fear
    Depression

Loneliness
Boredom
Ambivalence
EMOTIONS AND SELF-ESTEEM

Even more important than knowledge is the life of the emotions.

Bertrand Russell

8

Feeling: How Emotions Communicate

THE ROLE OF "NEGATIVE EMOTIONS" IN GROWTH

In this chapter we deal with a subject that has caused much confusion—emotions. This topic is often ignored in communication because of a *supposed* difficulty in dealing with such an abstract and complex matter. *Yet it is my belief that we cannot communicate well without consciously responding to our own feelings as well as to those of others.* Emotions are often suppressed, denied, rationalized, ignored, or confused. We feel embarrassed because we *think* emotions display our weaknesses, the things which control us, the responses which make us feel helpless. The most difficult aspect of dealing with emotions is admitting that our feelings are *ours!*

First we must recognize the *value* of studying our emotional tapestry and the dramatic roles our emotions play in communicating and relating. A great deal of the mystery about emotions can be eliminated if we adopt the attitude that they do not necessarily sweep over us, take hold of us, or well up inside us. *We have a choice about the attitudes we take toward our emotions.* Here is the attitude I choose: "I am responsible for my emotions. I am angry when I give myself permission to be angry. I am loving when I decide to be loving. I feel depressed when I allow myself to experience depression."

But why would anyone want to "allow" themselves to feel angry, afraid, depressed, lonely, or bored? I allow myself these feelings because they help me attune myself to my own personal experience of reality. My feelings belong to me. They are intimately connected to my self-identity—to my experience of myself as a unique person. They not only color my perceptions of my world and myself but also enliven my experiences of myself and others. I see myself as a deeply feeling person; therefore, I will allow myself to cry. A man who says "I never cry!" chooses *not* to cry as part of his identity. Therefore, his emotions fit his perception of himself as a person.

A low appraisal of emotions is part of our Western culture. Rewards are given for rational thinking, and we have been told that emotions must be controlled because they lead us down the "wrong paths." Sometimes perhaps they do—especially if we fear or ignore them. But when we take responsibility for our emotions and do not blame them on mysterious or external forces, we experience a tremendous sense of power over ourselves, our communication with our world, and our relationships with others.

In adopting a different attitude—a different reality from that we have been taught about emotions—we are in the position of having to give up "excuses." No longer can we blame others or outside forces for our emotions. We must take responsibility for them ourselves. *Many people may not be willing to go against what they have learned because they simply do not want to take control of their lives.* Yet we gain a great deal when we are willing to open up and examine our emotions, choose our emotional states, and determine our attitudes toward our own feelings. To choose an attitude is not to say that an emotion can be controlled by logic or reason. An emotion is *not* a thought process and usually cannot be overcome by logic.

We do not know as much about our own emotional states as we know about stars, nuclear reactors, or space travel. Yet if we choose the *assumption* of personal responsibility for feelings, we open up the possibility of seeing whether our *experiences* with our emotions are a matter of choice. Even if you cannot accept this proposition, you can increase your awareness of how emotions affect your life by exploring them.

The emotions we will deal with in this chapter are ones which students have indicated are the most problematic in their lives: anger, fear, depression, loneliness, boredom, and conflict. In Chapter 10, feelings of attraction, love, caring, and intimacy in relationships are considered. They often seem to be a problem too. In both these chapters, emotions are presented as *positive* tools for personal growth.

In a recent survey on the effects of feelings, it was found that 90% of dropouts leave high school not because of their intellectual difficulties, but because of their feelings. Similarly, 70% of people fired from jobs are asked to leave because of personality conflicts rather than any incompetence. The greatest percentage of people who commit suicide come from middle- and upper-class groups, indicating that education, money, success, and status do not necessarily help us solve our emotional problems.

The chemical and electrical makeup of the human body is not fully understood, yet we do know that emotional energy is essential for survival. Fear protects us from danger; anger provides energy to fight and survive; parental love provides energy to protect the child. All emotions—fear, anger, love, and so on—are accompanied by profound physiological changes in the body. The heart beats faster, the blood pressure rises, the sugar level increases, digestion ceases, the skin may sweat or react in other ways. Most of these body changes indicate the intensity of the emotion being experienced. The way we handle emotions deeply affects our physical well-being, which in turn affects the ways in which we communicate both to ourselves and to others.

Emotions and behavior may not be as closely allied as emotions and body responses. For example, we do not need to act out the anger we feel. (Conversely, it is possible to act angry without feeling anger.) It is possible for a person who *feels* shy to act gregarious and friendly. A man who feels a strong sex attraction to his best friend's wife need not *feel* guilty. He has some choice about his attitude toward his feelings as he has a choice about his actions. How we feel and subsequently act is more often determined by habit, training, or impulse than by conscious choice. As we learn to recognize, accept, and communicate the myriad feelings that constitute the tapestry of our emotional selves, we can all learn new ways of feeling and responding by choice.

Many people reveal only a little of what they feel—the rest we must often guess. Because feelings are so complicated, we often lose touch with them. *Feelings are sometimes mixtures of different shades of emotions. Moreover, feelings are often in conflict with other feelings, with thoughts or words, with actions or behavior.*

When we suppress our emotions, we often lose touch with them. *The first step in the study of emotions is to recognize them and learn how they influence our communication with ourselves and others.* Students helped compile the following vocabulary list for varieties of feelings, emotions, and moods. Read the list slowly. Dwell on words that catch your attention. Experience the emotions and what they mean to you. Take your time. On a piece of paper jot down those that are most meaningful for you.

abandoned	embarrassed	accepted	flexible
alienated	empty	adequate	free
ambivalent	envious	affectionate	friendly
angry	foolish	alive	generous
annoyed	frantic	aware	gentle
anxious	frustrated	brave	glad
apathetic	guilty	calm	good
betrayed	gullible	capable	happy
bitter	hated	cheerful	helpful
bored	helpless	clever	high
childish	hopeless	committed	honored
compulsive	hostile	confident	humorous
condemned	hurt	contented	inspired
confused	ignored	cooperative	involved
deceitful	impotent	delighted	joyous
defeated	inadequate	desirable	kind
degraded	inferior	determined	loving
depressed	intimidated	ecstatic	mystical
destructive	jealous	empathetic	nice
dishonest	lazy	energetic	peaceful
distracted	lonely	excited	pleasant
disturbed	miserable	fascinated	pleased

obsessed	scared	pretty	trusted
outraged	skeptical	proud	trusting
persecuted	spiteful	relaxed	understood
pressured	tense	rewarded	unique
rebellious	threatened	solemn	vital
rejected	trapped	spontaneous	vivacious
restless	violent	sympathetic	wonderful
sad	vulnerable	tranquil	worthwhile

The first step in communicating feelings is to become aware of them.

- Whenever possible in the next few days ask yourself: "What am I feeling?" Get acquainted with the vocabulary of emotions and begin to describe what you feel.

- Ask yourself: "How do I feel about that?" "How do I feel about that person?" "How do I feel about what she is saying?" "How do I feel about what he is doing?"

- Ask yourself: "How do I feel about what I am doing?" "How do I feel about what I am saying?"

- Find some time each day to get in touch with your feelings and verbalize them. Refer to the preceding vocabulary of emotions if you *intend* to be more precise.

Peter Koestenbaum, a philosopher, says that *our emotions can lead us to self-discovery*. He believes that we freely choose our emotions to give personal meaning to our lives. Although emotions are experienced within the self, they are intertwined with our experiences of others and deeply affect our communication. Although all emotions are experienced internally, they are expressed through our bodies even when we choose not to act them out or talk about them. In his book *Managing Anxiety: The Power of Knowing Who You Are*, Koestenbàum suggests that we study those areas of "negation" that are the most intense in our lives: "It is in these pains that the individual will be most helped by and responsive to philosophical insights about the meaning of his life." As you explore the meanings and experiences of anger, fear, depression, loneliness, boredom, and ambivalence, *be responsive to what these emotions tell you about "the meaning of your life."*

Anger

Anger and laughter are mutually exclusive and you have the power to choose either.

Wayne Dyer

There are many names for anger: aggression, hate, outrage, antagonism, wrath, hostility, defiance, or simply crossness. To describe people who are *feeling* anger, we use adjectives such as mad, bitter, annoyed, furious, hurt, irritated, cross, savage, vicious, dangerous, or offensive. To describe angry actions, we use verbs such as hurts, destroys, wounds, damages, breaks, ruins, demolishes, ridicules, shames, criticizes, bullies, crushes, or kills. *Language plays an intimate part in communicating our emotions to ourselves and to others.*

We need nouns to name the different qualities and quantities of anger. We need adjectives to describe our feelings, and we need verbs to describe behavior as related to feelings. The more *specific* we can be in communicating the intensity and color of our emotions and moods, the closer we can get to acknowledging, recognizing, and dealing with our feelings. Therefore, let us look more closely at the differences between frustration, aggression, and hostility as different forms of anger.

Living involves the experience of delay between something we desire and the fulfillment of that desire. We often make plans and then have to wait for the results. Although we know that life involves delay, we may feel uncomfortable tolerating it. When it is difficult or impossible to have a desire satisfied, many of us experience the emotion of **frustration.**

When toddlers begin to pull toys behind them as they walk, they often get a wheel caught on something and cannot figure out why the toy won't move. They cry in frustration until an adult comes along and untangles the toy from the leg of the chair. As we grow older, we often experience things that do not work: tools, machines, zippers, buttons, and so on. Children can scream when they want something that is withheld or when something does not work. But in our culture, as children grow older, we tell them that such behavior is not acceptable. They must learn to *control* themselves and endure the frustration.

Although most adults experience frustration, they learn to hide it, endure it, or convert it into something else. Some adults who have great difficulty handling frustration may continue to behave like children: temper tantrums, explosive behavior, destroying something; they may take refuge in self-pity or childish fears; they may seek sympathy or demand immediate gratification of their desires, even at the cost of manipulating others.

Adults who feel frustrated, yet do not express it in behavior, may learn that the reward at the end of a waiting period, the joy of fixing something, or the experience of adjusting an unrealistic desire to fit the real world can be a learning experience. They learn that the child's world of immediate gratification is a fantasy world and that frustration is part of the real world. The shift from fantasy to realism reminds us of *others*. Without them, there would be no warmth to share, no love to give, no companionship or relationship. *Clear communication helps alleviate the experience of frustration.*

Some people express frustration while others hide it.

Finding out what frustrates us most can be a valuable guide to self-knowledge.

- Recall some past experiences in which you felt frustrated. Be very specific: Name things you wanted and could not have; things that would not work; places you could not go; people and situations and relationships that frustrated you—at home, school, work; with family or friends.

- What things frustrate you now?

- What do other people do that frustrates you? Be specific: Name a person and describe the action.

- How do you handle (express or act out) your frustrations? Evaluate the results you get (desirable or undesirable, satisfying or unsatisfying, destructive or constructive) and describe alternative ways you might handle frustration.

Aggression *is a fighting instinct—a tendency toward hostile action as a protection against assault, intrusion, or invasion.* If well directed, aggression can give energy to much that is good and beautiful. We can find constructive and useful ways to direct our aggressions so that we strive toward growth and live life fruitfully. For example, assertiveness is a desirable quality to develop for those who have difficulty saying no to others or standing up for themselves in a competitive situation.

We can also direct aggression into acceptable channels such as athletics, physical exercise, games, and hobbies. We can work for grades and degrees, compete for better jobs and positions of authority, and strive for power. We can fight ignorance, crime, disease, poverty, or ugliness. We can conquer obstacles by creating machines, buildings, bridges, and roads. We can fight the elements to conquer blight and disease. We can also direct aggression into artistic expression through music, drama, painting, writing, gardening, or crafts. At times we convert aggression into wit and make light of our own humanness. Recognizing aggression in ourselves is the first step toward directing, controlling, and using it.

Although we have an instinctual drive toward the preservation of life, beauty, and creativity, we also have an opposing instinctual drive in the direction of destruction. Masochism, for example, is the tendency to direct aggression against ourselves to diminish feelings of guilt. Unconsciously, masochists may feel they need to be punished. Mass self-destruction takes the form of wars in which we all lose. In fact, war is human aggression in its most destructive form. *Balancing constructive aggression and controlling destructive aggression is a problem not only for humanity but also for each individual in daily living.* Through discussion and communication, each of us can become more conscious of the ways we handle aggression.

We all reach individual solutions to the conflict between aggression and the need for social relationships.

- When you feel cornered, do you fight or do you take flight?
- Describe a time when you attacked someone either physically or verbally.
- Describe a time when you felt you won in either defending yourself or attacking someone who threatened you (either physically or verbally).
- Do you see yourself as an aggressive person?
- In what ways do you hide aggression or divert it into other activities?
- Have you ever mocked someone to release aggression? How do you feel about being teased or mocked? What alternatives are there?

In 1972, Anthony Storr wrote a book called *Human Destructiveness.* The subject has been studied historically in many fields: penology, sociology, psychology, anthropology. The psychological roots of destructiveness are universal and timeless. Examples of human destructiveness can be found in persecutions, exterminations, mass murders, racism, witch hunts, and attacks on minorities. *We all experience hostility and destructive urges toward others and even toward ourselves.*

Hostility may stem from fear, frustration, or deprivation. All of us in infancy have experienced feeling utterly helpless and under the power of others—larger people forcing us to do things against our will or withholding from us things we want. This helplessness of the child is instinctively accompanied by some degree of resentment and desire for retaliation. Power struggles between children and adults usually involve aggression and fear of aggression. As we grow older, we may feel ashamed to admit our feelings of hostility or hatred. We may project these feelings onto others rather than acknowledge them in ourselves. Then we become *doubly* afraid. Having projected our own feelings of resentment onto others, we become paranoid, fearful that They are out to punish us, as if we were still children.

As long as adults are responsible for the life and welfare of children, the adults will restrict the children—confine them in fenced yards, feed them, bathe and clothe them, and keep them from harming themselves. Moreover, adults reward children who behave in acceptable ways and punish children when they endanger themselves or others. As children grow older, other adults begin to give them orders and direct their lives. We live in a hierarchical society with a dominance order depending on sex, age, education, and other individual differences. Historically men have been dominant over women. Older people often have domi-

Resentment or hostility may accompany demands from authority figures.

nance over younger ones. Educated people often have dominance over the less educated who take orders. Dominance and submission affect many relationships: parent/child, teacher/student, boss/worker, principal/teacher, government/citizen.

Obedience to authority, to superiors, is often prompted by fear and accompanied by frustration and hostility. Resentment, revenge, violence, and human destructiveness stem from the experience of being a powerless infant—on this experience is built a structure of hierarchy, authority, and power that results in fear and paranoia. Anthony Storr says: "We shall have to live with the fact of man's paranoid potential so far as the foreseeable future is concerned; and this means that we shall also have to live with human cruelty and destructiveness." In other words, destructiveness is part of the human condition. But if we become aware of destructive feelings and are able to understand their source, communicate them openly, and accept them as human, then we can at least be responsible for the choice to act or not act out those feelings.

We can learn to recognize hostility and understand its source.

- Describe a time when you felt hostility. How did you handle your feelings?

- Describe a time when someone larger or more powerful than you dominated you. How did you feel?

- How do you habitually handle hostility? What alternative ways of handling such emotions are available?

- How do you now handle the potential hostility in you in relationship to parent/child, boss/worker, teacher/student situations?

- Choose a partner. Make sentences using the word *they* referring to a power/authority group. For example:

  They (the academic system) won't let me . . .
  They (the establishment) won't let me . . .
  They (the government) makes us . . .

  Now change the word *they* to *I.* Discuss any changes in feelings or any insights.

How we deal with anger, frustration, hostility, aggression, and hate depends on many things—on the degree of the emotion; on whether we accept our emotions or hide and repress them; on whether we have learned to control destructive impulses or act them out. Our emotional reactivity may vary by genetic constitution, by environmental influences, and by cultural programming. We differ in the tendency to accumulate anger, express it, hold it, experience it. Studying how much anger we feel, when, and under what circumstances can help us deal with emotions intelligently and realistically, in our own best interests.

Emotions are complex. Anger or hate can be a cover for fear, for example. If we are afraid someone will not approve of us or if they appear to ridicule us, we may have strong hostile feelings that can develop into hate or resentment. When you feel hostility, hate, or anger, try to trace it back to its source. Perhaps it is a cover for fear or pain.

Ask yourself: "What am I afraid of?" If you overreact, your reactions get out of proportion to the stimulus. Look carefully to see whether you are covering pain or defending yourself against something. Is there some basic fear you don't recognize? Fear of rejection, criticism, inadequacy, failure, disapproval, or punishment can make us react with anger, resentment, bitterness, or hate.

There are, however, constructive ways of handling anger and human destructiveness. First it is essential to recognize, accept, and face the emotion—to "own" it. Next look at whom or what the anger is directed toward (which may not be the *source* of the anger). There are other useful actions which take off some pressure: to act it out harmlessly (as in athletics), to sublimate it in some other activity, or to compensate for it by doing something that will increase self-esteem. Avoiding the cause of the anger or adopting different goals that will produce less anger or frustration can also be effective. *In the process of communicating and understanding these emotions, they often become defused.*

Fear

Fear tells us when to avoid psychological danger, when to run away, when to take flight. If you experienced fear at the zoo when the tiger got out of its cage, that reaction would be considered normal because the danger was real. But fear reactions without a real and present danger need to be understood and managed, because they occur throughout life.

We all feel fear. Children feel small and insignificant in a world of powerful grown-ups—and we carry our childhood fears with us throughout life. Young people are often surprised to learn that adults (those people they think are in such great control over situations) also experience fear, anxiety, dread, anguish, and similar emotions. Adults often hide these feelings so well that they no longer recognize them even when they are experiencing them.

What do you fear most? A team of market researchers asked three thousand Americans this question and found that the responses fell into the following categories:

Biggest Fear	Percentage of Population
1. Speaking before a group	41
2. Heights	32
3. Insects and bugs	22
4. Financial problems	22
5. Deep water	22
6. Sickness	19
7. Death	19
8. Flying	18
9. Loneliness	14
10. Dogs	11
11. Driving/riding in a car	9
12. Darkness	8
13. Elevators	8
14. Escalators	5

Many people named more than one fear, which accounts for the figures adding up to more than 100%. According to the London *Sunday Times*, which reported this survey: "In general, women were more fearful than men." Perhaps women are more willing to express or experience fear. It is interesting to note that the greatest fear was speaking before a group. We need to recognize our fear of communicating.

Our fears often provide clues to self-knowledge and directions for personal growth.

- Which of the fears listed above are your greatest fears? Can you name others? List several in order of intensity.
- Write about experiences you have had with these fears.
- When you are communicating with others, do you experience such fears as being misunderstood or disliked? Discuss these concerns.
- Since speaking before a group was rated as the most common fear, relate to the class your own feelings about speaking before a group. What do you feel is the source of this fear?

Feeling afraid without knowing why is called **anxiety.** Anxiety may be an expression of an unconscious fear—something is wrong but you don't know what it is. You may feel like "climbing the walls" or running away, or hiding, yet you really do not know what is wrong. Anxiety is greater at some times than others.

Coping with anxiety is a common human experience.

When anxiety occurs too often or fails to wear off, you need to explore what is throwing you off balance. If small pleasures fail to give you satisfaction, if you are unable to think or work, you may be suffering from chronic anxiety. People who consistently fear other people or new situations, who are suspicious and mistrust old friends, or who often feel inadequate and filled with self-doubt need to become aware of the unconscious fears that are making them anxious.

Some philosophers say that we all must live with anxiety. Anxiety is universal, they say, because:

1. Our existence is limited (finite); we all must die.

2. We are all basically alone; each is a separate entity.

3. We are each responsible for our own lives, free to make choices that may not work out and with no way of knowing which choices are best.

Everyone suffers from a certain amount of anxiety. People say: "I feel nervous today and I don't know why." Others say they feel restless, irritable, or "blue." High school students responding to a questionnaire listed their five most prevalent fears:

1. Unpopularity—fear of being rejected by others.

2. Inadequacy—fear of not living up to expectations. (Expectations of parents and teachers had often become the students' own expectations.)

3. Loss of protection—fear of growing up and taking responsibility.

4. Personal changes—both physical and psychological fear of impulses and emotions (anger, love, sex).

5. New experiences—fear of being unable to cope with the unfamiliar.

After discussing these fears, the students were asked to translate them into fears they witnessed in adults. Students found "unpopularity" transformed into adult fear of rejection; anxiety about school was transformed into fears of being inadequate as parents, employers, or employees. Adults fear that they will not be able to achieve at some ideal level once set for them that they now demand of themselves. And adults continue to be anxious about experiencing, controlling, and expressing their own emotions of love, anger, and sex.

These young people came to the conclusion that powerful emotions are common to everyone at all ages and need to be recognized, accepted, and shared. Although at first these young people were often critical of adults—wanting them to try new experiences, quit unsatisfactory jobs, or live free of fear—when they compared their own fears with those of adults, they were better able to understand and accept these emotions both in themselves and in others.

Knowing that we all share fear can help us accept fear in ourselves.

- Which of these five fears do you experience: fear of rejection, fear of inadequacy, fear of safety, fear of emotions, fear of new experiences? Give some personal examples. Be as specific as you can.

- *Anxiety scale:* On a scale from 0 to 100, how do you usually rank your anxiety level for each item in this list?

Being silent

Meeting new people

Making poor decisions

Being considered stupid

Exposing your feelings

Having someone visit when your room is dirty

Having others see your children misbehave

Looking or acting "old"

Competing with others

Being ostracized

Hurting others

Not being able to support yourself

Applying for a job

Filling out a school application

Ending a relationship

Driving or taking a trip alone

Going to a new class or meeting alone

Continue the list, making up your own items. Discuss your anxieties in class and explore likenesses and differences.

There are many theories about anxiety. Freud believed that the source of anxiety was repressed sexual desires. Eric Fromm says the fear of separateness, of being alone, arouses anxiety. Karen Horney feels the source of anxiety lies in our hostile impulses—we suffer guilt and fear when we wish harm, punishment, or death on others. Bishop Fulton J. Sheen says the basic cause of anxiety comes with the worry that we cannot be saints or that we are sinners. Jacques Barzun says that mass society with its threat of overpopulation, machines, and mechanical living results in feelings of uselessness or hopelessness. Nathaniel Branden says anxiety comes from a crisis in self-esteem—a conflict between how we think we should behave and how we feel we can. We set up certain standards and when our feelings or actions cannot meet them, we feel that we are "bad" or "wrong." If we betray our own standards, we sense unknown retribution that might punish us.

Anxiety, Fritz Perls believed, is the result of living either in the past or in the future. "Stay in the here and now," he said. Anxiety may stem from that gap between now and then—what you "should" have done or what it "should" have been like. Or anxiety may stem from the gap between now and later. Whenever you leave the "here and now," you become preoccupied with the past or the future and you may experience anxiety. The future often represents some ideal standard of performance; anxiety is thus a kind of stage fright. You may have catastrophic *expectations* about what will happen. In the "here and now," the excitement of living flows into ongoing, spontaneous activity. Like the small child absorbed in life, you can be creative and inventive, totally experiencing the present.

The fierce drive to control the external world, to deal with uncertainty, and to manage life can cause anxiety. Each of us must find the source of our own anxiety. Becoming aware does not automatically dissolve the anxiety, but at least we have a chance of working it out and finding constructive ways of handling it. One of the most productive methods for dealing with anxiety is to talk about it with others. Through the process of communication, feelings can be examined and channeled toward positive goals.

- Which of the theories presented about anxiety do you think fits you? Write about specific situations, conflicts, or experiences in which you have felt anxious.

- Notice a time this week when you are feeling anxious. See if you can find the primary source of that feeling: "There is no one out there to help me"; "I'd like to get even with . . ."; "I'm not . . ."; or "If people knew who I really am, they wouldn't be able to stand me because I can't . . . ." What goes through your mind when you are feeling anxious?

- Make up a list of activities that work for you when you are feeling anxious—for example, watching TV, reading, going to the beach, going to a movie, sleeping, or talking it out with a good listener. Does making a decision and taking action help when you are feeling anxious? What works for you?

Destructive anxiety can produce strain, fatigue, exhaustion, weakness, and physical sensations such as trembling, perspiration, rapid heartbeat, headaches, backaches, breathing difficulties, and digestive disturbances. If we try to escape anxiety by denying it or running from it, we may suffer more. Burying these feelings in alcohol, drugs, social activities, work, or sleep may increase the problem. Communicating feelings, talking about possible solutions, making decisions and carrying them out—this process, for most people, is easier to bear than pretending the emotion does not exist. The following list offers suggestions for handling anxiety. Make up some of your own.

Talk it out with someone: in person, on the phone, in a letter.

Escape for a while in some pleasurable activity.

Work off your tensions: take a walk or play a game.

Do something for others. Get involved with another person.

Take one thing at a time. Stop pressuring yourself.

Stop trying to be a perfectionist. Stop castigating yourself for mistakes.

Avoid criticizing yourself or others. Your standards may be unrealistic.

Cut down on the competition. Try to cooperate with others.

Schedule your days so that you have time for recreation.

If your anxiety continues, it may well be that you must simply "go with it"—experience it fully until it dissolves. Allow the source of that anxiety to communicate itself to you completely.

Sometimes rational thinking or verbal phrases help relieve anxiety. It is irrational, for example, to think that everyone can like us or approve of everything we do. So when we feel threatened or rejected, we can say to ourselves: "Everybody isn't going to like me . . . any more than I like everybody." Fear of inadequacy can be partially overcome by expressions such as "So I can't win 'em all," "So I goofed," "So I'm not perfect," or "So that's the way it is." These expressions can help those who rarely forgive themselves. If overused, of course, they may become excuses or rationalizations for every mistake.

Become aware of your habitual ways of responding. Activity, commitment, developing talents, or enjoyment, learning, experiencing, and communicating can all provide methods for dealing with anxiety. To find the most appropriate methods for you, as a unique individual, can be an exciting exploration.

Fear can be converted into excitement. Those who conquer mountains, explore new territories, or fly into the unknown play with "fear." Fear, anxiety, and worry can be perceived and used in constructive ways. Concern about one's job, marriage, or family can motivate us to find solutions to problems.

Anxiety is the excitement, the élan vital *which we carry with us, and which becomes stagnated if we are unsure about the role we have to play. If we don't know if we will get applause or tomatoes . . . the heart begins to race . . . and we have stage fright.*

Fritz Perls

Fear and anxiety can be powerful motivations toward achievement.

- Describe a time when you turned fear into a positive experience or a time when you were anxious and your attention to the situation helped you find a solution.

- In your group, list ways that anxiety or fear can produce positive results. Give specific examples from your own experience.

Many famous and successful people turn anxiety into constructive energy: the actress who performs in spite of her stage fright and receives a standing ovation; the skier who braces himself for the decisive downhill run; the surgeon who inhales deeply before the first incision in a delicate operation. The list, long and varied, sends us the message: Anxiety can be converted to energy. How we use it is up to us.

Anxieties we choose have value for us. In her essay, "One Vote for This Age of Anxiety," Margaret Mead writes that "we have developed a society which depends on having the right amount of anxiety to make it work." Intense concern can result in constructive change that enriches our personal lives as well as our culture. Peter Koestenbaum regards anxiety as proof of our vitality and the search for meaning in life. He reasons that since our anxieties and our values coincide, we are anxious about losing what we value most. *Achieving what we want satisfies our search for meaning.*

Guilty feelings are a form of anxiety. Some people feel that God is counting sins against them. Others internalize guilt. They count "sins," imperfections, failures, or mistakes against themselves and condemn themselves for not living up to their own expectations. Some people put unreasonable demands on themselves or others. When we have not performed according to the Bible or some other set of rules or code of ethics, we often feel guilty or worthless.

If we have a picture of how a "good" mother should feel or behave with her children and we do not fit the picture, we may feel guilty. A husband who has been taught a definition of a "good" husband that involves feelings he does not have or behavior he does not perform may suffer from guilt. Almost all children have been taught to feel guilty when they disobey. Trying to make people feel guilty sometimes makes them behave the way we want them to. We use guilt to socialize both ourselves and others.

Some people feel guilty if they choose themselves over someone else. The working mother who has been taught that "mothers should stay home with their children" may choose to work because it fulfills her potential. Peter Koestenbaum says her experience of guilt tells her that she has freedom of choice—freedom to choose her own identity and her own definition of motherhood. *Understanding that feeling guilty is proof of our freedom to choose our own behavior can help us deal with the guilt we impose on ourselves.*

Guilt feelings can serve as guides to our own values and freedoms.

- Describe a time you felt guilty about something. How did it feel? What was the source of the guilt?

- Describe an incident in which someone used guilt to manipulate you (or vice versa).

- How has guilt motivated you to take some action you wouldn't otherwise have taken? According to your own values at that time, was the action positive or negative? Did the action become a new behavior pattern for you? Share these answers with your group.

Resentment is the opposite of guilt. It is a feeling of displeasure or indignation—a sense of having been insulted or injured by another. A mother who does not work although she really wants to often feels resentment. Even though she made the choice, she then pretends that it is someone else's fault that she is unhappy. Similarly, a husband who works all his life, giving up his time and money for others, at the end of twenty years may feel intense resentment: "After all I did for them, and now they don't even appreciate it or try to pay me back." This man *chose* others over himself in order to fit his model of the "good" husband or father and now he's angry. He gets to feel "injured" and can play the blame game instead of taking responsibility for his own choices.

Fritz Perls says: "The guilty and the resentful are, for the most part, *clingers.*" They hang onto others by nagging the self or the other party. "What is avoided . . . is actual contact with the other person as a person, whether this contact were to take the form of an explosion of anger, a generous act of understanding and forgiveness, enjoying the other's pleasure, being frank about oneself, or any one of a number of other actions."

Recognizing guilt and resentment is often a first step toward accepting responsibilty for freedom of choice.

- Notice with whom you feel guilty or resentful. What does this person do to trigger such feelings? Would the same action arouse the same feeling if performed by another person? What expectations of each other underlie this relationship? What alternative ways of interacting might you explore?

- Becoming aware of guilt and resentment "gets all the garbage out on the table." What do you do after you have become aware of these feelings?

  Be vindictive—blame others.

  Project my own feelings of guilt onto others in the form of resentment (resent them by refusing to accept the quality in them I have found in myself).

  Feel guilty and degrade myself before others, or be resigned and simply shrug it off.

  Use guilt as a form of self-punishment.

  Use resentment as a way to punish others.

- Discuss these two statements: Guilt tells me I chose myself over others. Resentment tells me I chose others over myself.

Jealousy is the jaundice of the soul.

John Dryden

Jealousy, *an emotion that is often very destructive, is a form of fear–fear of being supplanted by a rival.* The Bible tells the story of Cain's jealousy, which resulted in the slaying of his brother Abel. Shakespeare's tragedy *Othello* depicts the tortured mind of a jealous man who kills the woman he loves over *imagined* deceit. A wife fears a mistress will steal her husband. A child fears the new baby will take its mother's love. A successful actor, executive, or politician may fear some newcomer will take his or her place. It hurts to share a person we love because we believe sharing means that we will get less. It hurts to have someone take our place because we feel that they are "better" or more successful than we are.

Repressed jealousy comes out in disguised ways. Sometimes psychosomatic illnesses, breathing difficulties, headaches, and physical pain express feelings of jealousy. Another person may become destructive: break and drop objects, drive a car irrationally, or criticize or attack other people. One form of repressed jealousy is compulsive competition: beating everybody until finally one can only compete with one's own best efforts—yet never finding satisfaction. Another individual may shun all competition, quit every struggle, and never stand up for himself or herself. To say "I shouldn't be jealous" doesn't change the feeling.

Because jealous feelings have been forbidden, we often feel guilty about feeling jealous.

A researcher at San Diego State University devised a 48-item jealousy questionnaire and administered it to 66 male and 102 female college students. Responses indicated how the students felt and what they did when they were jealous. Women were more likely than men to respond to jealousy with such feelings as helplessness, insecurity, inadequacy, betrayal, and physical illness. It was common for a woman to cry alone, to unload her problems on a sympathetic friend, or to make plans to get even. Men, on the other hand, were more likely to turn their anger inward, to seek retribution, or to seek direct confrontation. They might try to appear unaffected, become more sexually aggressive or critical, or ask for an explanation.

Females tended to respond to jealousy with anger and feelings of depression. Males were more likely to respond by direct actions, such as going out with other people and getting drunk or "high." Both men and women who felt jealous paid more attention to the errant partner, became more sexually aggressive with him or her, and tried to monopolize the other person's time.

Becoming aware of jealous feelings in ourselves can help us control their destructive or self-destructive aspects.

- Describe a time when you felt jealous. How did you feel? What did you do?

- How does it feel when someone else experiences jealousy because you are with another person? Discuss these feelings with others in your group.

- Use role-playing to act out a jealous situation with someone in your group. Have the group observe and then suggest ways that the jealousy could be worked out. (Remember that you can pass any time.)

In our culture, some people believe jealousy is a function of love: "If he feels jealous, he must really love me." But a jealous husband does not necessarily love his wife more than a nonjealous husband. Often jealousy results from feelings of insecurity and inadequacy, from feeling dependent on another person. Jealousy may or may not have a basis in reality—we can be jealous when there is no real threat. We may even know that our thinking is distorted and still feel jealous. Secretly we know that the jealousy lies within ourselves rather than in the people we choose to see as threatening.

The answer to defeating jealousy lies within the individual, yet that makes it no easier to handle. All attacks of jealousy are painful for the sufferer and create difficulty for the partner. There are many ways of handling jealousy. We can cry and experience pain, talk to a friend, write about it, take a vacation, get involved in work or some project, volunteer to work with others. Ultimately we may have to experience the pain, but we do not have to act it out. *Acting out jealousy can be extremely destructive. But recognizing and communicating jealousy constructively can enhance self-esteem.*

Depression

Everyone is depressed at times. We fall into bad moods, experience the "Monday blues," have gloomy spells, or become morose. We accept mild depression as a natural part of living as long as it does not interfere with our daily lives. Yet some individuals experience more or longer periods of depression. Chronic depression is a serious, widely prevalent disorder, very unlike the mild depressions most of us experience. The impact of chronic depression on the individual and those around him or her can be devastating.

Mere awareness of depression will not cure it, but awareness can be a starting point. *There are many shades of depression.* A depressed person may feel sadness, a sense of emptiness, an impression that something is wrong, a growing conviction of unworthiness and hopelessness. These feelings can result in physical debilitation, exhaustion, inadequate personal striving, unresolved conflicts, and feelings of self-pity, impatience, or anger with the world. The victims of depression expect others to relieve their suffering. They often blame others for their unhappiness and consequently accuse and distrust everyone around them. Emotional symptoms may be feelings of sadness, nothing to look forward to, no reason to live. A depressed person may think: "What's the use? Life's not worth it. It's hopeless."

Depression can be a learned behavioral pattern. Helen De Rossis believes that anxiety is the basis for the feelings of depres-

Depression can result in finding new meanings in life.

sion. Anger, a common emotion, can be used to defend the self against anxiety. But in our culture, where it is not acceptable to display anger, particularly for women, the anger may be turned inward in the form of depression. Not surprisingly, then, women experience two or three times as much depression as men do.

"You have to get rid of anger in order to get rid of depression," says De Rossis. Doing something physical is one way to get rid of anger. Sedentary people are more apt to be depressed than the physically active, which may help to explain why there are more depressed women than men. People who feel ignorant or uninformed may feel they are unable to learn or are unworthy. Therefore, another method of combating depression is to develop oneself intellectually.

Depression expresses itself physically, emotionally, and conceptually. Common physical symptoms are fatigue, body aches, and body pain. Recent studies in depression show that depressive "illness" may have a chemical or biological cause. Two psychopharmacologists found that injections of lithium carbonate help severely depressed or psychotic patients. For the first time, scientists feel that a condition that was previously considered environmental or social may be biochemical. Lithium can have strong side effects, however, and is not recommended for the depressions that most of us experience.

The discovery that depression has a biochemical component does not relieve us of responsibility for feeling depressed. We still need to explore the feeling and make choices about our behavior, which may well include going to a physician. In doing so, we can give some thought to the biochemical makeup of our bodies. We need to pay attention to nutrition, rest, relief from stress, and good physical health, all of which are associated with emotional health. *The body, emotion, and mind are intricately interwoven.*

Peter Koestenbaum suggests that *depression reveals to us our freedom to say "no" to life.* He says: "If the self-disclosing individual drills deeply enough into depression, he will strike the wellspring of that negative decision. He will discover and experience the free decision of continuously saying 'no' to life. What then? Here is the important point: Once he is in touch with that decision, he has uncovered the freedom that can say 'yes' to life as well." Freedom means we can say either yes or no—that we have a choice. We can feel depressed or we can choose not to be depressed. Depression thus reveals the dormant power for self-affirmation in each of us. The following suggestions may help you shorten and work out depression:

Activity: Take a walk, bake a pie, ride your motorcycle, drive in the hills. Make a list of activities you like. Get into the water (swim, bathe, shower). Work, play.

Inactivity: Lie down, go to sleep, or rest. Admit that you are depressed. Experience it fully and then let go of it.

Run away: Distraction might make you feel better. Get involved with people, go away for a weekend, take a day off, go to the movies, make a change.

Talk to someone: Pour out your feelings. Share your emotions.

Write about it: List alternatives, describe your feelings, draw, paint, create, play music, walk in a forest, get involved with nature.

Treat yourself: Splurge, spend some money on yourself, order a banana split, buy some new shoes, a record, a book.

We all have available a variety of ways to communicate depression.

- Describe a time when you felt depressed. How long did it last? What did you do about it? How did it disappear?

- Describe a time when you knew someone else who felt depressed. What did you do? How did you handle the relationship? How do you feel when you are with someone who is depressed?

- Create a list of activities that you might use when you feel depressed. Share this list with your group.

Grief and depression are closely related. Loss of a loved one, loss of material things, or loss of an opportunity can result in a sense of emptiness. We may also feel guilt within the grief if we believe that our own actions have brought on the loss. Grief often invites empathy because most of us understand a reaction to loss. We expect sadness and offer comfort to those who have lost a loved one through death.

Grief may be followed by deep depression over a long period of time. In fact, it is not uncommon for an older person who has lost a mate to die within a year. Many of us feel helpless around a person who suffers grief, perhaps because we do not know how to deal with our own grief.

Yet grief can be a growing experience. People who transcend grief to find greater personal meaning can find a source of creative energy and courage in the experience. Deep sorrow is a means of finding out what is important and what is not. *Grief can bring a deeper understanding and a wider love of life to a person who experiences it.*

Loneliness

Being lonely calls for a taxing and straining of resources which toughens the individual for facing the realities of life.

Clark E. Moustakas

Loneliness, as most of us know, is not the same as being alone. In those moments when we feel "gratefully" alone, we can explore our thoughts, use our imagination in fantasy, and play in limitless ways. The ability to be alone is largely a matter of temperament. Some people seem to have more need to be among people. They find being by themselves difficult, at times even intolerable. Others prefer more time to themselves. Each of us differs in our responses to being alone. To explore our own intrapersonal com-

Loneliness is not the same as being alone.

munication patterns, we can ask ourselves: "Where do I feel most comfortable? In a crowd? Alone? With one other person? How much of the time do I want to be alone and how much of the time with other people?" Since we are constantly changing, our answers to these questions will change with age and time. Young people, as a whole, more often prefer to be with others. Older people often enjoy a great deal of comfort in time spent alone.

Some of us simply want to be "included." Bill Schutz, a psychologist, developed a measure called "inclusion"—the need to be included in social groups, in clubs and organizations, in

Being alone allows creativity to develop.

groups of people. Inclusion needs are not the same as needs for affection, which involve a deep relationship with another person. Inclusion needs involve a sense of belonging to a group and being accepted.

Being alone creates the space for fundamental learning and profound experiences in creating art and literature and a personal philosophy for living. By contrast, loneliness is a feeling of disinvolvement with other people—a sense of being friendless, despairing, and dissociated from the human race. Loneliness may include a complex desire to detach oneself from others because detachment avoids pain. We cannot be hurt if we avoid becoming emotionally involved with anyone: parents, children, other family members, friends. Subconsciously we may say to ourselves: "If I'm not involved, I don't have to be hurt—not even by the spread of crime, immorality, illness, and death which seems to be everywhere. I do not want to connect with a human being who is starving or in pain." But the price of not connecting with others is loneliness. To avoid it, we must find the courage to risk being hurt.

Some people feel they have so little to give that closeness would deplete them. They fear the loss of their individuality. Encased in emotional armor and shielded by aloofness, they shut out the world. Being in the world is a greater pain for them than loneliness. Others feel they are so unique that no one else could possibly understand them. Their loneliness is worn like a red badge of courage.

There is no permanent solution to loneliness. It is part of life. Neither age, personal history, wealth, nor marital status precludes loneliness. Sometimes people experience greater feelings of loneliness in a marriage or a relationship than they do when they are single. And lonely feelings are usually strongest during times of stress or change.

Some people who are severely lonely do not know they are lonely. They are so fearful of their feelings that they camouflage them by overeating, oversleeping or insomnia, use of drugs or alcohol, hypochondria, dependency on parents or relatives, promiscuity, psychosomatic illnesses, and hyperactivity. This conflict—needing people but being afraid of people—is quite common. We may cry out for a relationship, yet unwittingly put every conceivable block in the way of developing one.

One source of loneliness is the inability to recognize that it exists—the inability to reach out for closer relating. Another source of loneliness comes from the fear that becoming involved with another person would mean giving up freedom. And it would! Some popular people lose themselves in a merry-go-round of energy-wasting action in order to avoid sustained emotional involvement.

Much of our loneliness may stem from unrealistic expectations of what relationships or friendships ought to be like. Friendless children hope that their teenage years will be better. Lonely adolescents look forward to the promise of better things—university, the first job, marriage—a beautiful future that never comes. And so on.

Loneliness is not bad or shameful. It just exists and can be chosen or not chosen. Peter Koestenbaum suggests that *"Loneliness, although painful, leads to the realization that I cannot be replaced . . . I am unique; I am me; I am an individual . . . I am myself and not somebody else."* Knowing that loneliness will always be with us, we can choose at times to have the courage to risk being hurt, to reach out, and to share ourselves with others.

A middle-aged professional man, effective in his work, has become oppressed by a sense of emptiness and loneliness. He says: "You get so busy that you don't notice the children growing up. It's a surprise to find they're not little any more. The time's just gone. It's kind of frightening, but it doesn't last long because there's too much to do." This man is talking about *his own* deepest emotional longings and fears, yet he does not refer to himself once. He talks about "you" and "it." He describes his experience so that it is impersonal—his style of speech allows him to keep a distance from himself.

This loss of genuine awareness, this alienation from one's own being, is not uncommon. Some individuals are lost to themselves, to their families, to their relationships. They may use the narcotic of work to ease their fears and their sense of loss. *Detachment* allows them to be only another object in the world. And when we communicate that alienation to others by using impersonal words to describe ourselves, we encourage others to treat us as objects too.

We feel **alienation** when we try to live our own lives as though we were building a house or driving a car—by manipulating ourselves from the outside and by manipulating our external world. *We can overcome this alienation by owning our feelings.* The middle-aged professional man could say: "I allowed myself to become so busy that I wasn't aware my children were growing up. I was surprised to wake up and find them gone. I feel fright-ened that I have been so unaware and that I might continue to live unconsciously." He is now "valuing" the full range of his emotions, including his fear. Using the word *I* and owning his feelings of awareness and pain bring him face to face with him-self. *If we change our language patterns when we communicate our emotions, we can take personal responsibility for our feelings and our choices in the past, present, and future.*

Discussing loneliness and alienation can help us see how we experience and communicate these feelings.

- Write out and discuss a time when you experienced loneliness. After you've talked about it, either reread what you have writ-ten or have a partner tell you what kind of language you used to describe your feelings.

- Discuss some of the advantages of experiencing loneliness. What do you gain by being lonely? What do you lose?

- Make an effort this week to listen to how you and others use impersonal language to talk about feelings. Do you manipulate your life, your reality, and yourself by making an object of yourself as if you were another person? Do you substitute words like *you* or *a person* or *everyone* when you mean *I*? Do you emphasize reasons and logic when dealing with emo-tions? Do you use "why" and "because" explanations in place of "I feel"? How do these modes of communication affect the messages you give yourself and others?

- Do you deny or dismiss your own emotional pain or unpleasant feelings? What do you accomplish by these methods? What does it cost you?

When we express feelings and open ourselves up to satisfying relationships, we communicate connectedness.

Boredom

Boredom *is the feeling of being empty, being indifferent, as if noth-ing matters.* It is a lack of interest, expectation, desire, or caring. Some people believe it is fashionable to appear bored. Others are bored because they have too often relied on external stimuli to excite them, and in the absence of stimuli they are at a loss. Some are bored because they do not know how to compete. They feel they have lost too many times, so they simply "turn off" and "tune out."

Others use boredom as a test to find out who cares for them. If a little boy runs to his mother and says "I'm bored," she may make a suggestion: "Well, why don't you read or write or draw or play games?" Thus he gets her attention. She may also respond by playing with him every time he says he's bored. That is even a greater reward for being bored, and boredom can thus become a habit. Other people may see nothing worthwhile to work for because they are in a rut. Routine can kill interest and incentive.

Some people who feel bored blame others for their state: "He bores me." "That teacher bores me." "School bores me." Such people want others to be responsible for their boredom and do something about it. But boredom is a chosen reaction—only the bored person can do something about it. Boredom does not come from any outside source, such as a mate, friends, a hometown, a job, fate, or luck. Boredom comes from within—it is chosen for a variety of reasons. It is an effective anesthetic for people who do not want to feel anger, love, or any other emotion. Feeling bored can also be a defense against being hurt by others or by failure—a way of avoiding commitment to anyone or anything. It protects the individual who is afraid to feel, afraid of too much excitement or intensity of involvement.

Apathy, a lack of feeling, passion, or emotion, results in indifference to conflict, frustration, the world and its problems. Apathy and boredom can also be used to avoid change. Most of us have some fear of the unfamiliar, yet until we explore the unknown we cannot really change.

Life is not a continuous series of fascinating experiences. At times we all encounter periods lacking in excitement. We can learn to differentiate these calm, comfortable times when change is "on the back burner," cooking quietly, from those times when traumatic or insightful moments allow us to experience change. Compassion for ourselves during periods of boredom, anxiety, or depression helps to provide an atmosphere conducive to change. In *Man and His Symbols*, Carl Jung says that boredom is the sign that change is ready to occur. *If we recognize that boredom sometimes indicates that change is needed, we can use it to explore change.*

If you can look at, feel, talk about, and express your boredom, you may find that you are no longer bored. As the feelings change, you will begin to respond. If you do feel bored in a relationship, you owe it to yourself and to the other person to communicate this feeling—to recognize it as *your own feeling*, not something that others are responsible for changing.

Boredom is an uncomfortable feeling. Most of us want to feel alive, involved, committed to life and living. Superficial maneuvers and attempts at quick stimulation may bring brief periods of respite from boredom, but ultimately they may leave us more bored than before, just as increasing a drug simply creates less reaction.

Related to boredom is the painful feeling of meaninglessness. When we cannot find "truth" or some values to guide our lives, we may feel discouraged or empty or valueless. And we search outside ourselves for meaning (in what our parents told us, in church, and elsewhere). Ultimately we discover that we must create our own meaning and our own values. Peter Koestenbaum suggests that "meaninglessness shows each human being that he has the power of self-definition. He can create meanings for himself." *When we become aware that we must choose our own values, our own natures, and our own self-definitions, we then can move out of this state of meaninglessness.*

Exploring boredom can give us valuable clues to the need for self-made change.

- Describe a time when you felt bored or empty. What did you do about it? How long did it last? What replaced it?

- Why might it be necessary for some people to reject traditional values? Can you express feelings of apathy, boredom, and emptiness? Can you communicate those feelings to others?

- Try to recreate a situation in which you felt bored. Think of ways you could have:

  1. Changed your perceptions to make the situation more interesting to you.
  2. Communicated your boredom to put it outside you.
  3. Changed your environment.
  4. Chosen to appreciate this quiet time as a sign of impending change.

Ambivalence

A **conflict** *is a struggle between two opposing forces.* Most of us have little difficulty recognizing when we clash with others, yet many of us are not aware of ambivalent feelings. We must often make choices among opposing feelings, thoughts, or ways of behaving.

You cannot deal with the most serious things in the world unless you understand the most amusing.

Winston Churchill

"I hate you."

"I love you."

Ambivalence.

Some psychologists classify **intrapersonal conflicts** as approach-approach conflicts, avoidance-avoidance conflicts, or approach-avoidance conflicts. When you choose between two attractive alternatives, either going to the movies or to a dance, both of which you enjoy, you experience an approach-approach conflict. When you choose between two unattractive alternatives, such as cleaning your room or doing the dishes, neither of which you enjoy, you experience an avoidance-avoidance conflict. Then there are some situations or people to whom you are both attracted and repelled at the same time. You may want to fly a plane, but you are afraid. You like a particular person, but you're afraid that person won't like you. You want to go swimming, but the water's too cold. These represent approach-avoidance conflicts.

Generating alternative ways of dealing with conflicts can help us clarify our own needs and values.

- Describe in detail a conflict you are currently experiencing. If possible, classify the conflict (approach-approach, and so on.) Write down ways you have resolved conflicts in the past. Describe the results. List other alternatives.
- Put the list away for a few days. Then reconsider it and, if possible, talk to whomever else is involved. Make a decision.

Most conflicts are much more complex than these examples. The approach-avoidance conflict—the coexistence of opposite feelings about the same person or object—is called **ambivalence.** When you want some positive aspect of something but not the negative aspect that also goes with the choice, your decision may involve serious thought. You must be able to communicate well enough with yourself to establish criteria based on your values and feelings. Marriage, for example, involves making a commitment to another person but giving up a degree of freedom. Being single offers more freedom but involves giving up the deep commitment to another person. Usually people do not stand long at a midpoint. Talking about, writing about, and thinking about ambivalence can help us move in one direction or the other.

Ambivalence *or* **paradox** *in the form of polar opposites, both simultaneously desirable or "true," provides us with one of our greatest challenges.* The intrinsic contradictions of life—conflict in the very process of being, polarity in simply existing—create some of the strongest emotions with which we are forced to deal. Need for independence and dependence, for freedom and commitment, for individuality and society, for maturity and innocence, for rationality and feeling—all operate at the same time, pulling us in opposite directions.

But contradiction and paradox can also be a source of strength. If we accept the idea that conflict may not be resolvable, we can accept ourselves. There are unsolvable issues in every life. Need for independence and need for dependence pit the parent in each of us against the child in each of us. We experience this struggle throughout life. The only way to exist without one half is to kill one and live with the other. Some people manage to kill off one side of themselves in a desperate attempt to avoid conflict, but in doing so they become only half-alive.

When you are joyous, look deep into your heart and you shall find it is only that which has given you sorrow that is giving you joy . . . I say unto you, they are inseparable.

Kahlil Gibran

The adult in us—symbolizing rationality, maturity, freedom, and independence—can help mediate parent-child conflicts. The adult functions separately to find satisfaction in accomplishment and to earn self-respect as a unique and separate entity. The adult helps balance the need for freedom with the need to relate to others. We experience difficulty with these opposites unless we can verbalize them and communicate them to ourselves and others.

Ambivalence can be an invitation to self-knowledge.

- What form does ambivalence take in your life? What needs pull you in different directions?

- Give specific examples of times when you've wanted to be free (independent) and close (dependent) at the same time or a unique individual (concern for self) and part of a group (concern for others) at the same time. How did you handle the conflict?

- Make a list of needs that pull you in different directions. Leave a space between the opposite needs. Then attempt to find "adult" compromises that you can write down between each of the pairs.

- Have you experienced a love-hate relationship?

- Have you ever experienced attraction-repulsion feelings for some activity, project, or job?

- Share these experiences.

Conflicting urges toward independence/dependence, freedom/commitment, maturity/innocence, rationality/feeling, and adult/child exist in all of us. If we accept that not all contradictions can be resolved and that everyone experiences ambivalence, we will find these feelings more tolerable. *When we accept ambivalence or simply let it be, it can enrich our lives*—not tear us apart. These polarities make up the whole person. We cannot give up one part or the other without creating imbalance in the whole. There is challenge in realizing that values are usually ambiguous, that there is no absolute truth or "right" answer. We must act in spite of uncertainty, make decisions in spite of ambiguities, make commitments without knowing their future, handle contradictions and conflicts.

Those who learn to accept paradox and explore the polarity between inner and outer realities can reconcile themselves and bring order to their world. In communicating that order to others, they contribute to them. They can encourage others to stop attempting to reconcile the irreconcilable: the polarities of oneness and separateness, dependence and independence, internal and external, love and self-reliance, freedom and closeness. Polarity and paradox—like the oppositions of heaven and earth, spirit and nature, man and woman—bring about the creation and reproduction of life.

EMOTIONS AND SELF-ESTEEM

Individuality is founded in feeling.

William James

Why don't we know more about emotions? Mostly because we hide them rather than study them. Many people prefer intellectual processes. Yet who among us chooses their mates, friends, or relationships on the basis of the other person's ability to solve complex problems through analysis? Intelligent people often have difficulties with genuine, deep, fulfilling relationships when they do not recognize the immense importance of emotions in our lives.

All emotions are valuable in that they communicate to us something about who we are. Children are not born with feelings, but they are born with the potential to experience all feelings. As we grow, learn, and develop, we begin to respond more with certain feelings than with others. We adapt to pain with a "favorite" emotional response. As adults, we may continue to show a preference for functioning with this habitual emotional response.

Eric Berne calls such a chosen response a "racket"—we indulge ourselves in feelings of guilt, inadequacy, hurt, fear, or resentment by seeking situations that will create an opportunity to reexperience our favorite childhood emotions. Reexperiencing an old response maintains the status quo: the comfortable self-concept. Berne says people create "games" with others to recreate their childhood feeling states. Identifying the rewards for these responses might aid us in changing them. Perhaps we will find that as adults these responses no longer provide us with the rewards we want today.

Identifying a favorite emotional response is a first step toward letting go of it.

- Do you have a favorite emotional pain? What is it? What does it tell you about yourself?

- In your group, discuss some of the emotional games people play to recreate favorite roles. Which games do you recognize in your family? Friends? Yourself? What rewards do we get for playing games?

- After identifying a "chosen" emotional pain, look underneath. Is there another feeling beneath the feeling you now recognize? Anger, for example, may cover either pain or fear. Boredom or depression may cover anger. Like the layers of an onion, feelings often hide other feelings (see the figure below). Imagine that you are peeling off the layers of feelings. Look carefully underneath. Do you find another feeling beneath the one that shows?

- Make some decisions about how you might like to change certain emotional patterns. Be specific by listing situations, people, responses, and alternatives.

- Write a note to yourself on your calendar three months from now to recheck your decisions to change.

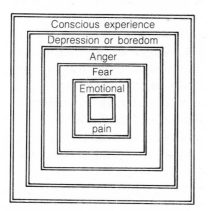

Cover emotions.

Pain of the body, the mind, the emotions, or the spirit is a guide—an indication that it is correcting itself. Focusing on the pain, just accepting it, sometimes leads to its source and brings about increased awareness of its cause. Genuine relief from pain comes through expanded awareness.

In Chapter 3 we found that people with high self-esteem have a positive opinion of themselves. Feelings of self-worth are intimately connected to our ability to handle emotions. Since self-esteem and self-acceptance can be learned, they provide a method for changing unsatisfactory childhood emotional responses. Our characteristic feeling states can be opened up for reevaluation and change. In exploring our favorite emotional responses, we can try to see what they tell us about ourselves.

If you feel secure about yourself, you are capable of responding honestly with your feelings. People with high self-esteem are able to respond authentically with anger, fear, depression, loneliness, boredom, and ambivalence. Yet they are less concerned whether others approve or disapprove of their expression of feelings. If we feel that we are valuable and interesting, we can accept either praise or criticism without being affected by either.

The possibility of change brings us back to our original proposition: We have some choices about our emotional states. We can experience a wide range of feelings without acting them out. Yet we are willing to own our feelings and welcome them because they are self-chosen.

A sense of self-worth creates a climate in which we can accept other people's feelings as genuinely representing who they are too. We can respond to them warmly even though they are different. The person of high self-esteem uses the processes of intrapersonal communication as a foundation for interpersonal relationships. When we feel valuable, we can express our feelings more precisely, open ourselves to the communication of feelings from others, and create more fulfilling relationships.

FOR FURTHER READING

Festinger, L. *Conflict, Decision and Dissonance.* Stanford: Stanford University Press, 1964.
> The author presents research about what we do when we are in conflict and how we resolve conflict within ourselves.

Hoffer, Eric. *The Ordeal of Change.* New York: Harper & Row, 1952.
> This collection of essays deals with our fear of The New—taking a new step, uttering a new word, moving in new directions.

Koestenbaum, Peter. *Managing Anxiety: The Power of Knowing Who You Are.* Englewood Cliffs, N.J.: Prentice-Hall, 1974.
> This refreshing book defines, describes, and analyzes many sources of emotional pain that result in positive growth when we accept such emotions as messages about ourselves.

Lorenz, Konrad. *On Aggression.* New York: Harcourt Brace, 1966.
> Lorenz studies the rituals by which animals control their destructive drives for the benefit of survival of the species.

Lynd, Helen Merrill. *On Shame and the Search for Identity.* New York: Harcourt Brace, 1970.
> The author explores the experiences of shame and suggests that such exploration can lead to self-discovery.

Menninger, Karl A. *Man Against Himself.* New York: Harcourt Brace, 1938.
> The author presents the theory that our war against ourselves is a struggle between the will to live and self-destructive tendencies.

Moustakas, Clark E. *Loneliness.* Englewood Cliffs, N.J.: Prentice-Hall, 1961.
> The author says that loneliness is a universal and timeless condition fostered by the way we structure our social world.

Actions speak louder than words.

9

Behaving: How Actions Communicate

INFLUENCES ON BEHAVIOR

Behavior *is anything people do that is observable by someone else. A unit of behavior is an* **act,** *and acts communicate messages.* Although we cannot see beliefs, attitudes, or values, observations of behavior tell us something about people. People may verbalize their attitudes and values yet not act them out. Behavior is not necessarily consistent with a person's language, thoughts, or emotions. *Often we believe what we say rather than what we do.* We may feel anxious or unreal if we become aware of the discrepancies between what we say and what we do. Other people can help us become more self-aware by noticing our behavior and sharing their perceptions with us. Although we sometimes hide things from ourselves, our behavior often gives us away.

A study of behavior is essential to the improvement of interpersonal communication. Behavior is influenced by our culture, education, family, past experiences, and habits. As we study the effects of this **socialization,** we will see how conformity, obedience, and consistency of behavior are acted out by the individual. Each of us has different motivations and needs. We act out different roles. With others we sometimes act out certain rituals, pastimes, and games as part of our interpersonal transactions. When we observe our behavior, we then have choices about ways to modify it to fit our goals.

Cultural Conditioning

Much of our behavior is a result of how we have been taught to act as children. Different cultures rear young children in different ways. American culture has emphasized the role of the family—particularly the mother—in raising young children. With the increasing number of working mothers, however, child care centers and private schools share some responsibility for childrearing.

Each culture differs slightly in its methods of childrearing. The American culture holds that a close-knit family is best suited to children's needs. One disadvantage of the family system is that children need contact with the outside world. In other cultures, extended families—including grandparents, aunts, and uncles—share the burden of childrearing. In Israel, the kibbutz provides yet another system for socializing children.

Each family also differs from others. And each parent has his or her own value systems, needs, and goals for raising children. These individual and family differences lead to wide variations in childrearing methods even within one culture.

Behavioral scientists suggest that human behavior can be guided through the use of punishment and rewards. Each parent develops a system of discipline unique to the situation and the individual child. Parental methods for dealing with children's behavior may be categorized as follows (in order of increasing coerciveness):

1. Acceptance

2. Explanation and discussion (evaluating behavior and giving reasons)

3. Natural consequences (letting the child suffer through his or her own behavior)

4. Giving information (evaluating without explanation)

5. Bribery (promising a reward for good behavior)

6. Reprimanding (scolding, berating, arguing, yelling)

7. Asserting authority (ordering, forbidding, demanding, stopping)

8. Threatening deprivation, natural consequences, or punishment

9. Compensation (having a child do extra work)

10. Deprivation (removing privileges, limiting actions, depriving the child of social contact)

11. Shaming (ridiculing, making the child feel bad)

12. Physical punishment (spanking, slapping, whipping)

Experts suggest that, generally speaking, rewards are preferable to punishment to get the desired behavior. Rewards can be physical, verbal, or material. Some children are more amenable to rewards than others. Each individual differs in his or her response to punishment and rewards. To get an adult to behave in a certain way, we offer better-paying jobs, more status, bonuses, special benefits, more time off, and other rewards. Some experts believe that such rewards are less successful in this day of affluence than in the past. Yet each culture devises a punishment-reward system to control and condition the behavior of the people in that society.

The Personal Past

Behavior patterns that we developed as children are difficult to change. W. H. Missildine, in *Your Inner Child of the Past*, says children whose parents had the following attitudes may have developed certain ways of behaving in response:

The maxim "nothing avails but perfection" may be spelled paralysis.

Winston Churchill

Parental Attitude	Childhood Response
Perfectionism	Preoccupation with physical, social, or intellectual accomplishment
Overcoercion	Dawdling, daydreaming, procrastination, and other forms of resistance
Oversubmission	Impulsiveness, temper outbursts, lack of consideration for the rights of others

Overindulgence	Boredom, lack of persistence, difficulty in initiating individual effort
Hypochondriasis	Anxiety about health
Punitiveness	Fierce desire for revenge
Neglect	Anxiety, loneliness, remoteness
Rejection	Lone-wolf feelings, unacceptance of others and self

However, children may also choose an opposite reaction to their parents. If you had a hypochondriac parent, you may have compensated (rejected the parent) by being very healthy. As adults we can take some responsibility for choosing or not choosing to continue our old childhood patterns, especially those which are self-destructive.

Each of us grows up in some social structure and has experiences in early life that affect our behavior when we are older.

- **Describe some early experiences that still exert some control over your behavior today.**

- **What habitual behavior, learned in childhood, would you like to change?**

- **What methods did your parents use to affect your behavior? How did you respond?**

- **What responses did you make to your parents' attitudes?**

There are many theories about how early experiences affect our behavior now. Erik Erikson says that each person passes through eight stages that influence future behavior. Most of these behaviors can be plotted on a continuum from one extreme to the other. Erikson says that in the first year of life a baby learns to *trust or mistrust*. The baby who finds no one to trust may need years of affection to undo the damage of that first year. During the second and third years, children pass through a crisis between *autonomy versus doubt*. Erikson says too much autonomy at this stage can be as harmful as too little. A little shame or doubt balances an inflated sense of autonomy. During the fourth and fifth years, children begin to talk and initiate their own activities. As a result, they experience a struggle between *initiative and guilt*.

If they are scolded too much for making messes or getting dirty, later in life they may experience persistent guilt about initiating their own activities.

From about six to eleven years of age, children learn a sense of industry and achievement at one extreme or a sense of inferiority at the other. The *industry versus inferiority* stage depends on experiences of success. From ages twelve to eighteen, adolescents encounter the problem of *identity versus role confusion.* They either develop a fairly strong sense of who they are, or they struggle continually to find themselves. Young adults need other people and they therefore develop, depending on their experiences, a sense of *intimacy or isolation.* During middle age, concern with others in the society beyond one's immediate family results in *generativity or self-absorption* with perhaps some bitterness. In the final stage of life, aged people look back on their lives with *integrity or despair,* depending on whether they feel they have taken or missed opportunities and directions.

If Erik Erikson's categories do not describe your personal stages of growth, substitute your own words.

- On these scales, place an × where you believe you function most of the time. Remember that some changes do occur in time and we do move back and forth within some limits on any scale.

Trust	————————————————	Mistrust
Autonomy	————————————————	Doubt
Initiative	————————————————	Guilt
Industry	————————————————	Inferiority
Identity	————————————————	Role Confusion
Intimacy	————————————————	Isolation
Generativity	————————————————	Self-absorption
Integrity	————————————————	Despair

- In your groups, share some specific early experiences that influenced where you placed yourself on the scale. In what stage of growth did these experiences occur?

Education transmits culturally accepted behavior.

Education is often defined in terms of varying degrees of success in teaching children to control behavior in socially accepted ways. This education takes place in the home, at school, at church, and in the neighborhood. In addition to punishment and rewards, there are many other complex influences on our behavior.

Physiological makeup is a primary force in the way we behave. Some individuals have greater energy than others. We may be restless or listless, nervous or apathetic, depending on our glandular makeup, basal metabolism, and chemical balance. Overall health has a great effect on behavior. Individuals also differ in **motivation.** Needs, desires, and drives are affected not only by the physiology of the body but also by emotions, values, and goals.

Self-perception also plays a major role in our actions. We act like the sort of individuals we perceive ourselves to be. *One overpowering motivation in life is to sustain the unity of the person.* Therefore most of us attempt to function in ways that are consistent with our self-image. Behavior overtly expresses the concepts we have about ourselves. And once we verbalize these concepts, we tend to act them out. (They become self-fulfilling prophecies.)

In summary, then, these are a few of the many influences on behavior:

1. Education: home, school, church, society

2. Physiology: chemistry, body structure, energy level

3. Emotions: feelings, values, attitudes, goals

4. Self-image: self-concept, self-esteem

5. Thoughts: beliefs, attitudes, expectations

6. Language: verbal concepts, words, symbols

Learning on an intellectual level, feeling level, and verbal level is intricately complex and expresses itself in behavior.

Habits

Although our behavior often seems to be innate because it is so habitual, it is usually subject to some degree of personal choice. Each of us can select behavior appropriate to a situation, depending on our awareness of our choices. *Sometimes habits lock us into stock responses.* Although habits simplify life so that we do not have to make new decisions continually, they are also difficult to change. When habits become unconscious, they restrict our options of behavior. Asking for feedback about habits can help us become conscious of stock responses that limit our freedom.

We develop habits of behavior so that we can concentrate on learning new behavior. While we are eating, we can talk and listen. Yet many people become creatures of habit who play out the same roles over and over with different players. Finding new solutions to old problems is difficult. It is easier to solve different

I never had a policy that I could always apply. I've simply attempted to do what made the greatest amount of sense at the moment.

Abraham Lincoln

problems in the same old way. Creative problem-solving requires us to give up old habitual behavior.

Scientists still do not know how habits are formed, either good ones or bad ones. Some research points to chemical changes in the brain cells. But the process must be much more complicated than simply chemistry. You don't often get rid of a habit by making a decision to stop it. If you've been driving a car with a gear shift and then drive an automatic, you will probably try to press a nonexistent clutch pedal to the floor. You have built up a habit system for shifting which must now be changed.

To replace poor reading habits, for example, you must begin with attitude and purpose—you must want to give up the old habits. Then you need *information* about how to replace the bad habits with better ones. But wanting to change and having the information are still not enough. Your old habits may be firmly set because you've used them so long. You must practice new habits until they overcome the old set patterns. Photographs show that eyes move and stop as they read across each line of print on a page. Actual perception—the making of pictures in the brain—takes place during the fraction of a second when the eyes have stopped. Reducing the number of fixations per line can improve both reading efficiency and memory because you get ideas rather than words. Other habits that slow reading efficiency are moving your lips as you read, vocalizing, regressing (going back over what you have read), and reading one word at a time. *These habits can be changed when a reader chooses an attitude, intention, and purpose to change them and then practices more efficient reading.* In a similar way other habits can be replaced with intention and practice.

Habits can limit our lives as well as help them flow more smoothly.

- Write a list of habits that help you function better and make your life work more smoothly.
- Write a list of habits that may hinder you (speaking, thinking, or acting patterns).
- In your small groups share these lists. Talk about ways you can replace habits with more efficient or satisfying behavior.

Self-Fulfilling Prophecy

Expectations can elicit behavior in others that results in those expectations coming true. Deeply suspicious people are convinced that others are not trustworthy, for example. They misinterpret a friendly gesture as an effort to put something over on them. As a result, they drive people away. People become wary and defensive. In effect, people respond as they predict—as enemies not to be trusted. We have all met individuals who look for the worst in others. They expect people to cheat, lie, or steal. Often they unconsciously draw people to them who fulfill these expectations. A parent or teacher who continually expects children to lie often finds this expectation fulfilled.

A self-fulfilling prophecy often begins as an expectation of a behavior or trait by a significant person that then becomes internalized as part of a person's self-image. It might simply have begun as a label. Sharon's mother may have told people (when Sharon was four years old) that "Sharon is bashful." By the time Sharon was five, she began to say to herself: "I'm bashful." When she is twenty, she may still have this self-image and act out the "bashful Sharon" role. Bill says, "I'm depressed." Then he drops his chin, hunches his shoulders, looks sad, and acts out his depression. The statements we make about ourselves act as suggestions. We can then become hypnotized by ourselves into behaving as we have predicted.

> *You will "act like" the sort of person you conceive yourself to be.*
>
> *Maxwell Maltz*

Give some serious thought to ways you "program" yourself to behave through self-fulfilling prophecy. *Ask others to help you change the words you use so that you can create behavior you want.*

- Go back to the "Who Am I?" exercise, in Chapter 3. Often words that begin "I am . . ." become negative self-fulfilling prophecies. Circle them. Examples: "I never have any control over my eating." "I always feel that I'm going to fail." "I never could spell."

- *Positive* self-fulfilling suggestions can help you create behavior you want. Examples: "I'm getting better at spelling." "I'm eating less today than yesterday." "I'm getting more disciplined in my study habits."

- "Programming" can be positive or negative. Choose one *positive* self-fulfilling suggestion. Affirm yourself for one week by writing out the same affirmation or positive suggestion at least ten times every day. Tape a 3 × 5 card with the positive suggestion on it to the mirror in your bathroom. At the end of two weeks review your behavior to see if any change has occurred.

SOCIAL BEHAVIOR

The psychologist Karen Horney says our needs lead to three kinds of social behavior: moving toward people, moving against people, and moving away from people. At different times in our lives and with different people, we all behave in all three ways. Yet each of us tends to favor one particular type of social behavior.

Moving *toward* people indicates a need for affection and approval—a need for a partner, friend, lover, someone expected to fulfill needs. Moving toward people may also indicate a need to be important to others, especially to a particular person. When the need to move toward others becomes overly important, people may become compliant pleasers who worry about how they can make others like them.

Moving *against* people indicates a need to excel, to achieve, to be recognized. This behavior begins with the need for survival and the pursuit of self-interest. Although all of us want to be recognized, when this need becomes exaggerated an individual may become *aggressive* and consider the best defense to be the best offense.

Moving *away* from people indicates a need for privacy. Each of us desires some privacy. At times we do not want to feel tied or obligated to others. In some cases, people who move away from others become *detached*. They develop the philosophy that if they stay away from people, they won't get hurt.

How each of us finds a balance between being with people, taking care of our own survival, and also having some privacy is an individual matter. First we must know what we want, where we are in our growth, and how we can best achieve that balance most appropriate at any given time.

- Write down the name of each person in the group, including yourself. Write down the word *compliant, aggressive,* or *detached* after each name as you *perceive* that person. Can you accept another person's choice to be compliant, aggressive, or detached?

- Do you tend to be compliant, aggressive, or detached? Can you trace the source of that behavior? Are you comfortable with that kind of behavior? Do you want to continue it? If you would like to move toward a different social response, which one would you choose?

- Share with the group your experience of yourself as compliant, aggressive, or detached. Ask others how they perceive you. Is there a difference of opinion in the group? What might be some sources of differences in the way people perceive you?

Conformity and Obedience

Conformity is behaving the way others around us behave. Children conform when they stay away from hot stoves or look both ways before crossing the street. Automobile drivers conform when they obey traffic signals. Hospital workers conform when they sterilize operating instruments. These cases of conformity make living safer and more productive.

Behavior intended simply to gain the approval, acceptance, or recognition of others, rather than because the behavior makes sense or is responsible, is conformity for the wrong reasons. People who drink, smoke, or use drugs *purely* for peer approval may be acting in opposition to their personal wishes. Pressure from salespeople and the influence of mass media, such as television or newspaper advertising, can persuade people to behave in ways entirely false to their own beliefs and values.

Perhaps the most difficult kind of conformity to avoid is obedience to authority. When obedience requires us to behave against our moral principles, it can be negative. *In our culture, we profess to teach children to obey primarily for their own welfare and safety.* However, sometimes teachers, parents, or employers wish others to behave in certain ways primarily for convenience. Sometimes we learn to obey so well as children that as adults we forget to think through orders to validate their worth.

He is happy as well as great who needs neither to obey nor command in order to be something.

Goethe

Obedience/conformity signs.

Psychologists have devised interesting studies of obedience. One famous experiment involves a naive subject who is asked by an experimenter to administer an electric shock to a victim. The subject is told that this is a learning experiment and when the victim gives the "wrong" answer, he or she is to receive a shock. But the shock generator (which has clearly marked voltage levels) is simulated, and the victim is actually a trained confederate of the experimenter. The experimenter tells the subject to increase the voltage when the victim gives wrong answers. As the experiment proceeds, the subject is commanded by the experimenter to administer increasingly intense shocks to the victim, even though the voltage meter reads "dangerous" and "severe shock." The victim pretends to be in great pain. Although some of these obedient subjects exhibit extreme stress, most of them continue to obey. This study has been reproduced a number of times. As high as 80% of the subjects obey the commands of an experimenter and administer "almost lethal" shocks to the victim. Even in this case, where the person in authority has no special powers to enforce commands, most of us follow instructions. Experimental evidence thus indicates that the majority of us when in conflict between hurting others or obeying would do what we are told.

As adults we are free to evaluate and change the obedience patterns set up in us as children.

- Describe a time when you conformed to some peer pressure and later wished that you had not.
- Describe a time when you talked someone else into acting in ways they didn't want to. What was the result?
- Evaluate yourself in terms of conformity and obedience. Do you think you would have been part of the 80% in the shock-test study?
- Describe a time when you insisted on obedience from someone and felt a surge of power when you were obeyed.
- Write down some of your thoughts and experiences about being obedient or demanding obedience from others. Share these in a group discussion.

Consistency

People tend to behave in a manner consistent with what they *believe* to be true. This sense of inner sameness helps us to synthesize behavior, self-concept, and belief systems to maintain unified self-images. Our beliefs and expectations largely determine how we think and act. We predict, guided by past experiences, what effects our behavior will have on both things and people. People who see themselves as humane and compassionate and who believe that others have these same qualities often trust and believe in the goodness of others. *Thus consistency or inconsistency will be expressed when we communicate with others.*

Many of us have experienced being the victims of our own actions, particularly habitual behavior. We think one way while repeating a habit that indicates its opposite. Recognizing these conflicts and coming to terms with them can help us to avoid saying one thing and doing another. We can also learn to accept the fact that *actions, thoughts, and feelings cannot and need not always be consistent.*

Another area of inconsistency is the **double standard.** When someone else commits a certain act, we may feel they are wrong or bad; but we may find some way of defending ourselves and preserving our self-image if we perform the same act. To make our view of ourselves consistent with our beliefs even when our behavior is not, we make excuses, find extenuating circumstances for ourselves, rationalize, blame others, or find other defenses equally self-deceptive. This continual effort to make one's world view emotionally consistent, even if it is not logically consistent, is called **psychologic.**

Giving and accepting feedback is a valuable way for group members to uncover inconsistencies in their behavior.

- Do actions speak louder than words? If a person does a kind act, is he or she therefore "kind"? What is the relationship between what you say and what you do? Give a personal example.

- Hypocrisy means "pretending to be what one is not or to feel what one does not feel ... acting a part." Tell about a time when you acted a part.

- What do you do when you notice that your actions say one thing and your words another? How do you feel? Give specific examples.

- What do you do when someone says one thing and then does another? How do you feel? Give a personal example.

- Ask your group for examples of discrepancies between what you've said and what you've done. Be conscious of your feelings as you listen to the feedback.

Our behavior depends partially on the changes in our society. We find new words to express behavior as the culture becomes conscious of it. Anxiety as a social problem became popular in the 1950s. The problem of identity became popular in the 1960s. Recently, the subject of apathy (alienation, withdrawal, indifference) has been emphasized. Rollo May says that apathy is the opposite of love. He argues that *love* and *will* both describe "a person in the process of reaching out, moving toward the world, seeking to affect others or the inanimate world, and opening himself to be affected."

May also suggests that violence and apathy are related. "To live in apathy provokes violence; and ... violence promotes apathy. Violence is the ultimate destructive substitute which surges in to fill the vacuum where there is no relatedness." Violence thus flares up as a necessity for contact. To inflict pain at least proves that one can affect somebody. *Hurting others as a way of communicating can be converted to other channels.* As we become more conscious of social changes in behavior, we can have more control over how these changes affect our own behavior.

Violence, even in the form of play, indicates a need to communicate.

Here is a list of behaviors that most people consider to be problems. Use this list as a source of topics for discussion and for the activities that follow:

impertinence, defiance, rebelliousness

disobedience

rudeness, selfishness

lack of reliability

carelessness in work, surroundings, or habits

cheating, lying, stealing

laziness

disregard for material possessions

profanity, obscene talk

cruelty or bullying

smoking, drinking, overeating, other compulsions

suggestibility, overobedience

temper tantrums, bursts of anger

interrupting, talking too much

silence, inability to relate, aloofness, shyness

resentment, expecting others to live up to your needs

thoughtlessness, insensitivity

nervousness, nervous habits

suspiciousness, distrust

excessive criticism of self or others, complaining

To improve communication through behavior, we must become aware of how and what our behavior communicates.

- In your groups, describe the kinds of behavior that irritate you (interrupting, talking too much, giving advice). Does any of your own behavior annoy you?

- Choose a partner. Assess your own *social behavior* and give your partner feedback on his or her social behavior.

  Do you make friends easily?

  Do you get along with the people you live with or relate to?

Are you satisfied with your social relationships?

Are you honestly interested in others?

Do you understand others (teachers, parents, employers) and empathize with them?

Are you more comfortable with people or alone?

- Describe (but do not label or judge) personality characteristics you display (for example, cheerfulness, thoughtfulness, impatience). Notice ambivalent responses—thoughts, feelings, behavior that do not go together. Ask your partner to share his or her observations of what you are saying and doing.

- Describe problem behavior in yourself or others. What behavioral strengths could you use to deal with these weaknesses? Give specific examples.

MOTIVATION AND NEEDS

A **motive** *is a need or desire coupled with the intention to attain a related goal.* Sometimes we are not aware of our desires, intentions, and goals. Some motives may be stronger than others, and some motives are more socially acceptable than others.

Needs and motives, however defined, are substantially influenced by learning and the external environment. Yet individuals are motivated even without external input or biological deficiencies. Most human beings, for example, have a need to be active and to explore new environments. We are energetic, curious creatures. According to this view, all behavior serves to satisfy some needs or drives, either directly or indirectly.

The psychologist Abraham Maslow, in his treatment of motivation, has arranged needs in five levels from "lower needs" to "higher needs" (1 is low, 5 is high):

1. Physiological needs (such as hunger and thirst)

2. Safety needs (such as security and stability)

3. Belonging and love needs (such as affection and identification)

4. Esteem needs (such as prestige, self-respect, achievement)

5. Need for self-actualization

Maslow believes that a lower need must generally be satisfied to some degree before the next higher need can emerge in a person's development—for example, a man does not usually become concerned about his safety if he is starving. Similarly, only after a degree of safety has been attained can a person relate to others with love or affection. Then an adequate degree of belonging allows one to develop esteem and self-respect. And finally, after all these preceding levels have been relatively achieved, a person can develop toward *self-actualization*. The figure below shows Maslow's hierarchy of needs.

We do not complete each step before going on to the next higher one. Rather, these needs behave like a succession of waves, in which different needs gradually shift from one need to another. Yet the natural course of development may go awry if there is insufficient gratification of needs at any given level.

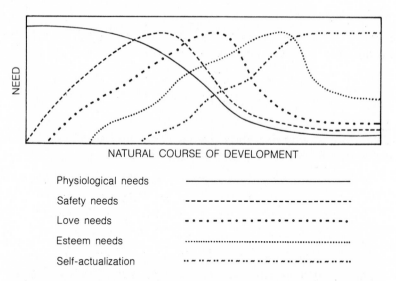

NATURAL COURSE OF DEVELOPMENT

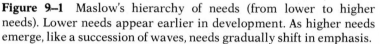

Physiological needs

Safety needs

Love needs

Esteem needs

Self-actualization

Figure 9–1 Maslow's hierarchy of needs (from lower to higher needs). Lower needs appear earlier in development. As higher needs emerge, like a succession of waves, needs gradually shift in emphasis.

For most of us, physical survival and basic safety needs are met. Some of us have experienced love or affection in a family or group. And a smaller number of people have, particularly as they get older, had certain ego-status needs fulfilled. Ultimately human beings move in the direction of self-actualization. Maslow describes certain observable characteristics indicating that an individual is moving toward *self-actualization:*

Superior perception of reality

Increased acceptance of self, others, and nature

Increased spontaneity

Increased detachment and desire for privacy

Increased autonomy and resistance to enculturation

Greatly increased creativeness and frequency of peak experiences

Increased identification with all mankind

Becoming aware of intangible needs is more difficult than becoming aware of tangible ones such as food.

- What motivates you? What are your needs? In terms of Maslow's hierarchy of needs, which needs on each level do you still need to fill?

- In your group, share your needs and discuss this statement: "All needs are relative."

- One psychologist says there are only four basic needs: *security, recognition, response from others,* and *new experiences.* In your group, discuss whether or not each of the needs in the following list could fit into one of these four classifications:

  1. To acquire possessions: property, money, goods
  2. To conserve: collect, repair, clean, preserve things, save possessions, be frugal
  3. To order: arrange, organize, put away objects, be clean and tidy
  4. To construct: organize, build
  5. To achieve: recognition, ambition, power; to do difficult things well and quickly
  6. To exhibit: excite, amuse, thrill others; to attract attention

7. To defend: the self against blame, belittlement, shame, humiliation, criticism, ridicule, punishment
8. To preserve: self-respect, one's good name, pride
9. To dominate: influence, control, persuade, lead, direct, dictate
10. To cooperate: admire, follow, serve, defer to a superior
11. To empathize: imitate, emulate, identify with others
12. To surrender: comply, accept punishment, apologize, confess, atone
13. To obey: be well-behaved, avoid ostracism, punishment, or blame
14. To punish: assault, injure, belittle, blame, accuse, ridicule
15. To be unconventional: unique, different, contrary
16. To be autonomous: resist influence or coercion, defy, seek independence and freedom
17. To affiliate: form friendships, greet, join, live with others, cooperate
18. To love: nurture, aid, protect, help, care for others
19. To seek love: protection, sympathy, help
20. To reject: snub, ignore, exclude, discriminate; to be aloof, indifferent
21. To play: relax, amuse, entertain, have fun
22. To inquire: explore, learn, satisfy curiosity, touch, look, listen, inspect, read
23. To teach: point out, demonstrate, relate facts, give information, explain, interpret, lecture

---

ROLES

In the theater, a **role** is the part an actor presents in a play. It consists of certain behaviors that make the person appear somewhat consistent or whole in personality. In everyday life, roles are created as a response to certain expectations placed on us by other people. When you were born, you were assigned your first role: boy or girl. The roles we choose influence our communication as well as our relationships with others.

We can become more aware, as we go through life, of playing many roles, changing costumes, wearing different hats. In the classroom, we put on our teacher/student hats; at home we put on our parent/child hats; on a date we put on our female/male hats. Each of these roles comes with a set of expectations and attitudes that define us as persons in a relationship. These many sets of behavior can become confusing at times. We often feel a sense of unreality about changing roles when we are in different situations with different people. It is possible to experience yourself as a unique, identifiable, whole person *within* the roles you play when you become conscious of what they are and how they contribute to your social interaction.

A role by definition is a repertoire of behavior patterns in an appropriate context. Roles are inescapable—they must be played or else the social system would not work. In the process of playing roles, however, we may lose ourselves: We may become alienated from ourselves. It is possible to know the self and still act out appropriate roles in appropriate situations. It is also possible to play out a role so successfully that other people do not really know the person playing the role. If we are willing to communicate our thoughts, feelings, beliefs, and experiences to others, then they get to know our real selves.

Deception in relationships often occurs because of **self-deception.** We frequently deceive ourselves while playing deceptive roles for other people. Such deception has its price—we may lose touch with our real selves. Sidney Jourard says: "People's selves stop growing when they repress them. This growth-arrest in the self is what helps to account for the surprising paradox of finding an infant inside the skin of someone who is playing the role of an adult." Alienation from the self not only stunts growth but also prevents relationships. Deception, repression, and alienation take energy and often result in tension and stress. Within each role, however, is a self that can be known, shared, and incorporated within the role.

Every man alone is sincere. At the entrance of a second person, hypocrisy begins.

Ralph Waldo Emerson

Sex roles today are far more flexible than in the past, and we are more free to choose how to express them.

- Circle the words that you feel best represent your sexual identity. Add your own words if you wish.

emotional	soft	logical	hard
inferior	warm	superior	cold
mystical	Yin (left hand)	heroic	Yang (right hand)
passive	intuitive	active	analytical
patient	moon	insistent	sun
home	submissive	work	dominant

- Traditional sexual identities are changing. Lists of male and female characteristics are beginning to intermingle. Write a page describing your sexual identity as experienced with another person in relationship (daughter/son, sister/brother, mother/father, man/woman, husband/wife).

- Write a page explaining as concretely as you can (using examples, illustrations, anecdotes, narrative, or description) how you came to recognize a particular aspect of your sexual identity at a given time in your life.

Traditional sexual roles are becoming more flexible.

TRANSACTIONS: RITUALS, PASTIMES, GAMES

There are other models of interpersonal communication in addition to the drama (role, act, setting). One is based on economic or business transactions. Another uses such terms as computer, channel, transmitter, code, encode, noise, feedback, and other mechanical terminology. Eric Berne's model of communication—**Transactional Analysis**—has three components: Parent, Adult, and Child. The Parent corresponds to one of your own parents or some other authority figure from your early childhood. The Adult is a state of mind in which you make objective appraisals of situations by using thought and analysis. The Child represents those reactions you had when you were very young.

People reveal noticeable changes in posture, viewpoint, voice, vocabulary, and other aspects of behavior accompanied by shifts in feeling that correspond to these three states of mind. **The Parent** enables us to be parents of actual children and to make automatic responses for self-survival. It includes both the protective parent and the critical parent who tells us what is "good or bad" and "right or wrong," as well as what we "should or shouldn't" do. **The Adult** is necessary for survival, for processing data, and for computing probabilities. **The Child** can be the intuitive child— spontaneous, creative, filled with joy—or the "adapted" child who modifies his or her behavior under parental influence and becomes compliant, whining, or rebellious. Each of these states is important and can be balanced within each individual, depending on the situation.

Begin to notice when your thoughts, body postures, and language slip into one of the three states of mind: Parent, Adult, and Child.

- Write down examples of Parent-Adult-Child thoughts and notice how posture, viewpoint, voice, vocabulary, and other aspects of behavior accompany these shifts in feeling states. Note, for example, how shaking the forefinger goes with the Parent; how laughing, giggling, dancing, singing, and joy go with the Child; how thoughtfulness and solemnity go with the Adult. Use the following model for your list:

Parent	Adult	Child
"Don't cry."	"I seldom cry."	"I often cry."
"That's bad/good."	"I ask questions."	"I joke a lot."
"You shouldn't do that."	"My actions have consequences."	"I will do whatever I want."
"I eat what my parents ate."	"I eat what's appropriate."	"I eat whatever I want."
"I never break the law."	"Some laws are inappropriate."	"I break laws frequently."
"Most parties are nonsense."	"I seldom joke at parties."	"I often joke at parties."

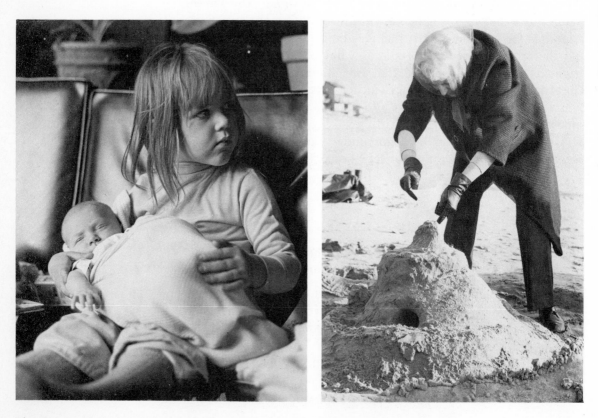

The Parent role is learned as a child. *The Creative Child* exists in us at all ages.

Berne says that when two people get together six states of mind interact. These interactions (see the figure below) can be complementary or crossed. **Complementary transactions** result in further communication; **crossed transactions** usually result in the communication being broken off. Suppose Person 1 says (Adult to Adult), "Maybe we should find out why you've been drinking more lately," and Person 2 answers (Adult to Adult), "Yes. I'd certainly like to know." In this case the communication is complementary. But if Person 2 answers (Child to Parent), "You're always criticizing me, just like my mother," then the transaction has become crossed.

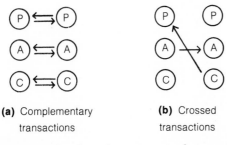

(a) Complementary transactions   **(b)** Crossed transactions

Figure 9–2   Complementary and crossed transactions.

Complementary transactions occur when two people communicate in the following states: Parent to Parent, Adult to Adult, Child to Child, or Parent to Child.

Parent to Parent

Person 1: "The state of the world today is awful. Taxes are impossible, the ecology is bad, and people just won't do anything about it."

Person 2: "You're absolutely right. The welfare system is pulling the country down the drain, crime is getting out of hand, and the government doesn't do a damn thing about it."

Adult to Adult

Person 1: "Do you know where my cufflinks are?"

Person 2: "On the desk."

Child to Child

Person 1: "I'd like to go to the beach today."

Person 2: "Hey! That's a great idea. Let's go."

Parent to Child

Person 1: "Did you remember to take your vitamins today?"

Person 2: "Yes, dear. I did."

Crossed transactions occur when a person speaks to another as an adult and gets a Child-to-Parent response. For example:

Person 1: "Do you know where my cufflinks are?"

Person 2: "Do I wear your cufflinks? How should I know where they are?"

Salesperson: "This one is better, but you can't afford it."

Customer: "That's the one I'll take." ("You can't tell me what to do.")

Complementary transactions in interpersonal communication satisfy our needs for recognition, time structure, social interchange, and human contact. When transactions are crossed, however, communication is short-circuited and needs are not fulfilled.

Berne's theory of communication transactions can offer useful insights to specific relationships.

- Notice some of your transactions this week. Describe in detail an example of a complementary transaction. Was it Parent to Parent, Adult to Adult, Child to Child, or Parent to Child? Diagram it.

- Write an example of a crossed transaction. For example, hearing an Adult comment as a command or criticism might result in a Child response, such as "You can't tell me what to do."

- Notice this week any response to a communication where someone *reacts out of proportion* to the discussion. For example, when another person responds to you in an emotional way which seems inappropriate to what you have said or done, note whether this inappropriate response fits the Berne model of a Child response to the Parent or a Parent response to the Child. Share examples of these communication experiences.

• Watch for *reactions* where someone's "buttons have been pushed"—some seemingly unimportant comment or behavior triggers an inappropriate response. Discuss this experience in your group.

Berne classifies more complex communication transactions into (1) procedures and rituals, (2) pastimes, and (3) games. A **ritual** is a series of stereotyped complementary transactions programmed by society. It includes such things as introductions and leave-taking rituals. The "Hi, how are you?—I'm fine—How are you?" conversation is a stereotyped series of complementary transactions programmed by external social forces.

Pastimes are typically played at social gatherings or before a formal group meeting (such as a class). Talking about cars, clothes, PTA, sports, and travel provides topics that can be classified as chit-chat. Berne labels some such conversations as *General Motors, Wardrobe, PTA, Who Won, How to, How Much, Ever Been, What Became Of, and Kitchen.* People at social gatherings provide structured time and mutual stroking through pastimes. Pastimes also serve as a social selection process for those candidates most likely for more complex relationships (games). Pastimes confirm roles and stabilize positions.

Pastimes or chit-chat are not usually productive for interpersonal communication. Instead of allowing one to share the self, pastimes often function as topics to hide behind. Topics that deal with past history likewise may be used to avoid intimacy. In interpersonal communication, small-group communicating and relating are most rewarding when people respond to each other in the here and now.

In your group, discuss the risks and gains of "here and now" communication. When is it appropriate to use rituals and pastimes?

• Sometimes briefly telling about something significant and emotionally charged that's going on in your life outside of class right now—or something that happened in the past that is very influential in shaping your life today—can help others understand you. In your group, practice talking about a feeling you have *at the moment* and relate it to an outside or past experience. Limit your discussion of external topics to about one-tenth of your whole discussion. (Timing it with a watch may help.)

• Write about your feelings when another person gets into a long discussion about something that happened "then" (in the past) and "there" (in another place). When you get into the past, make your discussion brief and be sure to show how it relates to the here and now.

Eric Berne, in his book *Games People Play*, says that people tend to play out certain "games" in their interpersonal relationships. He says these games have several purposes: to avoid reality, to conceal motives, to rationalize activities, and to avoid intimacy. *These games, if they are not destructive, are both desirable and necessary.* People can achieve a new self-awareness by analyzing their behavior in terms of games—and so learn to live their lives more constructively.

Games *are a series of transactions with predictable outcomes and concealed motivations.* Although every game is basically dishonest, most are often unconscious; and many are necessary because we cannot be intimate, spontaneous, and game-free with all the many people who move through our lives. Here is one of the many games Berne describes in *Games People Play*—*"Why don't you . . ." "Yes, but . . ."*:

Mary: "I am so plain and uninteresting. I never have any dates."

John: "Why don't you go to a good hairdresser?"

Mary: "Yes, but that costs too much money."

John: "Well, then, how about trying some magazine suggestions?"

Mary: "Yes, but I just can't fix my own hair. I've tried."

John: "Well, how about learning some makeup techniques?"

Mary: "Yes, but my skin is allergic to makeup."

John: "Maybe you could take some training in being a good conversationalist."

Mary: "Yes, but I'm always exhausted after work."

Mary is setting John up for the "Yes, but" game. As long as he tries to tell her how to solve her problem, she will continue with answers to prove to him that "he can't tell her what to do" (Child to Parent game). If someone asks your advice and then rejects every suggestion with "Yes . . . but," try saying: "I can hear what you're feeling about that. What do you think you might do about it?"

Another game is *If It Weren't for You,"* also a Parent-Child game. One person plays restricted child; the other plays domineering parent. Berne gives an example: Mrs. White complains that her husband won't let her go dancing. As long as her husband prohibits her, the game proceeds. If he refuses to play and says "Go ahead and go dancing," Mrs. White will experience depression, frustration, and bewilderment. She married him so that he would restrict her and give her the excuse not to go. If he allows her to go, she will find she is afraid of dancing and has social fears. Playing "If It Weren't for You" allows us to avoid feared situations—for example, "If I had not had children so early, I could have been a great dancer." Berne defines and describes about forty games people play. Some people model their entire behavior, communication, and relationships on one or two major games.

The word but *usually cancels whatever precedes it.*

- Choose a partner. Take turns making any statements you like. Use the word *but* in the middle of every sentence. What do you experience as you give and receive "but" statements?

- Take turns making any statement you like. Use the word *and* in the sentence. What do you experience as you give and receive "and" statements?

- In your group, discuss this change in words from *but* to *and.* How do the two different words affect communication?

- Go through your writing. Change the word *but* to *and.* Read the sentence both ways and experience the difference.

Berne suggests that real **intimacy** is based on spontaneous, game-free, candid, aware behavior. He says that awareness, spontaneity, and intimacy may be frightening for the unprepared—for most social interactions we will continue to play games. The procedure of liberation involves obtaining a "friendly" divorce from the Parent voices inside our own heads.

Roles, rituals, pastimes, and games give us an identity; moreover, they structure time and relationships. As forms of communication they are appropriate in some situations with some people, depending upon *intentions*. If we intend superficial interaction with others in a social situation, then rituals and pastimes are appropriate. We cannot be intimate and open with everyone we meet. When these forms of communication work, they are worth perpetuating. When they leave us feeling empty and alienated, we can give them up. *Giving up habitual communication patterns is related to intention and awareness.* Sometimes change happens rapidly simply with consciousness, but most often changing habitual communication patterns comes slowly. As you become willing to trust and risk intimacy, you will be willing to disclose who you are to others. Then you can give up labels, pastimes, and games with those special people for those appropriate times when your *intention* is to create true interpersonal communication.

- What's your label? What kind of behavior are you enjoying? Identify the "racket" or game you play (or someone you live with uses). For example: "I am shy." "I am sensitive." (Please don't hurt me.) "I am stupid." (So don't expect anything.) "I'm bored." The variations are endless: cheerful; critical; happy; helper; loyal friend; impatient; rejected; kick me; no hope; busybody; guilty; I don't know; just my luck; what's the use; trapped; unfair.

- Notice when you and others communicate by using pastimes (talking about cars, clothes, sports, children, cooking, movies, books). It is not necessary to change this kind of communication—simply notice it.

- Games include any *habitual* patterns of communication you use in your personal relationships. Although you can read Eric Berne's *Games People Play* to become more aware of the most common games, you can also become conscious of your own personal communication patterns to see what rewards you gain from structuring your communication. Describe some of these habitual patterns. Think about the "payoffs" for structuring responses with others in a relationship. What do you have to give up to be relatively game-free, candid, and open?

BEHAVIOR CHANGE

Any change in behavior, however slight, represents a break in routine, threatens our established habits, and challenges the familiar attitudes and images we have about ourselves. It demands that we think, examine, decide, or choose new ways. For most people, it is more comfortable to act in the old, safe ways. *We tend to resist change.* Most people prefer to keep old patterns of acting and communicating rather than feel insecure or afraid of what they do not ordinarily experience. Yet beyond resistance to change wait many possibilities for individual development as well as the advancement of humanity. *Change can be an exciting project.*

Many of us decide that our old ways of behaving need to change. There are as many ways to change behavior as there are people. In this book we have briefly mentioned autosuggestion, role-playing, Eric Berne's transactional analysis, biofeedback, and many other approaches. We will now look briefly at the natural process of *maturing, behavior modification, setting goals,* and *visual imagery* as four additional modes of behavior change. Probably most of us change through some unique combination of methods rather than any single one. Yet a clearly *verbalized* intention to change, in combination with a *conscious* choice of methods, communicates through language, thought, and action the desire for self-actualization.

Every act of birth requires the courage to let go of something . . . of all certainties, and to rely upon . . . one's own power to be aware and to respond; that is one's own creativity.

Erich Fromm

The Maturing Process

In theory all living matter has a powerful inherent potential for growth. Erik Erikson says: "If we will only learn to let live, the plan for growth is all there." The implication is that there are natural stages through which each of us grows and matures: physically, intellectually, and emotionally.

Jung said that personal growth is the uncovering of our own unique *individuation* process and that the unconscious through dreams and symbols can give us the inner keys for the goals we need in order to mature. Like a butterfly emerging from its cocoon, the young human being must emerge from the social incubator and learn how to fly. Because of our capacity for awareness, each of us at some age experienced that *existential moment* of awakening: "That was when I first began to think for myself," or "All of a sudden I realized adults were really only people and didn't know all the answers," or "It was at that moment that I realized I had to make my own decisions about my life."

Experiencing the complex process of finding a personal identity unrelated to parents and culture can lead to maturation. Freud, Erikson, and Piaget all studied developmental steps in the human growth process. The growth sequence begins with a moment of *discovery*, followed by the courage to *experiment* and learn, and concludes with some degree of *mastery* over one's own life. Maslow, Rogers, and others believe that human beings are capable of pursuing the highest values and aspirations and reaching higher stages of maturity and growth. On the other hand, B. F. Skinner believes we must be *conditioned* and *trained* to perform at these higher levels.

Behavior Modification

B. F. Skinner, an American psychologist, believes that human behavior can be reduced to a science. He says that laws of behavior must be stated precisely and changes in behavior clearly specified. Thus we can learn to control ourselves. Skinner developed a "science" called **behavior modification** which deals with behavior that is observable. His followers are called **behaviorists.** The behavior modification technique they often use is **operant conditioning** or **reinforcement.**

Although much of the original scientific work done by the behaviorists involved animals as subjects, conditioning has also been studied in education and child development. When a person is rewarded for a certain behavior, that behavior will be repeated. The **principle of reinforcement** states that the results of our actions or behavior determine whether or not we will repeat that

Behavior is reinforced through both subtle and apparent rewards.

behavior. If you smile at someone (your behavior) and they do something nice for you (result), then you will probably smile more at people in the future (repeat behavior). The behaviorists believe that the principle of reinforcement controls just about everything we do.

The term *reinforcement* refers to a reward that a person wants—money, attention, food, being caressed, or something that he or she will expend some effort to obtain. When a baby says its first word, a mother may smile and clap her hands. When a boy in the first grade reads his first words, the teacher smiles, says "good," and gives him a gold star. *Reinforcement is used to shape behavior.* Once the behavior is identified and the reward determined, children can be toilet trained, taught to dress and feed themselves, taught to read and write.

Although human behavior may be more complicated than the behavioristic model suggests, there is a good deal of evidence that behavior modification can change simple behavior. Therefore, let us explore the concepts further.

- Choose behavior or a habit you have that you want to change: for example, overeating, smoking, or taking pills.

- Now choose a "reward" for changing your behavior: for example, make a chart and give yourself a star every time you want to eat, smoke, or take an aspirin and *you don't do it*. The reward might be buying yourself something after you have accumulated twenty-five stars or treating yourself to some activity that costs money. Depending on the behavior you want to change, rewards can be edible (food or drink), prizes (toys, clothes), social (a party, attention).

- Set up an experiment to study the effects of rewards on someone you live with. Write out the behavior you want to change. Without telling the other person, watch for the kind of behavior you want; then reward that person with praise, kisses, hugs, smiles, or some other social rewards. Write up your experiment as follows:
  1. behavior to be changed
  2. reward (love, attention, grades, money, power)
  3. record of times used
  4. result

- Notice effects of punishment or reward in communication feedback given in the class. Write down examples in other classes when a teacher gives recognition either positive or negative to a student, and write down the effects on the student's future behavior.

Goal-Setting

Literally millions of people go through life without knowing who they are, what they want, or where they want to go. Knowing where you want to go involves *setting goals*. The more specific you can be in setting your goals, the more clearly you can define your purpose and the better your chances of arriving where you want to go. *Setting specific goals can direct your behavior.*

Attitudes influence behavior. If you have a negative attitude about reading and writing, a college degree as a goal may be difficult to attain. But sometimes *motivation* or a strong desire to attain a goal can help you get what you want. Another aspect of behavior that helps is *getting involved*. To get the most out of something you must participate. Participating in this class or getting involved with others can make the experience more exciting and rewarding. *Thus behavior can be affected by setting specific goals, by attitude, by motivation, and by participation.*

Some people are **goal-directed**—they set goals and then organize their lives around achieving what they want. Usually these individuals organize their time. They are apt to set up schedules and control their lives to include good diet, exercise, and adequate rest. Usually they develop a degree of self-discipline and flexibility. They don't tear themselves apart if their plans get upset. In fact they often find time to have a little fun too. But for the most part goal-directed individuals exercise control over themselves and their lives.

Setting goals is only one way of changing behavior. People who set clear goals for themselves often feel more centered or "together." Setting goals helps some people make decisions more easily and achieve the kind of success they want. They can often think of alternative ways to reach their goals. Flexibility is an important quality. Whenever goal-directed people get new information, they can change either the direction or the timing of their behavior.

Goals are more real if you write them down. When they are written, you can look at them and plan alternative ways to reach them. You can schedule time in order to reach them. If you rank them by priority, you are more apt to accomplish the major ones. Another good plan is to divide them into short-term goals (for this day or week), medium-term goals (for this year), and long-term goals (five years or longer).

Once you have identified your values, you can set goals and objectives.

- Based on your values, clearly state one of your objectives and

two or three possible actions you might take to reach that
objective. For example: I want to make two new friends this
month. Action:

1. Go to church on Sunday.
2. Sign up for a new class at the college.
3. Volunteer to work on a committee.

- Make a chart of goals. Write in pencil so that you can make
  changes. Date the changes you make. On this chart write these
  headings:

self-development goals   family goals
  (short-term, mid-term, long-term)   things to do
education goals   places to go
professional goals   health goals

- In your group, discuss your goals and the possible actions to
  reach your objectives. Ask for feedback. Are your goals realistic? Are the actions clear and specific?

Using Imagination

We first discussed imagination in Chapter 6 on how the *mind*
communicates. In Chapter 7, on how the *body* communicates, we
practiced relaxation techniques. Review those techniques before
you read further in this chapter. Relaxation may take ten to
fifteen minutes when you are first learning. Practiced visualizers
can relax in a few seconds. Each time you go through a relaxation
exercise you will relax a little more in less time.

Relaxation can help us cope with those morbid fears called
phobias. Many people dread being in confined places or high
places, flying in a plane or driving on the freeway, riding in an
elevator, or speaking before an audience. Each of us has at least
one fear that makes us uncomfortable at times. Imagination can
help us overcome such fears. The first step is to write a detailed
description (as accurate as possible) of the action to be performed. If you are going to take an oral exam, describe the building, the room, the professor, the subject matter, and some of the
possible questions. Write down a complete, detailed account of
the entire scene. Then lie down in a comfortable position and get
as relaxed as possible.

Now vividly *imagine* the scene as if you were actually participating in the test situation. In your imagination, see yourself looking relaxed. Notice how calm your face looks. Allow a feeling of self-confidence to fill you. As you breathe, the air fills you with confidence. Now see the professor asking you questions. (Do not verbalize—use no words.) Notice yourself like a silent movie: your mouth is moving and the words are the right ones. You can tell by the professor's face that you are answering the questions satisfactorily. If you experience any emotional state such as trembling or perspiring, allow that to happen. Anything that happens in your visualization is all right. There is no program here that tells you in advance what is supposed to happen in your visualization. You are an actor. *Visualize yourself acting your part with complete confidence.*

If you repeat this whole session a number of times, you will find that with each repetition your reactions become less intense until they spontaneously disappear or become very weak. This technique has helped many people get rid of all kinds of fears. It can also be helpful before a job interview. Although it takes time, some people have used visualization to lose weight, stop smoking, or break other habits.

One of the key concepts in visualization is that willpower to change behavior often has an *adverse* rather than a beneficial effect. If willpower works for you, you may not need visualization or imagery to change your behavior. If willpower does *not* work, then try imagination. The law of reversed effort, as stated by William James, says that "when the will and the imagination are in conflict, the imagination invariably wins." James cites many cases of people who tried unsuccessfully for years to rid themselves of anxieties, worries, inferiority, or guilt. Conscious effort only drove these people finally to give up the struggle. *Change sometimes happens by surrender and passivity, not activity; by relaxation, not intentness.* James suggests that when you resign yourself, a "greater self," a regenerative self, will take over. Similarly, Carl Rogers believes that when people fully accept themselves and their habits, fears, and emotions, then change occurs. When you try to change through willpower, you are saying: "I don't like myself the way I am. I want to be different." And something inside you says: "No! I won't change. You can't make me." So "the inside" you remains the same.

Visualization and fantasy techniques can also be used to develop an awareness of attitudes toward the self. Self-concepts can be made more constructive, satisfying, and realistic. Most of us feel and behave in accordance with what we imagine to be true. *The nervous system often cannot tell the difference between an imagined experience and a real one.* Visualize a fresh yellow lemon. Feel its skin: somewhat oily and bumpy to the touch. Visualize yourself taking a knife and slowly cutting through the center of the lemon. Now pick up one half of the lemon and rub the inside pulp across your tongue. Feel the juices of the lemon on your tongue, tart and lemony. (You may have salivated while simply reading this passage. If not, visualize the experience in more detail or when more relaxed.)

Realizing that your feelings and behavior are the result of your own images and beliefs gives you the power to change those images. Mental pictures offer you the opportunity to "practice" new traits and develop the self-image that you imagine. Set aside fifteen or twenty minutes a day when you can be alone and undisturbed. Relax and make yourself as comfortable as possible. It helps to have a calm voice speaking these directions. You can use a tape recorder. Make your own tape and give yourself these directions.

Close your eyes and allow your imagination to see yourself as you want to be. Imagine yourself with a great deal of energy and vitality. Visualize yourself with great industry accomplishing some very specific task (clearing out closets, rearranging the kitchen, changing the transmission in a car). *Be as specific as possible.* Picture all the vivid little details. Feel the objects as you pick them up and reorganize them. If you need to use a tool, visualize and feel it. See the colors and shapes. Notice small details, sights, sounds, touch, odors. Create in your imagination the very experience of the way you want to be—filled with energy and feelings of accomplishment. Notice in your imagination how automatic and spontaneous your energy and movements are. Feel the exciting flow of energy and pride that fills you as you look at your completed project. Practice this experience each day for two or three weeks. If you are serious about wanting a behavior change, you will make a commitment to change and self-acceptance will flow into you.

Imagination can help us develop new, desired qualities and roles. Again, use a tape recorder with a tape giving you these directions.

- Enter a state of relaxation.
- Think of a quality you desire: spontaneity, flexibility, serenity, openness, trust, self-confidence.
- Visualize its quality, its nature, its meaning.
- Visualize your face and body as you act out this quality.
- As you act out this quality, experience how glad you feel, how much you value being this way.
- Imagine yourself in a setting that evokes this quality. (Serenity, for example, might be a cool green glade.) Feel the quality and repeat the word several times.
- Begin to identify with the quality. See and feel yourself as if you *were* this quality.
- Tell yourself that you are going to remain like this throughout the day.
- Write the name of the quality on a sign and place it where you can see it daily. Whenever possible, visualize and recall the exercise.

This same visualization procedure with its two stages of relaxation and imagination can be adapted to interpersonal relationships with parents, superiors, mates, children, and others. First, lie on a couch or bed and relax completely. Then visualize yourself in an interpersonal encounter that may arouse fear, anger, aggressiveness, or defensiveness. Then visualize what attitude you would *like* to have in this relationship. For example, imagine yourself looking calm, smiling, being pleasant, feeling confident. No conversation is necessary. Simply see your face and body relaxed, natural, friendly, accepting, trusting, invulnerable. Repeatedly visualize yourself acting and reacting in this relationship the way you want to relate.

This same procedure can be used to modify your attitude toward others. It may take three weeks, fifteen minutes per session, to be able to make and maintain change. But even after a single session the next encounter in a relationship may already be somewhat changed.

Like mental skills, body skills can be developed through imagination. *Research Quarterly* reports an experiment concerning the effects of mental practice on improving skill in sinking basketballs. One group of students actually practiced every day for twenty days. A second group engaged in no practice at all. A third group spent twenty minutes a day *imagining* they were throwing the ball at the goal. All three groups were scored on the first and last days of the experiment. The first group (actually practiced) improved 24%. The second group (no practice) showed no improvement. The third group (practiced in imagination) improved 23%. This research experiment has been duplicated with similar results.

Many professionals in tennis, golf, skiing, and other sports use visualization to develop mind-body coordination. Professional dancers and skaters also use imagery to improve their performances. The Buffalo Bills of the National Football League spend daily "ritual time" with a psychologist who shows them how to relax and visualize their moves on the football field. This *rehearsal in the mind* lets tension peak before the game and then cool down. The players thus mold mind and body in such a way that the mind allows the body to do what it knows how to do best.

Some medical scientists are exploring the role the mind plays in healing. This concept has been called the **placebo effect.** Some patients when given a pill without any drug in it show significant improvement when they believe they are taking a drug. Visualizing drugs without taking them produced a 70% healing result in one experiment with peptic ulcer patients. This experiment did not even include the placebo (fake pill), thus more dramatically illustrating the power of the mind over the body.

Dr. Carl Simonson uses chemotherapy with cancer patients. In addition, he uses therapy with "imagery tapes." Patients begin therapy by answering the question, "What do I want this cancer for?" After a discussion of what they might be gaining by being ill, the patients are shown X rays of their cancer and given the chemical or drug to treat the cancer along with a fifteen-minute tape to play three times a day. In using the tape, patients are first trained how to relax completely. Then they visualize the chemical going down into their stomachs, dissolving, disintegrating, being absorbed into the bloodstream, attacking the white cells, and carrying off the cancer cells and eliminating them. Each week new X rays are taken.

In a high percentage of cases, cooperative patients find there is a slow and finally complete remission of the cancer. The remission rate for those patients who do not use their tapes or otherwise fail to cooperate is remarkably lower. This experiment does not, according to Simonson, imply that cancer can be cured with visualization. However, it does show a high correlation between remission rate and cooperation with the total chemotherapy program. So many variables enter into such research that no cause and effect results can be drawn. On the other hand, if you had cancer, you probably would not care whether the remission was caused by relaxation, hope, cooperation, believing, or the visualization process.

For those individuals who have unsuccessfully tried willpower or logic to change behavior, help may come from imagery, visualization, or fantasy. Moreover, the functions of creativity and

Imagery can be used to develop artistic skills and creativity.

intuition can be developed. These skills are cumulative and require practice, as do verbal and mathematical skills. It is not realistic to expect qualities inherent in right-brain functioning to appear overnight, yet a creative imagination can be worth the time spent developing it. *Evidence indicates that if people are willing to go with the experience, to practice, they will develop ability with imagery and can use this function to be more creative, solve problem situations or relationships, reduce blocks to growth or change, develop physical and artistic skills, increase energy and efficiency, and improve health.*

The study of behavior involves looking at the many ways our behavior is influenced: past experiences, education, physiology, values and attitudes, self-concept, language, habits, motivations, and needs. As a result of these many influences, we have developed certain roles and behavior patterns with others. Once we have brought to consciousness much of the specific behavior we act out, we can make some choices about which ones we want to change. Behavior change can be brought about through will-power, through goal-setting, through imagery and visualization, through punishment and reward, and through autosuggestion.

Whether we are conscious of our behavior or not, what we *do* communicates something of who we are and what we value. Our behavior may or may not be consistent with what we say or think, yet it communicates to others and affects our relationships.

FOR FURTHER READING

Berne, Eric. *Games People Play.* New York: Grove Press, 1964.
Berne shows how our stock responses to certain situations and people result in certain behavior patterns.

Erickson, Erik. *Childhood and Society.* New York: Norton, 1950.
Erickson develops a theory of stages of behavior through which all of us pass depending upon our responses to others around us and their responses to us.

Hayakawa, S. I. *Language in Thought and Action.* New York: Harcourt Brace, 1964.
The author relates the connections between the symbols we use to communicate, our thinking processes, and our behavior.

Maslow, Abraham. *Motivation and Personality.* New York: Harper &
Row, 1954.
> In this book Maslow develops his theory of self-actualization
> based on human needs and motivations.

Morris, Desmond. *Intimate Behavior.* New York: Bantam, 1971.
> Morris describes animal mating and nurturing behavior and
> compares it with human behavior.

Packard, V. *The Hidden Persuaders.* New York: McKay, 1957.
> The author investigates all the many elements in our culture,
> especially those of mass media, that affect our behavior.

Schutz, W. C. *Joy: Expanding Human Awareness.* New York: Grove
Press, 1967.
> Schutz discusses human needs and shows how they can be
> brought to consciousness through certain exercises and
> activities he suggests in this book.

Part Three

Growth through Communication

We began our study of communication with Part One, The Basis of Interpersonal Communication. We found that each of us creates his or her own meaning and through expanded awareness can go beyond our present communicating patterns. We looked at how we create our own realities and our own self-concepts. We explored ways to communicate empathy, support, and validation to others.

In Part Two, Aspects of Communication, we explored how language, thoughts, body, feelings, and behavior communicate. Although we dealt with each aspect in a separate chapter, we do not experience the aspects as separate. In reality, we integrate all the parts into a unified process. The complexities of all these aspects become more exciting as we expand our awareness of the process of communicating.

Now in Part Three, Growth through Communication, we will learn how to grow through loving and caring about ourselves and others in relationships. Much of our growth comes through expanding the process of communication and by resolving inevitable differences. Finally, we will explore different paths to personal growth, how you can choose your own path, and how you can expand your present boundaries in communicating and relating.

Relationship is a process of self-revelation ... in which you discover your own motives, your own thoughts, your own pursuits; and that very discovery is the beginning of liberation, the beginning of transformation.

J. Krishnamurti

10

Communicating in Relationships

CLOSE RELATIONSHIPS

In Chapter 4 we discussed communicating with others. In this chapter, we will explore communicating love, caring, and empathy in *close relationships.* The ability to communicate these feelings can lead to intimacy and constructive communication. *It is essential in close relationships for individuals to make commitments or agreements in building and maintaining these relationships.*

We have many reasons for interaction with others. We share our ideas, and we attempt to change attitudes and influence behavior. And since human beings are social animals we want love and affection; we want to interact simply to enjoy the company of other human beings. Underlying every relationship, regardless of its purpose, is the communication process.

Each of us searches for others who will understand us as unique individuals and be attracted to us for what we are. When we are truly understood, we feel satisfaction, trust, and relief from loneliness. We perceive that the other person experiences what we experience and accepts us. At rare times we even feel at one with a person who affirms our own reality.

Feeling understood is one of the great rewards of interpersonal communication.

• Recall a time when you felt that someone really understood you. Try to determine the one person who understood you better than anyone else. It is *not* necessary that the person understood you for a very long time or still understands you now—it is only necessary for you to reexperience that feeling. Try to determine what it was about yourself, the other person, or the situation (or any combination of these) that made this understanding take place.

• A gift you can offer another person is the experience of "really feeling understood." Recall a time when you contributed this feeling to someone else. What was it about you, that person, or the situation that fostered the experience?

• Recall a time when you felt *misunderstood.* What in that situation contributed to the feeling?

• Recall a time when another person felt angry, hurt, confused or alienated by your lack of understanding. What were the dynamics of that situation?

When we feel misunderstood, we often become frustrated, confused, rejected, or angry. When others misconstrue what you think or say or feel, they act in a way that says *you are not coming through the way you think you are.* Often you may feel judged or criticized.

When someone doesn't agree with us or see life the way we see it, we often feel that person is "against" us. By acknowledging that people can think differently and see reality differently and still like us as individuals, we can avoid feeling that we are disliked. *And, by acknowledging that misunderstandings are a common occurrence in daily communication, we may be able to minimize their effects on our interpersonal relationships.*

We want others to confirm us—to help us in constantly rebuilding our self-concepts and relationships. Communication plays a primary role in building a relationship; therefore, we try to avoid communication breakdowns which jeopardize relationships. Most of us would like to be able to build the best possible human relationships. Improving interpersonal communication contributes to this goal.

Examining relationships helps us learn how they have influenced our lives and how to develop relationships that produce growth. First impressions tell us about ourselves.

- What do you notice first when you meet someone (age, sex, shape, height, color)? What do you notice about movements, posture, voice, eye contact, clothes? Do you notice yourself coming to certain conclusions rapidly? On what do you base conclusions about people?

- When meeting a person for the first time, note how you start a conversation. Do you usually allow the other person to begin? Notice the content of your opening conversations. Notice the balance of time each one talks. Do you identify yourself as a speaker or a listener?

- Write a description of a person you meet for the first time. What details have you selected to write about?

- After meeting someone, write down the dialogue that took place. How well do you remember conversations? What makes some conversations more memorable than others?

- Write descriptions of someone you like and someone you do not like. What do these descriptions tell about you?

Relationships vary greatly, depending not only on the individuals involved but also on the social rules.

- Do you and those with whom you share a relationship play by rules? What rules?

- What do you think are the differences among your relationships with the following?

  a person of the opposite sex
  a person of the same sex
  your parents
  a person who interviews you for a job
  an authority figure (boss, teacher, doctor, counselor)

  How do the rules differ?

SELF-IMAGES IN RELATIONSHIPS

Our images of ourselves and others affect our communication in relationships. I have an image of myself, and I have an image of you. You have an image of yourself, and you have an image of me. I have an image of how you see me; you have an image of how I see you. The functioning of our relationships depends on how these six different images are attuned to one another. Discrepancies tend to produce tensions in our relationships. Sometimes people adjust to these distortions and develop patterns of relating. But distorted images of either oneself or the other person often result in communication breakdowns.

"I'm afraid."
"She's friendly."
"I think she thinks I'm stupid."

"I like people."
"He's attractive."
"I think he likes me."

All of us have images of ourselves and others and of how others see us.

Paradoxically, in order to develop and maintain a sense of personal identity, people need to relate to others. Relationship communication is based on statements that include messages about the two speakers. The purpose of communicating in a relationship is not simply to exchange information but to include human involvement with other persons that ultimately affects who we are. In relationship communication, a person is saying: "This is how I see myself. This is how I see you. This is how I see you seeing me." In the process of talking about another person, what we say often tells more about ourselves than about the other person.

Images in relationships affect the content of our communication.

- Write about one of your relationships. "This is how I see myself with this person. This is how I see that person. This is how I think that person sees me." Check out your perceptions with that person by having him or her describe these three images in writing.

- Ask several of your classmates to write a few sentences describing you and themselves in terms of the six images in a relationship. In return, write telling them how you see each of the six images. Compare and discuss these images.

Martin Buber said: "I discover who I am through exploration of all the relationships of my experience, for I am created only in the experiences of those relationships." And all our relationships strongly influence our individual growth and development. As we relate to others, we learn not only about them and their reality but also about ourselves and our own perceptions, responses, attitudes, and values.

Much of the information we have about ourselves comes from our interactions with others. Sometimes we tell other people what we know about ourselves. This *shared* information then becomes known to others. Some things about ourselves we decide not to share; some secrets we keep *hidden*. Often we have *blind* spots about ourselves: Sometimes we cannot bear to look at our feelings or admit to ourselves what we are doing or what our real intentions are. Yet others can sometimes see our self-deceptions or what we are not willing to look at. And, finally, we must accept that some parts of us will always remain *unknown*. The following excerpts from a student's journal illustrate these four areas of open and closed self-knowledge:

I share a lot with my husband. He probably knows about 70% of me. I hide about 10% of me. I don't know how much is unknown to both of us; but my husband often knows when I'm about ready to "blow up," even before I get there. I guess everyone has some areas of "self-deception" or some areas they just are not willing to see.

I don't share much with my teen-age son. I don't think he wants to be burdened with my feelings or thoughts. He probably doesn't know more than 30% of me. It's partly my fault for not sharing. I hide a lot; and because he doesn't know me he can't help me much with my "blind spots." But he *thinks* he knows me, yet the picture he has is really not me. My *not sharing* contributes to the problem.

Evaluate three different relationships you have in terms of what is shared, *what is* hidden, *what is* blind *(to self), and what is* unknown *(to both) in each relationship.*

We can increase our self-knowledge by sharing and opening ourselves to others. When others know more about us, they are better able to give us feedback about our blind spots. Sometimes we cannot admit to ourselves that we feel hurt or pain. A person may say loudly, "I don't care!" But an observer can tell from the tight muscles in face and neck or from the loud, clipped voice that the speaker really does care. *Self-exploration through relationships can help us experience ourselves as our own creators and accept the responsibility for what we are creating.*

To be out of touch, to be unable to feel, to avoid close relationships, is to be unable to communicate. Communication is an act of will and love, a sharing of self with others. It takes courage to trust and risk self-disclosure. To dare self-exploration requires bravery.

When we are communicating with others, we are more or less aware of the process: sensory awareness, thoughts, feelings, intentions, and actions. A woman talking to a friend sees that he is continuing to turn the pages of his magazine. What she sees is the sensory input. Her interpretation of his behavior can be varied:

Thoughts

"He's trying to avoid me."

"He doesn't want to listen to me."

"He is not interested in what I have to say."

"He's angry with me."

(Or she may be unaware of what she is thinking.)

Feelings

"I feel ignored."

"I feel upset."

"I feel hurt."

"I feel a mixture of these feelings."

(Or she may be unaware of what she is feeling.)

Intentions

"I want to be heard."

"I want attention."

"I want approval."

"I want him to enjoy his book *and* I also want to be heard."

(Or she may be unaware of what she wants.)

Actions

She says: "You are ignoring me."

She walks out of the room.

She says: "I'm talking to you. Listen to me."

She sits down and starts reading too.

She gently closes the magazine and says: "When I'm talking to you and you continue to read, I feel ignored. I want to talk to you and I also can't control your behavior if you choose to continue to read."

We can develop more fulfilling relationships by increasing our awareness of communication patterns.

- Choose a communication experience that occurs between you and another person similar to the example just given. Write a description of what you are sensing (what you see—including body language as well as the situation); your *thoughts* or interpretations of the situation; your *feelings* (which may be a mixture); your *intentions* (what you want); and your *actions* (behavior). What information about yourself does this description give you?
- What alternatives—other choices of interpretation, feeling, intention, and action—do you have in responding to the situation?

You will not want to analyze all your communication processes *all* the time; it would be too complex and time-consuming. But when something important is happening between you and another person, or when you are feeling dissatisfied, identifying your intentions and responses can be helpful. Keep in mind that sensations, thoughts, feelings, intentions, and behavior are all mixed and even contradictory at times. We need to know more about our intentions.

INTENTIONS IN RELATIONSHIPS

We tend to judge others by their behavior and our-selves by our intentions.

Albert F. Schlieder

Often our intentions are disguised or we have lost awareness of them. In Chapter 1, we said that intentions are different from purposes or goals. Purpose implies a direction. A goal is the end result. *Intentions* are wishes that move us toward or away from those goals. *Often behavior provides us with the best clues to what our real intentions are*—rather than what we think or say they are. Intentions, like feelings, are often mixed, and both vary in intensity. Conflicting intentions, thoughts, and feelings often result in confusing communication in a relationship. We need to become more aware of our intentions when they are in conflict so that we can set priorities on them and communicate those priorities to others.

Goals are usually long-range or short-range. *Intentions are usually immediate and short-term—things we want or do not want in a particular context with a particular person.* Since we have no real control over others, we often hesitate to tell each other what we want. We tend to disguise our intentions from both ourselves and others. In language, we disguise intentions by saying "you should" instead of "I want you to." Or we ask: "Would you like to . . .?" instead of "I would like you to . . ." Or we say: "You shouldn't" instead of "I want you to stop."

When we express our intentions clearly, we can sometimes avoid communication breakdowns.

- Choose a partner. Each partner is to express five intentions to the other. Use the following vocabulary of intentions (or add your own words) to complete the sentence "I want . . . you (or myself)":

to reject	to support	to be funny
to ignore	to cooperate	to persuade
to avoid	to praise	to approach
to defend	to be friendly	to clarify
to hurt	to help	to ponder
to conceal	to be honest	to accept

to disregard	to be caring	to play
to demand	to be responsive	to explore
to control	to listen	to share

For example: "I want to help you feel good about yourself" or "I want to avoid you."

- Choose five people with whom you have a relationship. After writing each person's name, write your primary intentions for that relationship. For example: "With John, I want a friend." "With Helen, I want respect and enjoyment."

- Write three statements using *should* or *shouldn't*. Then translate them into "I want . . ." or "He (she) wants . . ." statements.

- Write three questions or statements that are disguised wishes. Then change them to statements beginning "I want . . ."; "I don't want . . ."; "I'd like to . . ."; or "I'd like you to stop. . . ."

- Write three statements that hide intentions. Describe the situations. For example:

  Wife to husband in dress shop: "Oh! Isn't that a lovely dress!" Intention: "I want that dress."

  Husband to wife after dinner: "Margie makes the best pies!" Intention: "I want you to pay more attention to me like Margie does to her husband."

- Using a small card or sheet of paper, draw a symbol representing something you want (a pencil, loan of a book, a vacation, a dialogue, a date). Choose a partner and give him or her the card. The partner then chooses either to give you what you want or not. Discuss how it feels to get what you want. Discuss how it feels to risk having someone say no. Discuss how it feels to have someone choose *not* to give you what you ask for.

DYNAMICS IN RELATIONSHIPS

Many forces interact in the process of relating. In this section we will explore such dynamics as attraction, love, and caring; the degree of intimacy and commitment in a relationship; and methods for confronting differences. Each individual in a relationship is a separate person with unique needs. Moreover, the relationship itself develops into a third force. Therefore three separate needs must be met: mine, yours, and ours. Sometimes these needs or desires come into conflict. In conflict, we have many alternatives. In Chapter 11 when we read about conflict, we will find that we can fight, confront, or run away. Our choices will depend on the dynamics of the relationship.

Relationships go through stages: beginnings, middles, and endings. Each relationship has a life of its own: it is born, it grows, and it ends. Some relationships are brief and others last longer than a lifetime—*death may end a life, but the relationship may continue for a survivor.* A study of relationships includes initiating and forming relationships, making decisions about maintaining or ending them, and determining levels of intimacy and commitment. Most of us are concerned about the quality of our relationships, which are deeply affected by the quality of our communicating.

Loving can cost a lot but not loving always costs more.

Merle Shain

For some people, love is the most difficult feeling to express. To say "I like you" or "I appreciate you" or "I care about you" or "Thank you, I really appreciate your being here" with a genuine expression of pleasure may be more difficult than expressing anger, hostility, or resentment. For many of us, to *accept* feelings of love or affection from another can also be difficult—resulting in feelings of anxiety ("What does he want?"), embarrassment ("Oh, it's really nothing"), or depression ("He's only saying I'm nice, but I'm really not").

Part of our problem is cultural. We have been taught to describe our ideas clearly and accurately, giving examples and illustrations. Our educational system stresses precision in thought. But it does not stress precision in describing our feelings or emotions. One way to express feelings verbally is to name and own them—for example, "I feel warm toward you" or "I feel embarrassed." Another method is to use a metaphor—"I feel trapped," "I feel cornered," "I feel stepped on," "I feel light as a feather." A third way to express emotion verbally is to tell what kind of *action* the feelings suggest—for example, "I feel like giving you a big hug" or "I'd like to kick you" or "I'd like to smash him."

Actually we do not have a great number of ways to express our feelings verbally. Nonverbally, we can touch, hug, smile, frown, kiss, or hit. And through action we can show we care about people by fixing their cars, making their favorite dessert, buying them presents, or simply spending time with them and listening to them. Thus we can learn to express feelings *verbally, nonverbally,* or through *action.*

We can learn to express all feelings *constructively* in the here and now. It is easier to express feelings we had in the past about someone who is not present ("I really did love John"). The more distant and remote the feelings, the more comfortably they can be discussed. It is most difficult to express concern or appreciation directly to someone at the moment we experience our feelings because *self-disclosure involves the risk of rejection.*

Moreover, feelings may imply a demand or some kind of control. "I love you" can mean any of the following: "I desire you," "I want you," "I want you to want me," "I want to love you," "I want you to love me (or admire me, feel comfortable and safe with me)." Or it can mean "Please accept me as I am" or "Please like me."

Ease of expressing feelings is related to distance: distance in time (past/present) or space (person here or not here). The most difficult feelings to express are those in the here and now—directly to the face of another person. The following statements represent different levels of difficulty, beginning with the easiest, in the expression of feelings:

1. Mary liked John (past; neither person here).

2. Mary likes John (present; neither person here).

3. I used to like John (past; John not here).

4. I like John (present; John not here).

5. John, I liked you (past; both persons here; person to person).

6. John, I like you (present; both persons here; person to person).

Most of us need experience in directly expressing feelings person to person in the here and now.

- Choose a partner. Tell your partner three things you like about him or her and something that makes you feel uncomfortable with him or her. Then change partners and repeat the exercise with at least three different partners.

- In your group, have each person in turn use one of the following expressions of feeling toward any other person in the
  group. Add or substitute your own words if you wish.

  "I feel annoyed when you . . ."   "I like it when you . . ."
  "I feel anxious when you . . ."   "I feel pleased when you . . ."
  "I feel good when you . . ."   "I feel sad when you . . ."

Falling in love, caring about people, experiencing the warmth
and intimacy of close personal friendships—these are some of the
most exciting aspects of being alive. William James said: "We are
not only gregarious animals, liking to be in sight of our fellows,
but we have an innate propensity to get ourselves noticed, and
noticed favorably, by our kind. No more fiendish punishment
could be devised, were such a thing physically possible, than that
one should be turned loose in society and remain absolutely
unnoticed by all the members thereof." Much of human interaction is based on the liking that individuals have for one another.
Some words that describe interpersonal attraction are *liking, love,
empathy, affection, attachment,* and *fondness.* **Liking** *for another
person is a predisposition to respond toward a particular person in a
favorable manner.*

In a relationship, there are many feelings that need to be
expressed. And expressing warmth results in positive attitudes
toward the expresser. The communication of affection to another
person is desirable and even necessary for our well-being. It is
also one of the major sources of joy in life. But unless you are
clear about what your positive feelings are, you may not be able
to communicate them to others.

Attraction

The study of interpersonal attraction is the study of why people
want to be with a particular person. *Extensive research has
shown that the more two people like each other, the better they
communicate.* Among the variables that lead to attraction, the
most prominent is *proximity.* When you live near or work with
another person, you meet often. The more often two people see
each other, the more likely they are to become friends. Studies in
suburban residential communities and apartments indicate that
residents and neighbors often become friends. *Thus a high correlation exists between physical proximity and attraction.* Perhaps

Attraction usually reduces barriers.

people who expect future contact with another person generally try to be more pleasant. If they meet a person only once, they may not make the effort to begin a relationship. If people believe they will be in contact with another person in the future, they take the time to begin a relationship. They are more attentive, learn to predict the person's behavior, and pay attention to personality characteristics.

Yet we do not make friends with everyone simply because they live within a reasonable distance from us. We choose among those relationships that are the most rewarding. *We are more attracted to people with similar backgrounds, interests, beliefs, attitudes, values, and behavior.* We tend to feel more comfortable with people who act, feel, and think as we do; and we tend to distrust or fear people who are different. Computer dating companies try to match people who have common interests on the assumption that they will get along and enjoy each other's company. One interesting finding is that people like *friends* who are similar, yet people are often attracted to a member of the opposite sex with complementary traits. A dominant person often chooses a passive partner. A highly emotional person may choose a mate who functions logically. *In a mating relationship individuals often choose partners with those qualities they themselves have not fully developed.*

Ultimately, attraction is based on the degree to which the relationship is rewarding. We want to be with people who make us feel good, who support who we are, who make us feel positive about ourselves—we want to be with people who *like* us. These positive feelings need to be reinforced, and we search for people who contribute to a positive self-image. We feel most comfortable with people who feel comfortable with us. We reward each other with positive reinforcement.

When we are with a person whose beliefs are similar, whose interests are similar, who lives near us, and who likes us, we find communicating enjoyable. We tend to translate a person's warmth and friendliness into a measure of honesty and trustworthiness in our relationship. We choose others who are similar in age, experience, religion, status, education, and socioeconomic level. We like people who are like us.

In one research study, people were asked how important physical attractiveness is in choosing a date or a mate when compared to qualities such as sincerity, individuality, dependability, intelligence, personality, and character. Most people ranked physical attractiveness far down the list. Yet these same people bought tickets to a college "computer dance" at which the researchers distributed a questionnaire. When given a choice as to future dates, people continued to prefer those who were physically very attractive. Apparently, what people say and what they want often prove contradictory. Any person can, through dress, diet, and personality, appear more physically attractive.

Both Erich Fromm and Carl Rogers observed a close connection between people's self-evaluations and their feelings for others. Those who are least accepting of themselves find it most difficult to accept people around them. Self-accepting people may attract others into their circle where they too will be accepted. People also like to be able to reach their own goals. If we perceive that others are unlikely to reciprocate acceptance, we will probably turn our affection to someone else. We aspire to achieve realistic goals, so we tend to be attracted to a person who will return our interest for mutual goal achievement.

Interpersonal attraction, then, occurs between people who live near one another, who are compatible and satisfy each other's needs, who find each other physically attractive, and who reciprocate the achievement of a relationship. Interpersonal communication is enhanced through attraction as similarity provides two people with a measure of social reality, an agreement about how objective reality is constructed, and a reinforcement of each other's established ways of structuring experience. *When we relate to others whose construction of experience is similar to our own, interpersonal communication is facilitated.*

Loving

Another dynamic in a relationship is the balance of affection, caring, and love we have for one another. The one human resource all of us have to give, love and caring, may be the most difficult of all to communicate. We often experience confusion, anxiety, and helplessness with the inability to express caring feelings for one another. Some people have great difficulty giving and accepting loving feelings. Our abilities to support and nurture, to accept and value one another, can be developed and will broaden the foundation on which our relationships are built.

No one can become fully aware of the very essence of another human being unless he loves him.

Viktor Frankl

One of the chief features of the experience of loving is the feeling of unity with the other without loss of either person's own freedom or identity. The paradox of love is that letting go— permitting others to be free to go—is the only way we can be freely loved. To love people without needing to change or hold them requires great strength and courage. In *The Art of Loving*, Erich Fromm says that love in our culture is extremely rare. In our capitalistic, Western culture, persons are often used by others as need-satisfying objects, for status or role relations, or as an approving or disapproving audience. Similarly, Freud suggests that almost every intimate personal relation contains sediments of aversion and hostility, and that we use each other as objects that administer pleasure or pain. *Perhaps love is one of those goals toward which we can continue to strive without expecting to achieve its infinite potential.*

Whole books have been written on the subject of love, yet it remains a mystery that defies understanding. Each of us, however, has had the experience of feeling love, either loving or being loved. As a word, *love* has been overworked. Many people today are afraid to use the word. Others use it easily when they mean something entirely different. A child says "I love you, mommy" when he means "I need you." A mother may say "I love you" when she is asking "Please love me." A father may say "I love you" when he means "I want you to do what I say." A man may say "I love you" when he means "I want to possess you." Our desire to possess, to control, to manipulate, to be believed in, to be possessed, and to be controlled is often confused with love. Yet in spite of our difficulties with understanding the spirit of love, the quality of love, and the degrees of love (affection, warmth, concern, desire, caring), *we do know that love is crucial to human life.*

The moment at which two people become intimate—feel unity—is one of the most exhilarating of feelings. Too often, however, this feeling does not last. We can only experience *moments* of oneness. Yet we can learn to make love more permanent. Lasting love is an art that must be learned, according to Fromm, a theory to be mastered and practiced. Love, he says, is an action rather than a feeling.

Ideally, infants receive unconditional love. As we grow, we may experience love either with our own siblings (brothers and sisters) or with other children. Eventually sibling love develops into the kind of love we feel for all human beings—love among equals. Eventually most of us experience erotic love or love for a member of the opposite sex. Erotic love or romantic love is perhaps the most deceptive and puzzling form of love, perhaps the most overpowering, the least understood, the least amenable to control. Each of us may experience romantic love in a different form unique to the self in its interaction with another unique self. *For many of us the most difficult kind of love to learn is self-love.* We want to be free to care for, to respect, to be responsible for, and to know the self.

Parental love, sibling love, erotic love, and self-love are just a few of the kinds of love we can experience. Our capacity for love depends partly on the influence of our culture. Love in America may be a different experience than love in Europe; love in India is not the same as love in Japan. *The influence of culture limits the experiences of individuals and structures the expression of all emotions.*

The word *love* has no fixed meaning. Love is neither static (remaining the same) nor is it absolute (complete and perfect). We all must find our own definitions of the word and create our own experiences. Moreover, we all must be responsible for our own actions in loving and being loved. Even as we experience what love means, the meaning of the word will change, our feelings will change, and consequently our actions expressing love will change.

Love may be the single most difficult feeling to communicate—and the most important.

- How do you define the word *love*?
- What kinds of love have you experienced?
- One person says: "Love involves freedom. If people say they love you and yet deny you freedom, then they do not love you." Do you agree?
- Create some short expressions of love. For example: "Love is letting go."

One dictionary defines love as:

> A powerful feeling of personal attachment; a powerful and absorbing affection for and attraction toward another person which generates a feeling of responsibility for and concern about that person; a tender feeling more absorbing and impulsive an emotion than friendship or affection.

Actually love is a matter of emotion and experience rather than definition. And few of us express love every time we feel it. Yet words are an integral part of the give and take of love. Words are, of course, no substitute for loving deeds. No matter how you express love, if your actions are selfish, thoughtless, cruel, dishonest or unjust your expression of love is sure to be unconvincing. But words are an essential complement to actions.

A surprising number of people, especially men, cannot express feelings of love because that expression involves risk. Yet without communication, love faces a precarious future. We need to be able to use words to communicate love fully and effectively. Because love is never static, we need to share its development with those we love. We need a richer vocabulary: *love, adore, need, want, cherish, treasure, appreciate, enjoy, value.* We need to convey that the one we love is *interesting, attractive, intelligent, sensitive, warm, enchanting.* Such words as *dear, dearest, darling, loving, lovable, honey, sweetheart,* and *love* can be used. We need to tell loved people that they are *generous, affectionate, tender, practical, strong, determined, efficient.*

Expressing love is an effective way to build love.

- Make a list of words, beginning with those just listed, that reflect the way you feel about those you love. Use them to write a love letter. Begin to build a vocabulary that can be understood and used by you and those you love.

- Write a love letter to yourself using the vocabulary you wish someone might use to express their love for you.

- Discuss different definitions of love with your group.

- Discuss the feelings that prevent your telling someone you love them (rejection, feeling foolish, being afraid of insincerity).

All people have a tremendous striving for love, appreciation, companionship; yet we set up barriers to prevent us from giving these gifts and receiving them. Love often produces feelings of anxiety and fear—the fear of being dependent on someone else who may in the end reject us or leave us. Most of us experience ambivalence, feeling love and hate for the same person at the same time. A need for love creates a trapped feeling, which often results in resentment and hostility. Such conflicting feelings must either be resolved or tolerated. Eric Hoffer, a San Francisco longshoreman, says: "It is easier to love humanity as a whole than to love one's neighbor. . . . Some persons genuinely vowed to the service of mankind are full of loathing for the people they live and work with. . . . We cannot love our neighbor unless we know that, on the whole, the world treats us better than we deserve."

Love is usually experienced as a mutual pleasure in being with someone, a desire for fuller knowledge of one another, a yearning for mutual identification and personality fusion. People want to love one another, but they do not always know how. Frustrated and starved for a word, a touch, a smile, a shared experience that will satisfy this universal hunger, many people try feverishly to fill the void. Some people become so afraid they cannot give or receive love that they isolate themselves. But an isolated existence can become an unbearable prison: we need to unite in some form with others. *We are not only afraid of rejection but also afraid that love won't last. Yet perhaps our greatest fear, conscious or unconscious, may be that we do not have the capacity to give love.*

There are many theories about love. In *The Adjusted American: Normal Neurosis in the Individual and Society*, Snell and Gail Putney say that love is "neurotic," a desire to possess and be possessed. Putney denies that love is a need. He believes that our primary need is to have an accurate and acceptable self-image that must be expanded and verified through association with others. Similarly, Karen Horney says that people who are neurotic use love as assurance against anxiety.

A sense of personal worth—a positive self-image—is essential in giving and receiving love. Self-esteem comes through interaction with others. *People who feel they are worthy of love can usually accept and give it.*

Caring

Caring is a process. It is a way of relating to ourselves or someone else that involves development, time, trust, and a qualitative transformation in the one who cares. Caring for others helps them grow and actualize themselves. We all need someone to care for and someone who cares about us. Perhaps even more important, we need to care for and take care of ourselves.

Taking care of ourselves is different from self-indulgence. We must care for ourselves in a way that appreciates the possibilities of our world and the choices we must make. Some philosophers believe that caring in this way is at the center of human existence. Indeed, if we do not care, we, in effect, give our choices to others and let them decide for us. Taking *care* of our own language, thoughts, bodies, emotions, and behavior, must precede our ability to care for others.

We may care for ideas, an ideal, or a community. Caring creates order in our values, activities, and lives. Instead of merely drifting, when we care about something we have "a place" in the world. We are at home—not through dominating or explaining or appreciating, but through caring *about* something. Caring and being "in place" provide a fruitful way of thinking about the human condition. When we care about *something, ourselves,* or *someone else,* we find focus and meaning in our lives.

When we care about other people, we experience them as having potential and the need to grow—as having a worth in their own right. We do not impose our own values on them. Rather, we allow them to find their own directions, to develop values that will best guide them in their lives. When we commit ourselves to others and to their unforeseeable future, we may experience great anxiety for their welfare. Nevertheless, we are consistent and persistent in our support of them even under unfavorable conditions. To help them grow, we encourage them to care for something or someone apart from themselves and apart from us. Caring involves helping them to find and create their own interests. We encourage them to care for themselves, to be responsive to their own needs, to care for and be responsible for their own lives.

We cannot care for everyone because our lives are limited. Because we acknowledge that we will die—that our time is limited—we must selectively care for certain individuals. Milton Mayeroff, in his book *On Caring*, lists seven major ingredients of caring. First, he says, *knowing* is essential. To care for others, we must know them, their powers and limits, their needs and modes of expression. We must also know our own powers and limitations. Second is *patience*. We must allow others to grow in their own time and their own way. Caring includes tolerance of confusion and floundering. Third is *honesty*. We must see ourselves and others as they really are. Fourth is *trust*. We must trust others to make mistakes and learn from them. Trusting is letting go. It includes risk and a leap into the unknown. Fifth is *humility*. We commit ourselves to learn from our own mistakes and limitations. Then we are willing to learn more about other people and what caring involves. Sixth is *hope*. We hope for the growth and possibilities of the others, for their realization through our caring. And finally is *courage*. Since we have no guarantee of the future, we cannot know what will happen. Caring gives us courage to go into the unknown, to risk exploring, and to accept what ultimately happens. Thus the major qualities of caring are *knowing, patience, honesty, trust, humility, hope,* and *courage.*

Caring may or may not be reciprocated. In a friendship, caring is usually mutual. In a hierarchy relationship, such as that between parent and child or teacher and student, caring may not be reciprocated all the time. Sometimes we blunder or lack interest and sensitivity. Self-interest or distraction may affect our ability to care. *Yet we can only fulfill ourselves by serving someone or something apart from ourselves.*

Caring gives order and meaning to life. Caring enables us to experience commitment and involvement. People who move toward greater realization of their own potential become less preoccupied with *self*—with feelings of guilt, fear, and anxiety—and become involved with living in a broader sense. *Authentic concern involves a willingness to make commitments, to let things matter—to care.*

Interdependence

Another dynamic in a relationship is the balance between independence, dependence, and interdependence. As long as we are in a relationship, we depend on each other. To some degree, I depend on you and you are dependable. To some degree, you depend on me and I am dependable. As I change each day, my dependencies and dependability change. I must also be aware that you will change likewise. *Each day we must balance our mutual giving and receiving.*

Human beings do not relate well when one person does most of the giving and the other most of the taking. When we get too far into debt to another person, we are not at peace with ourselves. Our relationship must be reciprocal to some degree. Reciprocity cannot be measured, but it can be experienced over a period of time. I may feel vulnerable when I depend on someone since I must trust the other person to be dependable. Conversely, being dependable makes me feel strong, as the other person learns to trust me. In our mutual dependence and independence, we become interdependent. When we balance back and forth on this seesaw, at times experiencing dependence and dependability, independence and freedom, we experience a fair interchange of giving and receiving in a mutually interdependent relationship.

Dependency can be used to gain control over another. A child can tug the strings of responsibility, a lover the strings of sympathy, a spouse the strings of guilt so that the puppet will dance. Relationships without strings allow people to act the way they *feel* like acting toward each other. Most of us do not want others to do anything for us out of responsibility, sympathy, or guilt.

Independence in relationships allows us to be who we are. Carl Rogers asks: "Can I be secure enough in my own person that I can allow the other person to be?" When both parties can interact in such a way that each is free to become independent, each person is allowing the other person to grow. Unfortunately, many of us do not feel secure enough to allow others to be independent. It requires courage to allow others to be who they

In any relationship in which two people become one, the end result is two half people.

Wayne Dyer

since feeling is first
who pays any attention
to the syntax of things
will never wholly kiss you.

e. e. cummings

are. Yet when we allow others to be themselves, we can achieve greater intimacy. When people place demands on each other or manipulate each other, their relationship suffers. When a person says "I need you," he or she partially denies the other person the freedom necessary for a relationship to exist, and even denies his or her own freedom. When we allow the other person the independence to choose to be with us or *not* to be with us, then we can be together because we want to be together. When I say "I want to be with you, and you are free to choose to be with me," then intimacy in a relationship is possible.

Intimacy

In addition to some degree of interdependence, relationships involve varying degrees of intimacy, involvement, and commitment. At different times in our lives, we all want more or less closeness, more or less privacy. Some people choose isolation over intimacy because of the risks involved in becoming intimate. Some feel fulfilled by one intimate relationship; others can handle several at a time. We can be intimate friends, lovers, marriage partners, siblings, or classmates. Friends share intellectual and emotional closeness. Lovers share physical intimacy. Ideally, marriage partners share intellectual, physical, and emotional intimacy. In many successful marriages, however, these three kinds of intimacy are not equally present at any given time. One of our greatest problems with relationships is catastrophic expectations—unrealistic expectations that destroy intimacy. *Perhaps we cannot expect one relationship to fulfill all the intimacy needs of both partners simultaneously.*

Intellectual intimacy includes words, ideas, roles, games, and language. Although intellectual game-playing may be appropriate at a social gathering or professional meeting, between two individuals it can become a problem. Being aware of roles gives us the option to choose when to play them in relationships. The roles of teacher and student, for example, can be reciprocally fulfilling when the intellectual needs of both are met. In such situations, intellectual intimacy can be very exciting.

Physical intimacy begins with the friendly touch of a hand, a warm hug, a soft caress. It can be the same nonsexual touching we experienced in childhood, or it can be sexual. All physical touching, proximity, hugging, and caressing fit somewhere on the continuum of physical intimacy.

Intimate relationships are characterized by strong physical, emotional, and intellectual bonds.

Emotional intimacy includes trusting and disclosing one's feelings to another person. To express feelings honestly and to be accepted unconditionally and nonpossessively results in feelings of self-worth. The attainment and maintenance of emotional intimacy is a process that requires constant attention, time, and energy.

In class interaction, students can experience differing levels of intellectual, physical, and emotional intimacy with other members of the class. We cannot strive for intimate relationships with everyone we meet. Nor do we want to. Self-disclosure may not be appropriate for someone who does not want to interact intimately. To be effective or desirable, self-disclosure must be subject to the situation, the goals of an interaction, and the nature of each individual. These different kinds of intimacy will be experienced differently by each individual depending on the relationship. As a group becomes larger, the degree of intimacy changes. *The deepest and most intimate relationships usually exist between two people.*

It is possible to experience *one-sided intimacy* in the process of disclosing the self and trusting the other person, but the most satisfying intimacy is a two-sided experience with both parties involved. Because human beings differ in their values and goals, each will express and experience intimacy differently. If intimacy is one of my basic goals in interpersonal communication, and I want to be closer than my partner wants to be, I can allow my partner privacy. And I will hope that my partner will allow me to express intimacy without assuming that I am manipulating him or her to do the same.

When we achieve intimacy, our need becomes satisfied. Then we usually wish to move away into a space of our own. This skating back and forth between closeness and distance is rarely coordinated between two individuals. At times, the conflict between our differing desires for intimacy can become a problem. When those desires are communicated verbally—with no strings attached, with no demands for satisfaction—the mere process of verbalizing can result in a release of tension. *Communication that facilitates intimacy includes acceptance, disclosure, trust, confirmation, and interdependence.* Most of us can handle intimacy only a small part of the time. Yet moments of intimacy, of mutual caring and understanding, enrich both our lives and our relationships.

We all need some intimate contact with others in our lives.

- Write about your most intimate relationship at this time. What is the balance of physical, intellectual, and emotional closeness?

- Write about another satisfying relationship that is not as intimate.

- Describe a time when a person wanted to "open up," disclose, or share with you, which made you feel threatened or defensive. What was being threatened?

- Describe a time when you wanted to get close to another person and that person became defensive. Was that defensiveness appropriate?

- To what degree in your life at this time is intimacy one of your values? Describe, define, or give examples of the kinds of intimacy you would like to experience or have experienced.

COMMITMENT AND AGREEMENTS

To commit oneself to a relationship means to bind oneself by pledge or assurance to another. The act of committing or agreeing to a relationship often occurs simply on a feeling level without being verbalized or defined except by marriage or contract. A mutual agreement usually comes about as a harmony in feelings. *Agreements range from mutual feelings and implied understandings to binding obligations.*

Today many people seem less willing to commit themselves—perhaps because values in the culture itself are in such rapid transition. Yet each of us must deal with commitment. Sharing our definitions of commitment in a relationship can help us clarify our intentions and express our wants to others.

On some level, most of us make commitments to something or someone. A teacher makes a commitment to a class for a semester and the student does the same. When a student drops a class, he or she breaks his commitment. When two people marry, they make a commitment to the marriage. If they decide to break that commitment, the law provides the legal procedure of

Commitments range from implied understandings to legal obligations.

divorce. In business, certain procedures often prevail for the breaking of a contract. Commitments are usually made with the *intention* of keeping them for some period of time or until some objective is accomplished.

Commitments that are made informally without verbal agreement often cause discomfort when the parties involved have different perceptions about commitment. Yet we often hesitate to ask for verbal confirmation of a commitment; we rarely make formal commitments in writing when entering a relationship. When a child is born, we *assume* the parents make a commitment to support that child financially, physically, and spiritually until the child reaches adulthood as legally defined. But the dynamics in that unwritten commitment include the relationship between the parents as well as the relationship between each parent and each child. Ultimately commitments are a pledge made at a particular time with the intention to fulfill certain stated objectives. *As time, people, and situations change, commitments change.*

Each of us values commitments differently. Some people believe that commitments are made for "life" and must be kept regardless of the consequences. Others believe that all commitments, made with the intention of keeping them, can be changed as circumstances change. No one can be forced to keep a commitment. Keeping commitments is a matter of individual choice.

Commitments can be valuable and productive in relationships. Yet they are costly. They must be performed in a spirit of love and choice, not duty and obligation. When either person feels that his or her separate identity is being submerged in the commitment, then rebellion, frustration, or depression may be felt. Often when one person feels less committed, the other person feels the effects. Such a period of pulling apart can be a time to reevaluate and renew the commitment in a different form.

Every relationship goes through cycles of satisfaction and dissatisfaction. These cycles bring moments of tension and anxiety. Most of us are frightened by change from a safe, stable situation. We have difficulty shifting to an outcome which is uncertain. But these shifting moments of uncertainty can be "gifts" to the relationship—keeping it from becoming stale, dull, or too predictable. We can move out from a secure base to find ourselves. We can destroy the former comfort of an old commitment which is no longer appropriate. As both people grow and change, their commitments change.

Any commitment to a relationship restricts freedom. *Relating and caring require some submission of individuality for mutual gain in the form of physical and emotional nourishment.* A commitment is made by choice and needs to be renewed continually. Neither person is obligated to a relationship—only to be true to themselves. A relationship takes time, space, and energy. It cannot provide personal meaning or prevent feelings of loneliness. That is not its purpose. A relationship is a "place in time" to share, by *mutual* consent, and to celebrate the joys and sorrows of life with someone who cares.

Our struggles to be close yet free, intimate yet autonomous, dependent yet independent—all at the same time—present us with conflicts in our human relationships. We need human relationships to cope with loneliness, to satisfy our desire to be nurtured, and to experience intimacy and sharing. We need distance from others to satisfy our drive to be productive, to find self-esteem on our own, to satisfy our need for freedom, to function as individuals, to enjoy the virtue of self-interest, and to satisfy the need for privacy.

To make room for ourselves and still have room for others requires decisions that test the intimacy-autonomy relationship. Relationships grow when people enjoy each other's differences. In any relationship that matters, the struggle between intimacy and autonomy exists. How each person handles these conflicts affects the relationship. And each person must take responsibility for the ways in which he or she chooses to relate.

Commitments in relationships can be equal or unequal. Probably all commitments are by nature unequal since no two individuals are alike. If you say "I'm not going to be committed because he isn't equally committed," then commitment gets lost and feelings become defensive. You can choose to say, "I care for you and am more involved with you than you are with me at this time." To be able to enjoy your own commitment because it is freely given and freely experienced often results in the other person coming closer to you. When your partner is free to choose a comfortable degree of commitment, both parties can experience more enjoyment. *We can experience and be comfortable with unequal commitment.*

Think about and discuss these commitment issues:

- What does commitment in a relationship mean to you?
- How do you feel about formally agreeing to commitment? Informally agreeing?
- Describe three relationships in which you have experienced different levels of commitment.
- Discuss commitment with one person in your life today and find out what it means to him or her. How do your definitions of commitment differ? Discuss the issue of unequal commitment.
- Do you find that you make a greater or lesser commitment to a relationship than the other person? How does this imbalance affect you?
- In class discuss commitments between teacher and students; among the students; between your group and the whole class; and other relationships that are applicable.

If after thinking and talking about commitments you want to make verbal or written agreements in a relationship, certain steps can be followed. But keep in mind that every agreement needs to be updated to go with change and growth. Adjustments must be made. Jot down your thoughts about the relationship. Get to know what you want from the relationship and ask for it. An hour each week can be set aside to talk about the relationship. An anniversary can be celebrated by discussing the growth and changes in the individuals in a relationship.

In reevaluating a relationship, begin by spending time alone. Write down what you want from the relationship, what you want for yourself, what you want in life. Write down your needs, wishes, goals, values, attitudes, and biases. Write down your concerns: what you want, what you're afraid of in the relationship, what problems you foresee. Ask your partner to do the same.

Then set aside some time to discuss your lists together. The purpose is to allow each person to support the goals and opinions of the other person; to find a common ground; and to understand differences. Don't pretend to understand something you do not. Don't pretend something is unimportant to you. Go over items and ask questions: How much does this mean to me? Do I really need this? How long have I wanted this? Why haven't I gotten this before? *A relationship, however intimate, is subordinate to the self.* If either individual is not fulfilled in the relationship, it cannot be a good relationship for the other person.

Agree on broad goals—for example, continued growth and development as individuals, equal sharing of responsibilities, and individual rights: to grow, to be yourself, to have privacy, to be trusted, to be respected, to be happy, to be free, to defend yourself. *A relationship has no rights; only the people in it have rights.* Neither person gives up individual rights in an agreement. Add your own individual goals: loving and being loved; constancy, dependability, support; continuing intimacy. Some agreements should be specific—division of labor or roles, use of money (each may contribute to the mutual support of the household or the relationship), and territory (time and space). Mail and phone calls may be private, for example. Make your privacy needs known.

Sexual fidelity is an especially sensitive area for agreement. Although fidelity is not a reasonable standard for defining a relationship, both partners may choose to restrict their sexual activity for life. However, many people reach that decision only after experiencing other realities and other people. The best relationship is one in which individuals have *the right* to experience anyone they choose, but choose instead to intensify their relationship with each other. No "new" person can be a threat to a really growing relationship. To demand or promise to be "true" will not change feelings. Laws cannot regulate feelings. The basis of love is that it is freely given. To love is to care about the feelings of another person as you do about your own. The constancy of affection, the dependability of emotional support, the sharing of feelings, experiences, and thoughts—all can be enjoyed at the same time you give space, time, and freedom to each other to grow and change, to be yourselves, to be happy, to love whomever you want. When sex takes on a meaning far beyond its worth, the relationship suffers. Infidelity is feeling that the other person is no longer special to you. Sexual fidelity develops by choice, not by trying to own another person. We can learn to respect without idolizing, share without controlling, love without possessing. *A relationship gives each person support and freedom to grow as a creative self.*

One of the most appealing aspects of a new relationship is its newness. The excitement of beginnings, the discovery of another human being, the pleasure of being in love with love and finding new facets of the self—all these things can be preserved in a relationship with the freedom to grow. Continually falling in love, discovering new selves, seeing yourself as not perfect yet lovable, and loving the differences in each other can keep newness alive.

Commitments Change

A relationship is an ongoing interaction between individuals and is constantly in transition. Cultural changes in values, life-styles, and sex roles also alter relationships. As individuals change, they must adapt to changes in their interactions. A relationship changes whether or not the individuals recognize it. Becoming aware of these dynamics can contribute to the relationship. Periodic reevaluation and open communication can result in more satisfaction in the relationship.

A growing relationship is nonpossessive, separate, and supportive. It allows both partners to grow and change—even if that means they need to find new relationships. *Satisfying relationships that last must change.*

People change and grow at different rates and often in different directions. Sometimes all the energy goes out of a relationship—it has run its course. To continue a relationship out of habit or fear of being alone often results in apathy, depression, or discomfort. Sometimes the relationship is over for one person but not for the other. When one person feels the relationship is over, usually it cannot continue in the same form, even though one person may want it to continue that way. *To survive,* the person for whom the relationship is over may have to leave.

Not all relationships can become intimate. Not all people want the same relationships nor the same qualities or depths of involvement. *The development of an intimate relationship requires both commitment and detachment:* a deep involvement and a willingness to let go. If we try to mold a relationship to preconceived expectations, whether personal or cultural, the relationship may wither and die.

Relationships go through many stages: beginnings, middles, and endings. They go through phases that are high and phases that are low. They have periods of compatibility and periods of conflict. And identifying conflicts and working through changes requires successful communication.

People change ... It's a question of finding your own rhythm ... your pulse, your heart's movement, the movements of your soul, all these things combined, create your own rhythm ... If you can find your own rhythm, you find a lot of other things at the same time.

Ingmar Bergman

Open communication is essential in expanding relationships to accommodate personal growth and change.

- Write about the phases through which you have experienced a long-term relationship—for example, between you and one of your parents.

- Describe a relationship that has lasted about a year. Write about how it was in the beginning, the next few months, mid-year, and now. What elements of change do you notice? Ask the other person in the relationship to write about the changes. Share what you have written.

- Describe a relationship you have developed over a period of years. Share with the person how you first perceived him or her and how that perception has changed.

- List ways that seem to make relationships work for you. For example:

  doing things together or simply "being there"
  taking and listening
  touching
  empathizing
  sexual compatibility
  enrichment (sharing knowledge, best qualities)
  commitment to make the relationship work
  more freedom and less structure

Confrontation and Change

In our relationships, we sometimes feel angry with people we love when we think they are behaving in a way that is destructive to themselves, to us, or to other people. We can ignore the behavior of people we do not care about, do not have to live with, or with whom we do not intend to maintain a relationship. Constructively confronting someone you love with your feelings will change the relationship and will sometimes improve it. Such confrontation originates from caring—from involvement—and is a way of expressing concern. *Confrontation is a deliberate attempt to call to another person's attention the consequences of his or her behavior.*

If the person being confronted has the motivation and ability to change and feels secure in the relationship, *confrontation can make a relationship stronger.* Confrontation can be worded as a suggestion or request for a behavior change. The person you are confronting is the final judge of the behavior that is a problem for you. That person may not view the behavior as destructive; may not be willing to change; or may not be able to change at this time.

Confrontation communicates to others your perception of their behavior and should be worded in such a way as to communicate your concern and love. The confrontation can lead to insight and growth. But even if the other person's behavior does not change, empathy and authenticity in the confronter will communicate genuine caring. The confronter must be willing to see the issue as an interpretation—not a fact—and therefore tentative. The confronter must be willing, in the final analysis, to allow others to make their own decisions about their own behavior. The use of *I, me, my,* or *mine* (taking responsibility for your own feelings), *describing* behavior rather than judging it, restating the other person's position, checking perception, and constructive feedback can help you develop ability to confront those you wish to involve yourself with more deeply.

When there is a discrepancy between what others feel about their behavior and how they feel about themselves, you can share your perceptions of this discrepancy. Confrontation also allows you to express your fears constructively for the other person—or your anger with them. The genuine expression of anger, followed by reassurance of concern and warmth, often allows constructive emotional release.

Confrontation means standing face to face. When we talk to other people, their attention often seems to be elsewhere even though we are face to face. We may feel as if we were talking to ourselves—and that feels pointless or lonely. A blank, glassy stare, a vacant look, and dull or rapidly shifting eyes all show an inability to confront. An absentminded nodding of the head and an occasional grunt also make speakers aware that their listeners are not paying attention. *The ability to confront is the ability to maintain attention, to concentrate, to communicate.*

Interested listeners seem full of energy and attentive. They look at you as if they really see and hear you. They are easy to talk to because they are interested in you. They can pay attention to you without wandering off. They avoid turning in on themselves and their own problems. They respond to what you have to say. People who cannot confront others cannot communicate effectively. They usually avoid looking at problems. They do not want to deal with problems—yours or their own. They may have the idea that if they do not deal with a problem, it will go away by itself. They do not want to bring up an issue that might lead to misunderstanding. People who confront their own problems and are willing to listen to yours have learned that problems are best solved by direct appraisal. When you confront problems directly, they seem smaller and get resolved more quickly.

Effective confrontation depends on the ability to face people and problems.

- Choose a partner and sit about three feet apart facing each other. Close your eyes. Do not talk. Avoid moving, or any other form of body language. Just be with your partner comfortably.

- Now open your eyes. Sit and look at each other. Say nothing. See how long you can sit comfortably, confronting another person without blinking, fidgeting, giggling, or speaking. You do not need to "do" anything. Simply be with your partner.

- When you are satisfied that you are able to confront, say "thank you" to your partner.

Practicing confrontation in a group allows for valuable feedback.

- In your group, choose three people to play the roles of a confronter, a person being confronted, and an observer. Choose a real-life situation—a person you care about whose behavior you see as destructive or ineffective. For example:

  a friend who rarely speaks in a group

  a person who criticizes others

  a person who embarrasses others

  a person who makes jokes or teases

  a person who is polite or nice in an insincere way

> a person who is overenthusiastic and seems to need a lot of attention
>
> a person who acts as if he or she loves everybody indiscriminately
>
> a person who smiles all the time

- The confronter describes the situation to the person being confronted. Some expressions he or she might use are:

    "Are you aware that . . . ?"

    "The things you do that bother me are . . ."

    "Something you could do that would improve our relationship is . . ."

    "I have difficulty handling it when you . . ."

    "I perceive you as acting in such a way that . . ."

    "I feel . . ."

    "I perceive your behavior as . . ."

    "When you act like that, I feel as if the result is . . ."

    "I see you doing . . . with . . . kind of a result. It bothers me."

    "When you do this, I feel as if you want . . . or mean . . ."

    Remember that confrontation is based on your own perceptions, which are highly subjective. Take responsibility for sharing those perceptions and feelings in confirming ways that express concern and caring. The person being confronted is to respond as genuinely as possible. The observer is to make notes about other options possible in such a confrontation and evaluate the skill of the confronter.

- Ask the observer to evaluate the experience. Then switch roles to allow others to practice confrontation skills.

Commitments End

As we experience changes in relationships, we become better able to handle change in the future. When we take responsibility for our relationships, we recognize that we are creating them. If we know at the beginning of a relationship that change is inevitable and endings are inevitable (either by death or separation), we can make agreements with ourselves to *accept a relationship for whatever it has to offer for however long it lasts.*

We have some options about our attitudes toward endings. We do not have to experience the end of a relationship as a rejection. If one person does not want the relationship to continue, then it cannot be good for either person. We can then recognize an ending as a choice. If we are not good for someone at this time in their life, then the relationship cannot be good for us either.

In the fertile void between relationships, we can take whatever time we need before we begin another relationship of any depth. Relationships are almost always available, and one choice is simply to wait. A relationship has a price: It takes time, energy, commitment. It means giving up freedom; and it means considering another person, changing one's life to accommodate another person. No one can say it is better to have a relationship, good or bad, than to be alone. When we have a relationship because we want one, then we are with another person because we *want* to be. When we are not "needy," we can handle endings, communicate about endings, and create better relationships.

Everyone is different in their responses to endings. Yet there are some common patterns in the dissolution of a relationship—depending on the individuals, the duration of the relationship, its intensity, and whether the ending is by choice or beyond their control. Anything from a mourning period to a surge of relief can follow an ending.

In an intense relationship or one that has lasted a long time, the love that existed between two people doesn't usually die quickly; rather it dissolves gradually, perhaps with lack of kindness, consideration, or respect. Sometimes anger is followed by depression and helplessness. It sometimes feels like an unreal experience, like a movie or novel in which both people are acting out lines they have heard before. They feel as if they are playing roles.

Most of us pass through certain phases: an initial reaction of pain, sadness, emptiness; then an overwhelming feeling of being alone, feeling hollow and disconnected; and finally a healing process. Isolating the self may be necessary to make a space for a new relationship. In this space we have time to develop personal strength, recall the past, and learn from it. We can look at what was missing in the relationship. We can experience guilt or resentment; cling to a negative self-image; or blame the other person. If the relationship ended by death, we may feel anger at the one who left us; or the illusion of a "perfect relationship" can interfere with future relationships. Although we may go through similar patterns, each individual experiences a unique loss and goes through a unique healing process. *When we look at this process, we may find we have some choices about the attitudes we want to take toward the ending of a relationship.*

All relationships end—either by choice or by death. Exploring possible endings can lead to making conscious choices.

- Describe a relationship in which you are feeling some conflict. Is it more important to build this relationship or to stay the way you are? Or to have your own way? What thoughts do you have about ending this relationship? Share these possibilities with your small group to get their perspectives.

- In a relationship, it is important to be aware of "the point of diminishing returns"—the point at which the relationship is stifling the growth and development of one or both individuals. Describe a relationship in which you reached that point. What did you do?

- In a relationship we must constantly weigh things anew. The situation and the people are all in transition. Describe a relationship that you or another person decided to end. How was it ended? In what other ways might you have handled the ending? Share this experience with your small group.

- Have you experienced an important relationship that was ended by death? Write about the changes in feelings and phases you experienced. What attitudes are you *now* choosing toward that death?

FOR FURTHER READING

Bach, George, and Ronald Deutsch. *Pairing.* New York: Avon, 1970.
   The authors outline methods for people to use in building relationships with others.

Buber, Martin. *I and Thou.* (Translated by R. B. Smith.) New York: Scribner, 1923.
   Buber says that when we treat each other as objects, we negate each other. We can respond to each other as persons whose essence is in the process of enfolding.

Fromm, Erich. *The Art of Loving.* New York: Harper & Row, 1956.
This small book is a classic in defining different kinds of love
and ways to practice loving.

Lewis, C. S. *The Four Loves.* New York: Harcourt Brace, 1960.
These six essays discuss four basic kinds of human love:
affection, friendship, erotic love, and love of God.

Lowen, Alexander. *Pleasure: A Creative Approach to Life.* New York:
Coward McCann, 1970.
Lowen believes that pleasure sustains the creative force, the
source of all good feelings and thinking, and that we can relate
to others through the body as a source of pleasure and love.

Mayeroff, Milton. *On Caring.* New York: Perennial Library, 1971.
This book outlines the qualities that demonstrate caring between
individuals and the values that caring brings to relationships.

Ogden, Thomas. *Game-Free: The Meaning of Intimacy.* New York:
Dell, 1974.
The author presents ways to create and experience intimacy in
relationships through interpersonal communication.

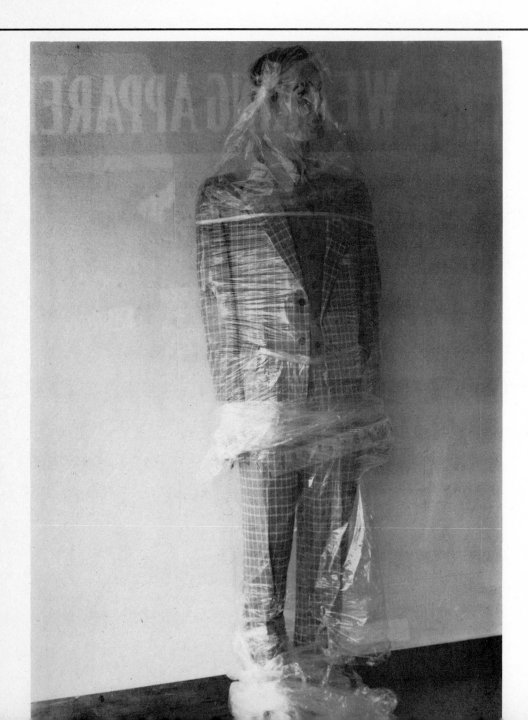

Something there is that doesn't love a wall,
That wants it down.

Robert Frost

11

Expanding the Process of Communication

GETTING THROUGH BARRIERS TO COMMUNICATION

Most of us can develop and enjoy relationships, but we have some difficulty sustaining them. In this chapter, we will explore ways of expanding the process of communication. We need to know ways of getting through barriers to communicating and relating. Certain conditions seem to suppress our lives. Certain ordinarily unnoticed laws often determine the persistence of conditions that keep us from enlightenment. These unconscious forces challenge our willingness to expand our consciousness.

We can begin here to explore ways to break through some of these blocks. *Perception sets, belief systems, and behavior patterns often prevent us from growing personally and socially.* This problem pertains to the world as well. For example, the belief that hunger and disease are the result of natural conditions such as scarcity and inevitability, or that there are "no solutions," actually creates and perpetuates the conditions. Look into your own personal perceptions, belief systems, and behavior patterns to expand your awareness of ways that you limit your growth. Through integrating much of what you have learned in this course on interpersonal communication, you can break through personal, social, and world barriers.

First our socialized responses, such as *suppressed feelings*, and programmed responses need to be examined. When we are afraid that others won't approve of us, we often become defensive and self-protective. Jack Gibbs, a communication expert, writes about **defensive communication.** When we become defensive, we often try to manipulate others. Everett Shostrom in *Man the Manipulator* suggests ways to replace manipulation with self-actualization and growth. We will be looking at what Gibbs and Shostrom have to say.

RELEASING SUPPRESSED EMOTIONS

To be nobody-but-yourself in a world which is doing its best, night and day, to make you everybody else—means to fight the hardest battle which any human being can fight; and never stop fighting.

e. e. cummings

We have the capacity to bury information we do not want to experience. It is possible to be afraid, angry, or jealous without being aware of it. Often we disguise feelings we have been taught are "not nice." Depression can be camouflaged as guilt or resentment. Fear and pain can often be covered by anger. In these cases, depression or anger becomes a secondary emotion used to hide the primary feeling that is too painful to acknowledge. If we hide feelings from others too often, we may not recognize them ourselves.

When we block off feelings of anxiety, fear, and conflict, we often immobilize ourselves so that we cannot function effectively. *We use energy to distort our perceptions so that we cannot perceive our experiences accurately.* Then we feel alienated from our real selves. Frozen emotions within us impede our flow of energy, growth, and change.

Thinking blocks, mood and feeling blocks, and blocks to action or speaking can occur at any time in life. A small child may reach out for approval or love and find no response. A teenager may experience failure or punishment. An adult may experience rejection or alienation. Whenever we need love, approval, or affection and it is not given, one way of handling our frustration is to set up barriers to the resulting pain. We become attached to these emotional patterns when they protect us from future pain. We resist giving up these defenses, and sometimes we think of them as part of us. For example, "I never cry" may be the response-identity of a person who has been badly hurt and who has blocked the pain.

The poet Robert Frost said: "Something there is that doesn't love a wall, that wants it down." To find what we have walled off inside us that keeps us from expanding requires *consciousness*. Buried emotions rule the unaware life. Once we recognize a feeling or behavior pattern, we can learn to move through these barriers—or around them. We need not know the original "cause" of the block; we need only recognize that it exists. When we begin to notice the response, it loses its power. For example, words to which we react may be the clue to past events that we have frozen. We can explore our own word blocks to open up our feelings. When we uncover the feelings behind such words, we can unblock our communication. Some responses are almost automatic. We become conditioned to react in a certain way. Although words can stand for whatever we agree to make them represent, we tend to become rigid toward certain words as if they had only one meaning. We have become *conditioned* to respond to certain words in certain ways depending on our past experiences. Once we become aware of this conditioning toward certain words, we can choose to change our automatic responses.

Free association can help uncover some of our blocked feelings.

- Use a tape recorder or choose a partner in class to read you the following list. Write any words that come to you in response to the words on this list. Test, feel, and experience any emotion that goes with a particular word. Notice when a word makes you feel defensive.

intimacy	hope	snake	God
criticism	morals	establishment	heavy
teacher	conflict	rock music	black
love	race	rights	mother
war	religion	pot	spiders
father	stereotype	abortion	"F"

- Share your association to these words with your group. Notice how different people respond to certain words in different ways. What experiences do you think have affected your responses? How do you think your behavior is affected by these experiences?

- Begin a personal list of "trigger" words that release blocked feelings. Exploring emotions behind these *symbols* may unblock something suppressed.

There are other ways to let out blocked emotions. When you have a strong emotional response to something, ask yourself: "What does this remind me of? What does this feel like?" If you have a strong emotional response to a person, ask: "Who does this person remind me of? If this person were a color, what color would he be? What food? What animal? What part of the body?" Analogies such as these can give us clues to hidden feelings.

You can also convert a feeling into a physical action. For example, pretend a pillow is a person (mother, father, husband, child, boss, friend). Do something with the pillow. (Don't stop with a hit or a hug . . . let the feeling come.) Feel it through. After hugging or hitting, something else may follow. Feelings are often complicated and ambiguous. Perhaps you will just carry on a conversation.

Another method is fantasy. Lie down, shut your eyes, and relax for about three minutes. Allow your mind to daydream. Let images form. Imagine a big cave. Walk through the opening. Go in and see what happens. Spend a few minutes in the cave and then walk down into one of the tunnels . . . down . . . into the cave. Allow your imagination to take over. Let go. What you imagine freely can offer valuable clues to feelings.

In all these approaches, allow your imagination to roam. You need not analyze, interpret, or understand what happens. Don't expect "revelations"—simply enjoy the imagery experience for its own sake. If no picture or sound comes to you, then feel what it is like to experience nothing. Feel the flow of nothingness and accept it.

Blocked emotional states can become physical disorders. When we swallow emotions, ignore them, hide them, or control them in some other way, we often suffer actual physical pain. Our emotional energy is diverted into the inner organs of the body, and we may develop such problems as breathing or digestive disturbances, heart or circulatory diseases, muscle problems, or headaches. Many patients have recurring illnesses for which doctors can find no demonstrable organic explanation. Such people may gain rewards by being sick. Pain can be used to avoid responsibility, such as going to work or school. It can be used as a defense mechanism to keep people away or as self-punishment for a person who feels guilty. And it can be used to get attention—flowers, cards, gifts; a rest or a change from everyday life; the fun of being in the limelight.

Many doctors recognize the following complaints as possibly psychosomatic in origin: muscle spasms, shortness of breath, palpitations (rapid heartbeat), vomiting, dizziness, impaired vision, arthritis, chest pain, lung problems, mental illness, jerking movements, high blood pressure, insomnia, skin problems, sex problems, back problems. The emotions that may be related to these physical disturbances originate from family troubles, worries, guilt (need to punish self), resentment (desire to punish others), fear, and so on. Passive aggression can result in laziness, indifference, helplessness, procrastination, or failure to finish anything. Some people, driven by unconscious feelings, act out such compulsions as excessive eating, drinking, smoking, washing, sex, or drugs.

Emotions can drive people in self-destructive directions. Karl Menninger in *Man Against Himself* says: "No one evolves so completely as to be entirely free from self-destructive tendencies." Our self-destructive tendencies can lead to psychosomatic illnesses, personality disorders, compulsions, and accidents. People who do not get enough sleep, eat poorly, or overstress their bodies set up situations where they have less resistance to bacteria and infection. In this way they "cooperate" with such diseases as pneumonia and tuberculosis that are around all the time. People who take care of their health have greater immunity to disease.

Another theory of psychosomatic illness is that each of us uses some organ or system in our body through which we communicate to ourselves that we are in stress. One person may get blinding headaches; another may develop a stiff neck; another may develop ulcers. *Our characteristic illnesses may be trying to tell us something about our life problems.* Biofeedback machines can help us train ourselves to give up our habitual body responses to stress and emotional upset. This is a matter of individual choice, of course. We may choose to have a headache rather than go to work. But we cannot choose freely unless we know we are choosing the reward of a physical ailment over being well.

Many medical people today are interested in **holistic health.** Holistic health suggests that optimal well-being involves personal responsibility for one's own body. These medical professionals believe that health is an integration of psychological, physical, and spiritual aspects of each individual. *We communicate our well-being to others through our bodies, but our thoughts, feelings, and perceptions influence what we communicate.* Therefore the values of our culture have some effect on our bodies.

In our culture, which often stresses objectivity and thinking, many concepts have been developed that tell us it's unacceptable to talk about feelings. Some of the ideas that prevent us from becoming aware of our emotions (which in turn affect our bodies) are:

Emotions are bad: "I have a feeling, but it would be destructive to tell what it is. I must be polite."

Feelings must be logical or not expressed: "I have a feeling, but it's irrational or unjustified."

Inappropriate feelings are not acceptable: "I have a feeling, but it's not appropriate."

Feelings have to refer to something specific here: "I have a feeling, but it isn't about anything or anyone here."

Feelings must be significant to be mentioned: "I have a feeling, but it's trivial."

Feelings must be all worked out and in polished form before they can be presented: "I have a feeling, but it's fuzzy."

Hostility or anger are the only two emotions that count: "I don't feel hostility or anger toward anyone." (Boredom, disappointment, and annoyance are often fleeting, yet they are very important feelings in group interaction.)

Once we become aware of our emotions, we can often choose not to be ill. When our emotions are no longer suppressed, they have less power to affect our bodies.

- How do emotions affect *your* body and create physical patterns of responding to stress? Do you use certain parts of your body to express stress? (For example: headaches, breathing difficulties, stomachaches, backaches, digestive problems.)

- Can you think of two or three other people—friends, relatives, acquaintances—who have physical problems stemming from what appear to you to be emotional stress?

- Give examples of times when you have suppressed your emotions and felt physical discomfort (tension in the head or chest, choking in the throat).

- The assumption that human beings need one part of their body through which to express stress can be a self-fulfilling prophecy. If we assume this notion to be *false*, what might happen? What happens when you change the word *need* to *choose*?

AVOIDING DEFENSIVENESS

When we feel threatened, we often find some way to protect ourselves against attack. Most of us feel the need to protect our own self-concepts: the self we think we are, the self we would like to be, and the self others think we are. Our private selves and public selves differ. *We may spend a good deal of time and energy protecting our private selves.* At times we wear masks or put up a front so that others won't know who we really are. We can become aware of our personal methods of defending ourselves—our defense mechanisms—and also how and when we put others on the defensive.

Karen Horney suggests that the basic anxiety against which we defend ourselves is "the feeling a child has of being isolated and helpless in a potentially hostile world." It is impossible for parents to raise a child without some kind of domination, moments of indifference, and inconsistent behavior. Parents, teachers, and others cannot *always* be in touch with a child's individual needs. Nor can they find that perfect balance between too much admiration or too little, too much responsibility or too little, too much protection or too little. *Every child suffers from injustice, discrimination, unkept promises, and a host of other imperfections in an imperfect world.* As a result, every one of us has experienced feeling "isolated and helpless in a potentially hostile world." The defense mechanisms we learned as children were useful to us then; they helped us survive. But when they persist in our adult lives, they may block our communication with others.

Some people spend much of their adult lives trying to survive. They become "surviving machines"—hiding, fighting, or justifying their behavior even though their parents are no longer telling them what to do. The parent voice is now in their mind.

Should's always contribute to disturbance in human relationships in one way or another.

Karen Horney

Threats, doubts, and fears may become more real than reality itself. The defense mechanisms that helped preserve and protect them as children can now lock them into a perpetual unhappy childhood, unless they choose to let go of their defensive posture.

Karen Horney suggests that we move *toward* people, *against* people, or *away* from people. These patterns determine how we defend ourselves. By moving *toward* people, we may accept our own helplessness and try to win the affection of others by complying, belonging, and agreeing. When we move *against* people, we take hostility for granted and respond by fighting. Aggressive individuals find that fighting is their best protection and also helps them get revenge for past pain and hostility. We can also simply move *away* from others. If we feel we do not have much in common with others, we may build our own world.

In each of these three responses, one element is overemphasized: helplessness in the first, hostility in the second, and isolation in the third. Each of us tends to use one of these three responses more than the others. If we become aware of our pattern of defense, however, we can choose to be more flexible. At times we can give in, at times fight, and at other times keep to ourselves. These three responses can complement each other and be appropriate in different situations.

Sources of Defensive Communication

Communication as a "people process" rather than a "language process" needs some fundamental changes in order to improve interpersonal relationships. Jack Gibbs says we need to reduce our defensiveness—behavior that occurs when a person perceives a threat from another person or group. *Defensive people devote a large portion of their energy to defending themselves and their position, so they have less energy to listen.* They keep thinking about how they appear to others, how they may be seen, how they may dominate, impress, or escape punishment, how they may avoid attack. Defense postures, both verbal and physical, create defensiveness in others and become circular. Moreover, defensive listeners distort what they hear. They project their own anxieties, motives, and concerns onto others. According to Gibbs, behavior listed in the left-hand column tends to arouse defensiveness, whereas that listed in the right-hand column allows a safe, supportive "space" for better communication:

Defensive Climates	*Supportive Climates*
1. Evaluation (judgments)	1. Description
2. Control	2. Problem orientation
3. Strategy	3. Spontaneity
4. Neutrality	4. Empathy
5. Superiority	5. Equality
6. Certainty	6. Provisionalism

The first item under defensive climates has to do with making *evaluations* or *judgments*. A judgment expresses an opinion and also implies approval or disapproval. As we discussed before, judgments overladen with emotion often tell more about the judge than they reveal about the person being judged. The statement "He's conceited" is not a fact, for example. To *describe* the same person, you might say "He failed to stop and talk to me." Perhaps he is shy or perhaps he didn't even see you. Most of us make judgments. In order to make decisions in life, we have to evaluate *situations*. However, we can be aware that when we judge people we are expressing personal opinions, not facts.

Judging ourselves and others often leads us into communication breakdowns. *Critical attitudes that express disapproval or dislike block communication.* Even positive evaluations can be threatening. We express our critical attitudes nonverbally with contemptuous facial expressions—frowning, a skeptical look, raising the eyebrows. A scornful laugh, sarcasm, and ridicule can block communication. Reading a book, ignoring what another person says, a bored expression, a superior attitude—all communicate "I reject you." Criticism and judgments are used by those who feel it is not safe to express anger, annoyance, or irritation directly. Direct expressions of feelings—"I feel critical; I want you to change and be different" or "I feel judgmental"—are not judgments. *Description* of behavior we do not like and direct *expression* of feeling creates a more supportive atmosphere.

Gibbs' second point is that *control* is often a hidden element of defensiveness. In other words, *we may defend ourselves by trying to control others.* We may also believe that everyone has similar hidden motives. Sarcasm can be used to avoid direct expression of feelings, which make us open and vulnerable. The

Judging, blaming, and criticism put others on the defensive and block communication.

tone of voice, a toss of the head, or a disdainful look may hide anger, irritation, annoyance, or hurt. These nonverbal cues are often used to control others, to threaten them, or to make them feel guilty. The defensive response is "I'm not that bad" or "I'm not guilty." The destructive use of humor to belittle another person is difficult to fight because it has a certain social acceptance. Wit and teasing are often disguised forms of hostility, though. And when the victim reacts defensively, the "joker" can say "Hey, can't you take a joke?"

The aim of *control* is to get the other person to change: to do or be something different. The use of such words as *should* and *ought* may accomplish its purpose, but the relationship and the communication suffer. *The most productive behavior change comes about through accepting others the way they are*—giving them the opportunity to bring about any change that springs from their own feelings and desires through *problem-solving* rather than from the wishes and standards of others. When we use each other as backboards to bounce ideas against, we use the *problem-solving process.*

Third, Gibbs suggests that defensive communication involves the use of *strategy*—planning ahead what to say and do. Implicit in all attempts to change others is the assumption that those others are inadequate, ignorant, uninformed, immature, unwise, or wrong. We then set up some strategy for making them change. If we can anticipate how the others will act, we can *plan our attack*. Having the "right" answers to all objections in advance can help the strategist "win." When we come to a person willing to let the group make the decisions, however, we spontaneously respond to whatever happens. *Spontaneity* requires trust in others—the belief that they are wise, mature, informed, and able to help in the planning.

The fourth element in defensive communication, *neutrality*, comes across as not caring. Being objective and removed may allow us to pretend that we are invulnerable. The objective person rarely gets involved emotionally. Being human, however, is to be vulnerable to pain. In a supportive atmosphere, one in which a feeling of *empathy* prevails, each person involved has an emotional stake in the outcome.

The fifth element in defensive communication, says Gibbs, is *superiority*, which puts people on the defensive. When we do not regard others as having value, we may block them from seeing themselves or their contributions as valuable. In an interpersonal communication class, for example, a group of five students (seeing any other individual from five perceptual realities) can often come up with more insights than any single communication expert. In some fields, experts do have more information, and they earn their living by being more informed. Yet authorities who believe that their listeners have something of value to contribute create a supportive environment in which listeners are perceived as *equally* valuable and can actually give positive contributions.

Gibbs' last point is that *certainty*—perceiving oneself as having all the right answers—can force defensive reactions. Knowing what is "right" implies that others are wrong and increases defensiveness in a relationship. Genuine authorities suggest answers as *provisional*, do not see theories as facts, and regard conclusions as temporary, based on all the information available and open to new data. People feel safer with authorities who regard answers as provisional rather than absolutely right.

In review, the defensive climate created by *evaluation, control, strategy, neutrality, superiority,* and *certainty* can be altered to a supportive climate in which *description, problem orientation, spontaneity, empathy, equality,* and *provisionalism* occur. These dimensions are not really separate but interconnected. The person who intends to create a supportive climate describes, asks others for help in solving problems, is spontaneous and empathic, treats people as equals, and views his or her ideas as possibilities.

Withholding judgments and blame can help us communicate more positively.

- Choose a partner. Decide who is going to be "good" and who is going to be "bad." Play these roles for about five minutes. You can use statements such as "I'm a good girl; I always eat everything on my plate" or "I'm a bad boy; I never make my bed." Listen to tone of voice, loudness, and emotion. Switch roles—"good" now plays "bad" and vice versa. How did you feel in each role? Which one did you like best?

- To your partner say: "I should . . . ." (Finish this statement.) Have your partner say: "No, you shouldn't." Continue this dialogue for a few minutes. Then switch roles. Try "I shouldn't feel (or be) . . . ." Have your partner say: "Yes, you should." Switch roles. How does each role feel?

- To your partner say: "I'm right about . . ." (finish this statement) "and X is wrong." For two minutes say as many things as you can about which you feel you are right and someone else is wrong. Your partner now has two minutes to say "I'm right and . . . is wrong." Does it feel good to be right? Does it feel good to make someone else be wrong?

- To your partner say: "It's his fault. He hurt me when he. . . . He *should* have. . . . He used me. It wasn't my fault." How do these communications feel to you and your partner? Discuss how you usually defend yourself against judgment or blame.

One philosopher says: "We do not require agreement or the absence of disagreement to survive." During a disagreement, ask yourself:

Is it more important to be right than to build a relationship?

Is it more important to have my own way than to build a relationship?

Are some things more important than being right? What are they?

When am I willing to sacrifice a relationship in order to be right?

We have experienced "win/lose" communication from the time we were born. Defining the self and establishing an identity means finding the differences between the self and others. School emphasizes winning contests, attention, recognition, and prestige. Winning usually involves others losing. So in a conversation, instead of listening, we may spend time thinking what we are going to say next, preparing to tear down an opponent's argument, finding ideas that seem superior to the other person's—in short, playing "I am smart and you are dumb."

No relationship can withstand continual competitive battles in which one person is downgraded for his or her ideas or personhood. One-upmanship becomes such a habit that it may take the competitive person a long time to unlearn stock responses. Most relationships are built on cooperation rather than competition. Competition in sports, politics, or other "races" may be appropriate, but in relationships we must share in winning, in achieving common goals, in working out solutions, in developing ideas. *Genuinely nonmanipulative listening and sharing result in cooperation and win/win situations.*

Benjamin Spock says: "Much more dangerous than the open antagonism of one individual toward another . . . is the readiness of a majority of human beings to mistrust and hate . . . . Displaced hostility . . . is derived from the antagonism that was first built up in all of us in early childhood toward family members." We were taught to feel deeply guilty about hating our own family, so we learned to displace this *hostility* onto whole groups of people. Another self-deceptive maneuver, called *projection*, is the readiness to project what are really our own hostile feelings onto any other person toward whom we feel antagonistic. A man may not like his neighbor, so he says "My neighbor doesn't like me." He then interprets any comment or action of the neighbor as hostile—which gives him a perfect excuse for disliking or attacking his neighbor. A third reaction is to *provoke* a conflict. During a divorce, for example, one married partner may provoke the other into some kind of retaliation; then both can tell their friends how bad the divorced mate really is.

Disguised hostility—in the form of displacement, projection, or provoked attacks—is only one way of releasing long-held anger. These powerful feelings are kept in balance through our desire to be loved and to be kind to others, which are derived from the loving and caring we received as children. Each of us lives in some kind of equilibrium between our loving and our hating sides. Talking with someone whose company we enjoy, sharing our feelings, indicating respect for the other person's likes and wants, pleasing another person simply for the sake of creating trust—all are expressions of love and caring.

We express love when we listen to others' troubles and try to make them feel comfortable. When we accept others' anger without attacking them in return—not because we are afraid but because we want them to feel comfortable in releasing painful feelings—and when we give them positive feedback, we have begun to create safety, security, trust, and love. People who do not need to praise, attack, or control themselves are often able to give others this kind of support.

Awareness of Manipulation

In *Man the Manipulator*, Everett Shostrom defines manipulators as *people who exploit, use, and control themselves and others as "things."* They camouflage their real feelings and thoughts. Manipulators need to control and be controlled, often using moralistic rules ("good/bad") to run the lives of themselves and others. The opposite of a manipulator is an actualizer. *Actualizers appreciate themselves and others as persons rather than things.* They turn self-defeating manipulations into self-fulfilling potentials. They trust their feelings, communicate their needs, admit to desires and misbehavior, enjoy worthy foes, offer real help when needed, and are honestly and constructively aggressive. Each of us falls somewhere along this continuum from manipulator to actualizer, moving back and forth depending on the situation and the relationship.

Shostrom suggests that there are two sides to manipulators: *top dog* (active, commanding authority) and *underdog* (passive, compliant). The paradox, says Shostrom, is that usually the underdog wins. Shostrom has grouped manipulators into four kinds of top dogs and four kinds of underdogs. He says that a person who is most strongly one type projects his or her opposite onto others. Such a person seems different to different people because he or she exposes only certain manipulations to some and other manipulations to others.

Top dogs and underdogs come in pairs:

1. *Dictators* (top dogs) exaggerate their strength, dominate, order, quote authorities, and act as Mother Superiors, Rank Pullers, and Bosses. *Weaklings*, who appear to be dictators' victims, develop skill in coping by exaggerating sensitivity, forgetting, not hearing, or being silent. They act as Worriers, Confused, Stupid-Like-a-Fox, and Giver-Uppers. Weaklings tend to choose dictator spouses and then control them by subversive devices.

2. *Calculators* exaggerate their control, deceive, lie, and try to outwit their partners. They are the high-pressure salespeople, seducers, poker players, con artists, blackmailers, and intellectualizers. *Clinging Vines* manipulate Calculators by exaggerating dependency. They want to be led, fooled, taken care of. They let others do their work. They play the roles of Parasite, Crier, Perpetual Child, Hypochondriac, Attention Demander, and Helpless One.

3. *Bullies* exaggerate aggression, are unkind, and threaten others. They act as Tough Guys, Threateners, Bitches, Naggers, or Humiliators. *Nice Guys* manipulate Bullies by exaggerating kindness and caring. They are hard to cope with because one cannot fight a Nice Guy, who is a Pleaser—a virtuous nonoffender who "never asks for anything."

4. *Judges* are overly critical; they distrust, blame, resent, and are slow to forgive. They are the Know-It-Alls, Blamers, Resentment Collectors, Shamers, Comparers, Vindicators, and Convictors. *Protectors* manipulate Judges by exaggerating support; they are nonjudgmental to a fault. They spoil others and do not allow them to stand up and grow for themselves. They are overprotective and oversympathetic. They act out the roles of Mother Hen, Defender, Embarrassed-for-Others, Fearful-for-Others, Sufferer-for-Others, Martyr, Helper, and Unselfish One.

Shostrom says the cause of manipulation is distrust. Not trusting ourselves, we believe our salvation lies in trusting others. Yet, not trusting others, we manipulate them to make them do what we want, feel what we feel, think what we think. We literally try to transform others into things for our own use.

Children can become master manipulators. They play underdog roles and often win. Three-year-old con artists can hustle their parents for anything: food, attention, a curfew extension at bedtime. They are masters of what speech experts call "communication strategies." Children can use words for acquiring what they want and avoiding what they don't want. Children often use nonverbal weapons when they cannot win with words—body movement, voice tone, and strategic timing often win. Royce Rodnick Gardner and Barbara Wood of the University of Illinois Speech Department explored devices employed by children two to eleven years old. They confirmed the never-ending war in which "parents are lucky if they win an occasional battle." Gardner and Wood studied communication tricks children applied to eating, playing, and sleeping. Nonverbal techniques were most used by younger children. The older ones no longer needed to manipulate parents. They transferred their techniques to their schoolmates, the teacher, and finally to the job market.

If we can become aware of our subtle ways of manipulating others, we can stop controlling through fear, distrust, competition, and withholding approval, support, and love. *We all at times attempt to control others through conscious or unconscious manipulation.* Teachers, parents, employers, even friends may try to enforce their value system on others through hidden means. Students, children, and employees, as underdogs, have found ways of winning the manipulation battle. Carl Rogers, as mentioned earlier, suggests the paradox that power is gained only through giving it away. *When we share power, our control of others becomes self-control, and we can then grow toward more actualization and less manipulation.*

Becoming aware of our characteristic styles of manipulation can help us break down this major barrier to open communication.

- Review Shostrom's classifications of manipulators. Are you a top dog or an underdog? Do you project the opposite onto others around you? Do you find that you expose some kinds of

manipulation to some poeple and other kinds to other people?
Give examples.

• Using Shostrom's role labels, give examples you have experienced of manipulating or being manipulated.

• Where do you usually operate on the following manipulation
scale? Give specific examples.

Manipulating	*Actualizing*
untrusting	trusting
closed	open
deceptive	authentic
bored	alive
unaware	aware
cynical	realistic
restrained	free
rigid	flexible
insecure	secure
competitive	cooperative

RESOLVING CONFLICT

In interpersonal relations, problems come up daily because of
differences in perception, interests, needs, goals, and personalities. We cannot live without conflicts both internal and
external. There is no life without discord. Since we already *know*
this, why do we suffer so much when we are in conflict with
another person?

First, we have been taught that "it's not nice to fight"—"Be
polite! If you love somebody, you are nice to them." We've been
taught that it is bad to disagree, argue, or confront others. We've
been taught to feel hurt, angry, or disappointed whenever we
aren't getting along with someone. When others disagree with us
or our ideas, we feel that they do not like us. Therefore we often
avoid a conflict, pretend it does not exist, or fight to win. As you
know from personal experience, these methods of handling
conflict simply do not work.

*Don't walk in front of me,
I may not follow.
Don't walk behind me, I
may not lead.
Walk beside me and just
be my friend.*

Albert Camus

Conflict may be as much a driving force as hunger and thirst.

Because of all this programming, we need to become conscious of the ways conflict drives us. Some psychologists believe that conflict is the same sort of driving force as hunger, thirst, and pain—a condition that produces learning, a basic drive that motivates us to act. If we reeducate ourselves to new methods of resolving conflict, we can learn constructive ways to deal with our differences.

We often communicate without conflict through agreement. But we cannot have conflict (disagreement) without some form of communication, verbal or nonverbal, that indicates we are in opposition. *Human conflict is not only inevitable but also valuable.* It can result in the growth and change of a culture if differences are managed through communication rather than killing. Laws and courts were created to handle conflict peaceably. Out of conflict can come evolutionary ideas and values.

Adlai Stevenson said: "It is better to discuss a question without settling it than to settle a question without discussing it."

Disagreement need not be unpleasant, unfortunate, or embarrassing. Arguments can reinforce a group or family when there is a respect for the right of people to disagree. We need to observe our quarrels and think more about them.

When we are in conflict, we test our own ideas and values. We learn something new about ourselves when we are forced to review certain concepts and habitual ways of thinking, feeling, or responding. Habits—automatic responses—are necessary and valuable when they simplify life so that we do not have to make new decisions every moment. But habit also diminishes attention and resists change. As feelings and thoughts become automatic, habits can be obstacles to growth, limits to development, and blocks to exploring new areas of awareness. *When we allow ourselves to be in conflict, we can review old habitual responses and free our minds for more intense work.*

Conflict prevents stagnation of both the individual and the social order. Conflict can also result in growth and development of relationships. When disagreement results in new forms of interacting, solutions to problems can be found. Struggles between groups—consumers and manufacturers, labor and management, government and individuals—result in the creation of new products, improvements in technology, and better social conditions for more people.

In addition to motivating growth, education, and improved living conditions, conflict in our daily lives provides us with a source of stimulation. If all our needs were met, we would create new ones. Human beings need goals—something to strive for, challenges to make life move forward. Growth and education require the examination of old ways of thinking or acting that are no longer appropriate. Reforms are vital not only to the individual but also to social institutions. Change is inevitable. Each individual is in a process of unique evolution. *As humankind evolves, our social structures must grow; conflict is the source of that evolution.*

Conflict can be resolved through consensus (agreement) or coercion (manipulation). Of course, conflicts cannot always be resolved so that both individuals "win" the same goal. The less powerful must fight for their rights unless the most powerful are willing to give up their power (economic, political, social, or individual).

The meaning of each conflict is subject to the individual's view of reality. Our desire for consistency, stability, and an integrated self in a consistent world may result in internal conflict. As we change and grow, we experience identity crises. When our self-esteem is threatened by inner conflict, we may protect ourselves through a number of defense mechanisms such as repression, projection, rationalization, or blaming others. Individuals experiencing self-conflict may create interpersonal, group, or social conflicts.

Conflicts in relationships arise from many sources. Many of us, for example, are afraid of unconsciously giving in to others or being manipulated. Moreover, most of us do not know what we want from each other. And if we do know, we may not feel free to ask or to risk denial. Parents may have to say no ten times to one yes. In fact, many parents just automatically say no and then think it over later. Parents, afraid they will be overindulgent, are often on the defensive against the thousands of requests they get from children. Therefore, in the process of growing up, we soon forget how to ask for things from other people.

Managing conflicts constructively requires accurate perception, accurate communication, a climate of trust, cooperative resolutions, and an awareness of the conflict. *Selective or distorted perception operates in most conflicts.* Assumptions that the other person's feelings are totally hostile make us defensive, and then our own hostile expectations become fulfilled. Both participants feel, at the same time, they are *innocent victims* presenting truth and justice while being attacked maliciously by an evil enemy. Moreover, we tend to perceive all underhanded and vicious acts of the other party while seeing all identical acts by the self as right and fair. What is legitimate for ourselves is illegitimate for others. And, finally, we tend to oversimplify conflicts and polarize everything as "good" or "bad," "right" or "wrong," with nothing in between.

Hostility, defensiveness, polarized thinking, selective perception, and distortion usually operate in the realm of the "half-conscious." Ordinarily we sense that something is wrong, but it gets out of our control—out of our consciousness. Simply becoming more aware of the elements that escalate conflict to hostility can result in more constructive conflict.

All conflict occurs in a context—a particular situation where roles are usually defined and limited by mutual agreement. When one person in a relationship perceives the other person as not living up to role expectations, conflict arises. Some conflict is inevitable, for example, when different perceptions of roles exist between husband and wife, parent and child, teacher and student, employer and employee. All of us are familiar with religious, economic, social, and political conflicts. And many of us have different values in regard to abortion, drugs, welfare, busing, or tax reform. Therefore the first step is to be aware of the conflict as it exists in context: personal, interpersonal, social, or political.

The situation and the relationship, as defined by roles, can be explored first. Some relationships are sustained over a long period of time; others are short-lived. Some relationships are intimate and complex; others are casual and uncomplicated. *The more involved the relationship, the more conflict one will experience.*

To avoid irreversible damage through conflict, we must be clear about what it is we are doing that does *not* work and what it is we want to change. It is possible for one person in a relationship to change in such a way that the other person cannot continue in the old patterns. Once we break the roles and destroy the pattern, the game cannot go on. The risk we take is that the other person will leave us to find someone who will continue the game. A game can also contribute to psychic stability. Some people will prefer to continue the patterns in their lives that are comfortable and controllable. For example, a woman whose father was an alcoholic may marry an alcoholic. If her husband stops drinking, she may divorce him without being conscious of her need to continue her own role in this game. In such cases, one may have to choose between giving up the relationship and playing the game. Refusing to play games can create conflict because not all individuals want autonomy.

There are different kinds of conflict. A confrontation based on message accuracy is **content conflict** over a fact, an inference, a definition. These conflicts are the easiest to resolve. Facts can be looked up, inferences can be tested, definitions can be verified. Even when content conflicts cannot be resolved, they are still much easier to cope with than other kinds of conflict because they are more logical than emotional.

The second kind of conflict, which is often more difficult to resolve, is **value conflict.** Value conflicts occur when people differ in their views of life, such as religious, political, and social attitudes. Values cannot be verified and are based primarily on belief systems. We either believe in God or we do not; we believe in welfare or think it is destructive; we believe in democracy or think people really cannot rule themselves. Good friends can enjoy good verbal combat knowing they will probably not change the other person's values. Long-term intimate relationships may be affected by basic differences in values. Such differences as the value of cleanliness, order, or time can produce conflict if they interfere with agreements on space, living arrangements, or schedules.

When we need to win, when our personal image is in danger, **ego conflicts** may arise. Judgmental statements about a person's self-concept (intelligent or stupid, graceful or clumsy, pretty or ugly, diligent or lazy) may threaten self-esteem and result in conflict. These conflicts are the most damaging and the most difficult to resolve. People with a strong sense of self-worth are far less vulnerable to attack than those who have not yet found their own value—although time alone does not make a person less vulnerable to attack from others.

Most of us are familiar with ego conflicts in the family. The parent/child conflict revolves primarily around dependence/independence needs. As children grow, they develop values of their own. Losing control of children is a frightening experience for parents. As children grow in size, strength, and intelligence, parents get left behind. By the time a mother learns how to treat a twelve-year-old boy, he is already fourteen. As parent and child both learn to depend on each other, yet at times be independent, conflicts inevitably arise.

To make room for the self and still have room for the other person involves conflicts, choices, and decisions that test us as long as we live—first in the child/parent relationship, then in the student/teacher relationship, again in the friend/friend relationship, and eventually in mating and work relationships. And many of us finally come full circle back to the parent/child situation, where our role in life is now that of parent.

How we respond to conflicts and resolve them can make our lives enjoyable or miserable. A relationship grows when two people enjoy each other's differences and celebrate each other's uniqueness. We need to retrain our feelings in conflict. We need to learn not simply to permit differences but actually rejoice in them.

Quarreling can be destructive or constructive, depending on your reactions, your awareness, and how you handle the conflicts.

It can give you a chance to look at your feelings and get them out. It can open up sharing, self-exploration, and growth. In *Teacher*, Sylvia Ashton-Warner wrote:

> A woman said to me once so proudly, "My family *never* quarrels." I was young at the time and our children were young and I thought, "How wonderful! If only I could say that." But I'm not young now and I know better. When I look back on that family who never quarreled I remember their passivity; the slow eyes that did not flash; on the parents' faces, no grooves that tears had scoured. I know now that it takes passion and energy to make a quarrel . . . of the magnificent sort . . . magnificent reconciliations; the surging and soaring of magnificent feeling.

When some students were asked how they felt about quarrels in a family or with friends, they said:

"I don't like the feeling of someone being angry with me; and I don't like feeling angry at someone else."

"I haven't learned to accept someone else's hurt feelings."

"Sometimes when I anticipate an argument, I start it."

"I sometimes see how far I can go with someone I love."

"I like to have someone disagree with me. When I get in an argument, I always learn something. I wouldn't like everyone to agree with me all the time. I wouldn't like everyone to disagree with me either."

"When I know I'm right and they won't listen, I feel angry."

"I don't mind as long as they don't try to make me believe what they're saying."

"I try to find people who agree with me because it makes me feel that I'm right."

"I drop the subject. I don't like disagreements."

"I couldn't care less!"

These responses show that most of us experience conflicts as painful. Can we retrain ourselves? Can we learn how to appreciate conflict and grow through our differences?

There are as many ways to resolve a conflict as there are people, situations, and problems. Whatever the situation, individuals have some concept of their roles and the positions they hold. Within the structure of these roles, the first step in conflict resolution is for all those involved to *define the conflict*. In an interpersonal conflict, each person sees the problem differently. Initially, those involved need to spend some time clarifying the conflict so they reach some agreement about the nature of the problem. Until there is agreement about what needs resolving, the conflict is not amenable to solution.

In addition to defining the problem, the individuals involved must have the *desire* to resolve the conflict. Some people enjoy conflict (even if they do not realize it) just for the sake of the excitement it stirs up. For many of us, conflict is more desirable than boredom. But when a conflict interferes with a relationship, the attitude for resolution as a goal must be agreed on. Without cooperation, the conflict cannot be resolved. Certain *agreements* can help resolve interpersonal conflict:

"Whatever the outcome of the conflict, we will continue to care about and respect each other."

"We will carry out the resolution of our problem with a spirit of warmth and support."

"We will strive for a constructive solution that will be beneficial in some way for all parties involved."

"We will review solutions periodically."

"We will openly and honestly express feelings without intending to manipulate each other."

"We will avoid distortions, destructiveness, and physical or verbal violence."

"We will spend whatever time and energy are necessary for the conflict to be explored fully. And when a resolution has been found, we will view it as temporary to see how it works in practice."

"After the solution has been tested, we will set aside time to review the problem, to make any needed changes, and to explore our feelings about the whole process."

In our culture, sales, athletics, and business are based primarily on competition. Competitive agreements often produce a higher level of performance than cooperative agreements. In competition, only one person can win the goal. Only one team wins the World Series. Only one boxer wins the world's heavyweight championship. Only one aircraft company is awarded the government contract. Competitors strive for a mutually exclusive goal. In many cases, competition can be friendly; but when winning means making a million dollars, few competitors can remain friendly. Yet even in cutthroat competition, there are still defined rules for the game.

In interpersonal relations, people may resolve to win at any cost. The newspaper tells about daily examples of conflict in families that result in death—both murder and suicide. There is a growing problem of battered mates and battered children. These examples of interpersonal conflict illustrate how destructive a struggle between individuals can become: The price is physical or emotional death.

Physical violence is a conflict pattern learned in childhood and repeated in adulthood. Emotional violence through the use of language, verbal and nonverbal, is also common; it is learned in childhood and repeated in adulthood. These patterns are difficult to unlearn. Therefore we need to help each other. Review the cooperative agreements; discuss them with those who are important to you. And if everyone agrees, you can *make a commitment* to resolve conflicts through cooperative methods.

If we break the agreement, we can take responsibility by saying "I take responsibility for breaking my agreement." Nothing more need be said: no recriminations, no advice, no scolding. Simply to acknowledge breaking an agreement and then to renew the same agreement or a different one can lead to change. The question is: Are we willing to pay the price? Setting aside the time, the space, and the situation to work out mutual problems is essential.

Conflicts can be resolved through discussion:

1. First, all parties to a relationship must agree on the goals of "cooperative agreements" in handling conflicts.

2. Each individual who thinks that he or she has a problem in a relationship must be able, clearly and specifically, to state the behavior in the other person that causes him or her trouble (perhaps in writing to make it more concrete).

3. All parties to a relationship (couple, family, group) must set aside a mutually agreed-upon time, with beginning and ending defined, to share problems (for example, Wednesday evening from 7:30 to 9:30). Allow enough time for a complete discussion to express feelings fully and resolve differences—a time when no one will be embarrassed and there will be no interruptions. (Take the phone off the hook.)

4. Share the problem by reading what you have written or by clearly stating what is troubling you. Give specific examples of behavior.

5. After you have shared the problem and how you feel about it, ask the other(s) in the relationship to paraphrase what you have said. You are now ready for hard work. Yet it is a relief not to have to discover the truth of everything by yourself. That's what conflicts are for.

6. Usually, in stating a problem, you have made a request that someone or some situation be changed in some way. Verbalize the change you want.

7. Have the others in the relationship acknowledge your request: "I hear you saying you want . . . ." Conflicts can be explored while the self-esteem of both parties is protected.

8. At this point, all those in the relationship must consider ways of implementing the change or deciding that what is being asked cannot be changed. Ideas and options can be discussed. This is a brainstorming session and takes time.

9. Decision-making based on all the alternatives is the next step. A joint decision on the best option is now made by all those in the relationship.

10. Set a future meeting to discuss how the plan is working.

The irony of such a plan for conflict resolution in a relationship is that the plan itself can become a game for people to get "their own way," to win the changes they want, to get others to change their behavior. If true autonomy for each individual in the relationship is the goal, each person must be in touch with his or her own motivations and intentions.

Conflict can result in growth. Some of the positive results are these:

To find the truth about myself.

To have different perceptions of the world.

To find out the truth about the other person.

To find my distortions or self-deceptions.

To share different views of reality with another.

In any conflict, we must take responsibility for ourselves and for our willingness to risk. *Sometimes our needs distort our perceptions.* Most of our self-deceptions protect us from something we are not ready to accept about ourselves. We may be pretending we do not want something we really want very much (telling ourselves "It's not nice to want that") or pretending we do not have a trait we consider imperfect—in short, pretending we are different from the way we are. Sometimes we hide from ourselves.

Unwillingness to confront is usually motivated by fear, need for approval, relief from guilt, or the avoidance of some other anxiety. Saying no to another person defines the self—tells who we are and what our limits are. *Conflict brought out into the open confronts another with our real selves.* If we do not care about the others, of course, there's no need to confront them.

In every relationship some differences may be irreconcilable. To avoid endless dispute when the conflict becomes unresolvable at the moment, we can say: "I feel that we cannot resolve this issue. I want to let it go at this time. We can disagree without jeopardizing our relationship. I do not want to merge my identity with yours on this issue at this time. I need some separate views of my own. I am concerned about our disagreement, and I feel bad about your anxiety. I think we share a great deal that is positive, and I enjoy being with you. I love you very much, and I would like to let this issue go at this time."

Two people can agree to confront each other as painlessly as possible for the purpose of realigning both realities—to share the meaning of each other's views of the world when they are different, to give each other, through confrontation, the gifts of growth and love.

INTEGRATING COMMUNICATION

But the gathering of facts does not make for the understanding of life. Knowledge is one thing, and understanding another.

J. Krishnamurti

We have performed an anatomy on our communicative behavior. We have found that *language* gives us the ability to send and receive meaning. The *mind* gives us the ability to think critically. The *body* gives us the ability to work and to play. Our *emotions* provide us with the ability to care, to love, and to enjoy. *Behavior* is the ability to make a commitment and put it in action. Now we must integrate what we have taken apart.

The human spirit gives us the ability to find something in life—to give it *a larger meaning*. As we integrate what we know about communication, we can learn how to give love and how to resolve conflict. We can learn to get along with others regardless of their beliefs, origins, or appearances. *With an expansion of awareness, we learn to communicate our humanity to others and develop, together, positive interpersonal values.*

There is a good deal of evidence that humanity is now on the threshhold of vast new possibilities. We have just begun our consciousness evolution. We are in the process of moving beyond our present state of communicating and relating.

In the last week or so before this class ends, think about all the things you will have left unsaid. Is there anyone in the class with whom you have something you want to complete by saying something else? For example: "If I had one gift to give you, I would give (self-confidence, serenity, patience, trust)." As people get involved with one another, they develop unfinished business—that is, they have things they would like to talk about further but which were interrupted because of lack of time.

Find a free moment inside or outside of class and approach someone. Here is a vocabulary for unfinished business:

"I have some unfinished business with you. Do you have time to talk?"

"I have a question I'd like to ask you."

"I have something I'd like to work out with you."

"I liked it when you . . ."

"You seemed like me when . . ."

"I was wondering what you meant when you . . ."

"How did you hear me when I said . . .?"

"How did it come across to you when I . . . ?"

Unfinished business can be positive, negative, or neutral—or just an unresolved issue, an unanswered question, an unfinished conversation. Many people want others to tell them how they are perceived. They want feedback. People need each other to help resolve conflicts, clarify values, and find out about themselves. The gifts of listening and responding are gifts we give each other to show that we care and are cared about.

One way of integrating communication is through the process of designing a communication model—a pattern that gives a graphic illustration of how communication works. You can synthesize what you have learned by creating your own model. Follow these steps:

- List all the components you think are essential to a chart of how communication works.
- Go through the text and find words that fit the different parts of your model. Include whatever terms you wish. For example:

  Perception: seeing, hearing, touching, smelling, tasting

  Sender: source, attitudes, values, expectations, knowledge

  Message: verbal, nonverbal, oral, written, signs, symbols

  Channel: TV, radio, film, books, newspapers, air, telephone

  Receiver: biases, listening ability, empathy, accuracy

  Feedback: responding, acknowledging, supporting, affirming

  Barriers: noise, defensiveness, interference, prejudice

  Environment: time, location, surroundings

- Visualize some organization of the parts that, when put together, would include all these components in a relationship.
- Begin to sketch your model, labeling all the parts and using arrows to show direction or process.
- After drawing and labeling the parts of your model, write an explanation of the relationships between the parts.
- Share your models in groups of five or six.

FOR FURTHER READING

Bach, George, and Peter Wyden. *The Intimate Enemy*. New York: Avon, 1968.
> The authors believe that conflict is not only healthy but essential to any good relationship when the individuals involved can work out their differences in constructive ways.

Chapman, A. H. *Put-Offs and Come-Ons*. New York: Putnam, 1968.
> Chapman describes games that people use and ways to stop playing them so that relationships can be more satisfying.

Ginott, Haim G. *Between Parent and Teenager*. New York: Macmillan, 1969.
> The author gives helpful suggestions for interpersonal understanding in family transactions.

Lederer, W. J., and D. D. Jackson. *The Mirages of Marriage*. New York: Norton, 1968.
> This book presents some misconceptions about marriage and presents ideas that can help improve communicating in a marriage.

Satir, Virginia. *Peoplemaking*. Palo Alto: Science & Behavior Books, 1972.
> Satir develops systems and rules for developing self-worth and improving the quality of family interactions.

Shostrom, Everett. *Man, the Manipulator*. New York: Bantam, 1968.
> The roles we play create their opposites in those with whom we relate—thus producing top-dog and underdog manipulators. Once we are aware of these interactions, we can change them.